TORWALI

AN ACCOUNT OF A DARDIC LANGUAGE OF THE SWAT KOHISTAN

TORWALI

AN ACCOUNT OF A DARDIC LANGUAGE OF THE SWAT KOHISTAN

GEORGE A. GRIERSON

BASED ON MATERIALS COLLECTED IN TORWAL
WITH A NOTE ON TORWAL AND ITS PEOPLE AND A MAP
BY

AUREL STEIN

GYAN

Published by

GYAN

Gyan Publishing House
5, Ansari Road
Daryaganj, New Delhi-110002
Phone: 011-47034999, 9811692060
E-mail: books@gyanbooks.com

Distribution Network
gyanbooks.com
India, USA, Canada, UK, Australia, France

ISBN : 978-81-212-3081-0 (PB)
First Published, London, 1929

2nd Impression 2020

Printed at: Gyan Press, Delhi.

Torwali
Author: George A. Grierson

TŌRWĀL AND ADJACENT TRACTS
IN
SWĀT AND INDUS KOHISTĀN

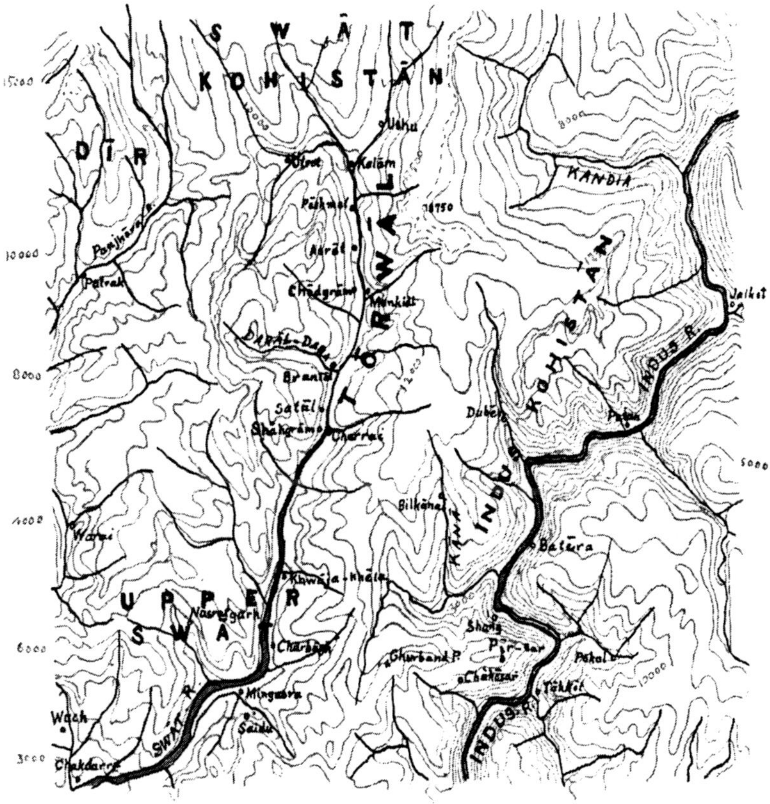

Scale:

Miles 10 5 0 10 20 30 Miles

PRIZE PUBLICATION FUND

VOL. XI

TORWALI

AN ACCOUNT OF A DARDIC LANGUAGE OF THE SWAT KOHISTAN

BY

SIR GEORGE A. GRIERSON,

O.M., K.C.I.E., PH.D., LITT.D., LL.D., D.LITT., VAGISA, F.B.A.
HON. VICE-PRESIDENT OF THE ROYAL ASIATIC SOCIETY.

BASED ON MATERIALS COLLECTED IN TORWAL

BY

SIR AUREL STEIN, K.C.I.E.

WITH A NOTE BY SIR AUREL STEIN ON TORWAL AND ITS PEOPLE
AND A MAP

PRINTED AND PUBLISHED BY THE
ROYAL ASIATIC SOCIETY
AND SOLD AT
74 GROSVENOR STREET, LONDON, W. 1
1929

CONTENTS

CONTENTS

INTRODUCTION

WHEN Sir Aurel Stein, in the course of his inquiries regarding the track of Alexander the Great in his march to the Indus, visited the valley of Tōrwāl, he recorded the three folktales and the list of typical words and sentences that form the basis of the present work. These he very kindly placed at my disposal, and I found that the linguistic information to be gathered from them was so full and of such importance, that it was impossible to refrain from subjecting them to a minute investigation. The results of this are contained in the following pages.

Very little has hitherto been known about Tōrwālī, the language of Tōrwāl. Biddulph, in his *Tribes of the Hindoo Koosh*,[1] called it " Torwâlâk ", and devoted a page and a half to the main features of its grammar, and about twelve pages to a very useful vocabulary. In the *Linguistic Survey of India*,[2] I have given a somewhat fuller account of the grammar, based on materials supplied by the late Sir Harold Deane. In neither case was the information sufficient for giving a complete description of the language. The folktales provided by Sir Aurel Stein now enable me to deal with it in much greater detail, and my account, if not pretending to be complete, can at least claim to be full enough to enable us to classify the language, and to describe its main features with some accuracy.

Tōrwālī is one of a number of languages generally grouped together under the name of " Kōhistānī ", as being spoken in the Panjkōrā, Swāt, and Indus Kōhistāns lying to the north of the Pēshāwar and Hazārā Districts of British India. Other members of the group are Gārwī, spoken in the Swāt Kōhistān above Tōrwālī, and Maiyā̃, spoken in the Mayō district of the Indus Kōhistān. Both of these are described

[1] Appendix D.
[2] Vol. viii, pt. ii, pp. 514 ff.

in the *Linguistic Survey*,[1] and are Dardic forms of speech. They belong to the Dard group of that linguistic family, being more nearly connected with Ṣiṇā and the Indianized Kāšmīrī than with the Khōwār of Chitrāl spoken to their immediate north. The materials in the following pages show that Tōrwālī in this respect is in entire agreement with the other Kōhistānī languages and that, like them, it also shows traces of a relationship with the Kāfir languages closer than that between it and Khōwār. Indeed, if the account given in the second folktale is to be accepted, the Tōrwāl country itself was once inhabited by Kāfirs that were conquered by Tōrwāls coming from Badakhshān. Such a legend must, however, be treated with reserve, for the word " Kāfir " is very loosely employed in Dardistān, and may well mean " any one who is not a Moslem ", instead of referring to the group of tribes in western Dardistān known by that name.

The claim that Tōrwāl tribes came from Badakhshān is of greater interest. Such traditions of national origin as exist in Dardistān all point to the Eranian country to its north and north-west as the original home of the Dards. The traditions of the Ṣiṇā tribes are confused, and do not help us, but the *Nīlamata*, the legendary history of the closely related Kāšmīrīs, which probably goes back to the sixth or seventh century A.D., states definitely[2] that Kashmīr in early times was invaded by tribes coming from " the Sand Ocean " to its north. So also, in Chitrāl, one of the largest tribes, the Ashimadek, claims to have come from Shighnān and Badakhshān, and Biddulph[3] puts their arrival as occurring in the beginning of the seventeenth century, a theory which is not inconsistent with the Tōrwāl account given in the second folktale. Lastly, as Dr. Morgenstierne[4] has shown, the Bašgalī, or Katī, Kāfirs, who inhabit the country to the west

[1] Gārwī, vol. viii, pt. ii, pp. 507 ff. Maiyā, id., pp. 522 ff.
[2] See *ZDMG.* lxvi, p. 74.
[3] Op. cit., p. 63.
[4] *Report on a Linguistic Mission to Afghanistan*, p. 41.

of Chitrāl, came to their present seat from Ktivi in northern Afghanistan some twelve generations ago. We thus see that every definite tradition of the Dards tells of migrations into Dardistān from the north or north-west in comparatively recent times ; but these can have been going on for unrecorded centuries, and the case of Yüdγā, an offshoot of Munjānī, now spoken in the Chitrāl country, shows that this Eranian infiltration is still going on at the present day.

On the other hand, south of Dardistān lie the plains of north-western India, in which Indo-Aryan languages are spoken. I have on previous occasions maintained that the Dardic languages cannot be classed as definitely Indo-Aryan, and, though my conclusions have been contested, I still see no reason for changing my opinion. At the same time I freely admit that from very early times there must have been infiltration of Indo-Aryan colonists into Dardistān.[1] This is borne out by linguistic evidence. The Indo-Aryan element in the Dardic languages is naturally most evident in the southern parts of Dardistān nearest India, and grows weaker as we go farther north into Chitrāl and Kāfiristān. It is in Kashmīr that the infiltration was strongest, and, through the influence of Kāšmīrī, its cognate Ṣiṇā, immediately to its north, shows more purely Indian traces than do the Khōwār of Chitrāl and the Kāfir dialects.[2] One of the most southern of these Dardic languages is Tōrwālī. As Sir Aurel Stein shows below, it is spoken in the Swāt Kōhistān, and we must expect it to show many signs of Indo-Aryan influence. This is the fact. In all its most typical features, it is a true Dardic language. Its speakers count in twenties, not in tens as in India ; the Old Present has become the Future, as in Eranian ; intervocalic occlusives are not necessarily

[1] In the case of Kashmīr, this infiltration is recorded in the *Nīlamata*, and has been so strong that it would almost justify us in calling Kašmīrī, although it has a Ṣiṇā basis, an Indo-Aryan language.

[2] Dr. Morgenstierne himself (op. cit., p. 68), although he maintains that all the Dardic languages are Indo-Aryan, sees traces of Eranian affinities in Bašgalī Kāfir.

elided, there is frequent interchange of surds and sonants, sonant aspirates are disaspirated, consonants are epenthetically affected by a following palatal sound, conjunct consonants are simplified without lengthening a preceding short vowel, initial *r* always becomes *ž*, intervocalic *r* is always elided, and so on for other typical Dardic phonetic changes enumerated in § 7 below. On the other hand, we see Indo-Aryan influence in the fact that while Dardic languages preserve conjunct consonants containing a sibilant or *r*, Tōrwālī treats these as they are treated in India proper.[1] Here, I am stating facts only in the most general terms, and for details I must refer the reader to the pages of the present work that deal with phonetics, which are summed up on pp. 20 ff.

Tōrwālī is spoken in a mountainous country, where intercommunication is not easy, and which has been the scene of frequent intertribal conflicts. It is natural that it should change from valley to valley, and should exhibit many dialectic variations. It is therefore not surprising that the three accounts of the language—that of Biddulph, that of the *Linguistic Survey*, and that given in these pages—should not always be in agreement. We do not know what particular dialect was described by Biddulph, but Sir Aurel Stein's inquiries showed that the account given in the *Linguistic Survey* correctly represents the form of Tōrwālī spoken in Chihil-dara, while the present folktales are in the dialect of Braniāl, a village which may be looked upon as the capital of the tribe.

Sir Aurel Stein has kindly provided the map of the Tōrwāl country prefixed to this volume, and also the note on Tōrwāl and its people, that immediately follows this Introduction. For convenience of reference, I have divided this work into four parts. Part I consists of Sir Aurel Stein's Note ; Part II deals with the language ; Part III consists of the Folktales and Typical Sentences; and Part IV of the Vocabulary and its connected Indexes.

[1] See § 8, below.

PART I

Note on Tōrwāl and its People

By SIR AUREL STEIN

Tōrwāl, where the Dardic tongue recorded in the stories dealt with by Sir George Grierson is spoken, comprises that alpine portion of the valley of the Swāt River which extends from Kalām down to the large village of Churṛai. It was visited by me as the first European in April, 1926. A descriptive account of the observations then made by me on my passage through the main valley will be found in chapters xii, xiii of my personal narrative of that tour in the dominion of the Miāngul of Swāt.[1]

The name Tōrwāl applies in a more specific way to a collection of hamlets counting about 120 households, and situated near the mouth of a side valley that debouches towards the right bank of the Swāt River about 5 miles above Braniāl, the present chief place of Tōrwāl. The alpine tract for which the name Tōrwāl is commonly used, in a more extended sense, includes the narrow side valleys that descend to the above indicated portion of the Swāt River course from the high snowy ranges forming the watershed towards the Indus on the east and towards the Panjkōrā on the west.

The whole of Tōrwāl forms part of the extensive but very sparsely inhabited mountainous area usually designated as the Swāt Kōhistān which is drained by the headwaters of the Swāt River. The hill tribes inhabiting it from the high glacier-crowned range towards Chitrāl in the north down to the open river valley below Churṛai in the south represent the remnant of that ancient Dardic-speaking race

[1] See Stein, *On Alexander's Track to the Indus*, Macmillan and Co., London, 1928.

which before the Paṭhān conquest may be assumed to have formed the main stock also of the population throughout the great and fertile territory now known as Upper and Lower Swāt.

Owing to the facilities for defence which the narrow and, in places, very difficult defiles passed by the Swāt River on its course here present, Tōrwāl appears for a long time past to have constituted a separate tribal territory, independent alike from the Yūsufzai clans established throughout the Swāt valley to the south and the Kōhistānī communities of Kalām, Ushu, and Utrōt. This accounts for the survival there of a separate form of Dardic speech, distinct from the Gārwī spoken in the Utrōt valley and about Kalām. In physical features the types presented by the Tōrwālīs of whom I obtained anthropometrical data, during my visit in 1926, distinctly recalled those I had observed among Chitrālīs and Tangīrīs, fair hair and light-coloured eyes being frequent.

The political dependence of Tōrwāl from Upper Swāt dates only from the year 1922, when the Miāngul ruler of Swāt extended his sway over the territory, using the opportunity offered by the absence of the fighting force of Tōrwālīs whom a feud with their northern neighbours had drawn off at the time to Kalām. No close estimate of the population of Tōrwāl was obtainable, but it can scarcely exceed 2,000 households in all, including semi-nomadic Gujars and a few small settlements of Chitrālī immigrants in Chihil-dara, Gurunai, and higher up.

The closer relations now established with the Paṭhān population of the open Swāt valley below Churṛai and the increasing trade intercourse under the Miāngul's beneficent rule are bound to lead to a steady spread of Paṣḥtō among the hill people. This will probably result in time in their becoming bilingual, as has been the case with several of the small communities of " Dardic " speech in the Indus Kōhistān.

The stories edited and translated by Sir George Grierson were taken down by me from the mouth of Muqadar, an intelligent inhabitant of Braniāl, occasionally acting as a reciter, with the help of my friend and old travel companion Rāja Shāh Ālam, nephew of Rāja Pakhtūnwālī, late ruler of Darēl and Tangīr.[1] I am indebted to this well-educated and capable scion of the Khushwakt family, now an exile, for much useful information.

[1] See, regarding Rāja Shāh Ālam and the help rendered by him during my passage through Darēl and Tangīr, *Innermost Asia*, i, pp. 15 sqq.

PART II

The Language

PHONETICS

1. Sir Aurel Stein, in recording these folktales, most rightly refrained from any attempt at securing uniformity of spelling, but, within the limited time at his disposal, wrote down for each word as nearly as possible the sound that he heard in each particular case. In recording a language that has no standard, and that has not been previously reduced to writing, it is found that the actual pronunciation of each word varies each time that it is uttered, according to its collocation in the sentence or to the mood of the speaker. In this way we often find the same word recorded as pronounced in different ways at different times. This is chiefly noticeable in the case of vowels, in which there is in the folktales, as recorded, great inconsistency, not only in the marks of length allotted to them, but even in their timbres. Thus, the word *ašū* " was ", is sometimes written *āšū*, and the agentive case of *pō* " a boy ", is at one time written *pōē*, and at another, *puē*. In the following pages I shall therefore confine myself to discussing the phonetics of consonants, and shall offer only one or two remarks on the subject of vowels.

2. We have Aphesis of *a* in *wā* " down " (Av. Skt. *ava*), in *wālī* (< *avapādita-*) " brought ", in *wat* (< *avâpta-*) " arrived ", and in *šū* instead of *ašū* " was " (§ 155). We have Aphesis of *ā* in *tanū* " own " (< *ātmanaḥ*), and *yē* (< *āyāti*) " comes ". On the other hand, we have Prothesis, or Metathesis of *ū* in *ūgū* (< *guru-*) " heavy ". In Kāšmīrī we find a Sanskrit *ū* regularly represented by *ǖ*, the pronunciation of which nearly resembles that of long *ī*, and which is represented by ي in the Persian character. Similarly, in Tōrwālī, we have *c̈iš* (? *cīš*) " the female breast " (< *cūcikā*);

dīmī " smoke " (< *dhūma-*) ; *sī* " the sun " (< *sūrya-*) ; and *pin* (? *pīn*) " the full moon " (< *pūrṇa-*).

3*a*. Turning to consonants, I begin with some general remarks. First of all, it must be noted that Biddulph, in his vocabulary, makes no distinction between cerebral and dental letters. This is no doubt due to the fact—more than once recorded by me—that the distinction in sound between these two classes of letters is not nearly so marked in Dardic as it is in Indian languages. Sounds that in India would be called cerebral are, in Dardic, merely alveolar.[1] Even natives of India, when recording Dardic words, are not always certain as to whether this sound is cerebral or dental. For this reason, we need not be surprised that so accurate an observer as Biddulph has failed to distinguish between these two groups of sounds. Sir Aurel Stein also informs me that, in the case of some Tōrwālī words, he has been doubtful whether a *t* or a *d* was cerebral or dental. It must therefore, in the case of words cited on the authority of Biddulph, be remembered that a *t* or a *d* may possibly be a *ṭ* or a *ḍ*, respectively.

3*b*. The peculiar Dardic cerebral sounds represented by *c̣*, *j̣*, *ṣ̌*, and *ẓ̌*, respectively, are no doubt heard in Tōrwālī, but their existence is not noted by Biddulph, nor had it been brought to the notice of Sir Aurel Stein when he recorded the specimens. They both, therefore recorded these sounds as ordinary *c*, *j*, *š*, and *ž*, respectively. That the *c* in such words as *cā* " three ", or *pūc* " a son ", is a palatalized cerebral is reasonably certain when we compare them with the Ṣiṇā *c̣e* " three ", and *puc̣* " a son ". In Ṣiṇā, an original *kṣ* is usually represented by *c̣*. In Tōrwālī it, as well as *ṣ*, is represented by *š* or *c*, as in *buš* " hunger " (< *bubhukṣā*) ; *kac* (< *kakṣē*) " near ", and other words noted below (§ 5*d*).

[1] Cf. Dr. G. Morgenstierne's remarks on the so-called " cerebral ", but really " alveolar ", *ṛ* of Kāfirī (*Report on a Linguistic Mission to Afghanistan*, p. 41). In Wai and Ashkund, not only does this alveolar *ṛ* occur, but also, alongside of it, there is heard the true cerebral *ṛ* of India.

Other Ṣiṇā words with these palatalized cerebrals are *sũçu* " straight ", and *ẓigu* or *jigu* " long ". The corresponding words in Tōrwālī, as recorded are *šũš* (Biddulph) and *jig* (Stein).

3*c*. Another general fact must be borne in mind—that in Tōrwālī, as in other Dardic languages, the Prakrit custom of eliding an intervocalic single consonant does not necessarily obtain. Thus, we have the intervocalic *t* preserved in such past participles as *sabāt* (< *saṁbhārita-*) " arranged " and others ; in *gīt* (< *gīta-*) " singing " ; *pattang* (so Bid., ? *patang*) (< *pataṅga-*) " a butterfly " ; *žit* (< *rīti*) " brass " ; *šet* (< *śarat-*) " autumn " ; *ned* (< *nada-*) " a river ", and so for other letters, as will be seen below. It is true that, as we shall also see, intervocalic consonants are sometimes elided, but in most cases they are retained. When so retained, they are liable to undergo other phonetic changes, such as the changing of surds to sonants, the change of *d* to *l*, of *j* to *ž*, and so on.

3*d*. The last remark leads us to one prominent peculiarity of Tōrwālī—that there is a very frequent, though not necessary,[1] interchange between surds and sonants. This is not confined to intervocalic consonants, though, naturally, the change of surd to sonant occurs most often in regard to such. With this must be considered another fact—that in Tōrwālī, as in other Dardic languages, with a very few exceptions, sonant consonants cannot be aspirated. Hence, when an aspirated surd (such, e.g., as *th*) is changed to a sonant, such a sonant is disaspirated, so that, e.g., the resultant of *th*, is *d*, not *dh*. The following are examples of the change of surds to sonants :—

-k- > *-g-*, in *agāš* (< *ēkādaśa*) " eleven " ; *bōgul* (< *kapōla-*, through **pōkala-*) " the cheek " ; *biginūsa* " to sell " ; (< *vikriṇītē*) ; *kāg* (written *kāgh* by Bid.) (< *kāka-*) " a crow " ; *kugū* (< *kukkuṭa-*) " a cock " ; *Sulaimānik*, N.P., sing. ag. *Sulaimānige* ; *tāgat* (Psht. *tāqat*) " strength " ; *nikūsa*,

[1] Cf. such cases as *pata-ge*, as well as *pade-ge*, backwards.

Past *nigāt*, "to emerge"; *siga* (Psht. *sika*) "lead"; *sugä* (< *sukarā*) "easy"; *sigal* (< *sikatā*) "sand". Cf. the remarks on *ke* or *ge*, the suffix of the Dative in § 29.

-kh- > *-g-*, see § 3*e*.

-c- < *-j-*, in *loj* (< *ruci-*) "light"; *śijū* (< *śuci-*) "clean"; *saj* (< Pr. *sacca-*) "truth".

-ṭ > *-ḍ* (*-ṛ*), in *gud* (? *guḍ*) (Psht. *guṭ*) "a corner"; *lāṭ* "a fight", Sing. Obl. *lāḍa*; *luṭ* or (Bid.) *lud* (? *luḍ*) "small", cf. Ksh. *lŏkaṭ*^{u}.

-ṭh- > *-ḍ-*, see § 3*e*.

t > *d*, in *āded* (Psht. *'ādat*) "accustomed"; *tē*, the postposition of the Instrumental, > *dē* after a vowel or *n* (§ 24); *kadak*, "how much?", cf. Ṣiṇā of Ḍāh-Hanū *katāk*; *pat* "behind", but *pata-ge* or *pade-ge* "backwards"; *śat* or *śad*, Auxiliary Verb (§ 169); *set* or *sed* (< *sahitē*) "with": *śidal* (< *śītala-*) "cold"; *sipad* (Psht. *ṣifat*) "praise"; *tid* (< *tikta-* > *titta-*) "bitter"; *žet* or *jada* "on".

th- > *d-*, see § 3*e*.

p > *b*, in *bariś* (< *pārśva-*) "a side"; *abōsa*, Past *āp* (< √*āp-*) "to come"; *ṭubak* (Psht. *ṭōpak*) "a rifle"; in √*pōw-* (< *prâpayati*), *-p-* has become *-w-*.

-s > *-z*, in *es*, Sing. Obl. of *ē*, this, but Sing. Loc. *ez-ma*; so *tes*, *tez-ma* (§ 96).

-ś > *-ž*, in *paś* or *paiž* (> *paśca-*) "behind"; *χužā* (Psht. *χuś*) "pleased"; *laś*, fem. *laž*, "bad"; *māś*, Sing. Nom. (before a vowel) *māž* (I, 2), Plur. Obl. *māža* "a man".

On the other hand, in some words a sonant becomes a surd, as in:—

g- > *k-*, in *kud* (? *kuḍ*) (Psht. *guḍ*) "lame".

-g > *-k*, in *jik* or *jig* (? *jik*, *jig*) (< *dīrgha-*, through **drīga-*) "long".

-gh > *-k* (? *-kh*), in *mek* (? *mekh*) (< *maigha-*) "hail".

-d > *-t*, in *umēt* (Psht. *umēd*) "hope"; *yāt* (Psht. *yād*) "remembrance".

-b > *-p*, in *ep* (Psht. *'aib*) "a fault".

-z > *-s*, in *awās* (Psht. *āwāz*) "a sound".

It will be observed that in Tōrwālī all these are final consonants.

3*e*. It is well known that Dardic languages possess no sonant aspirates. This is true, in the main, for Tōrwālī; but it does possess a few words, in which, probably for special causes, an original sonant aspirate has been retained. Such are :—

gh, in *ghō* " a horse ", borrowed from the Indian *ghōṛā*. The *gh* is evidently retained, in order to distinguish the word from *gō* " a bull ". Biddulph also gives *kāgh* " a crow "—a very doubtful word, unless he intends to represent *kaγ*, which is possible.

ḍh, in *ḍhē* " the belly ". A borrowed Indian word.

dh, in *gadhō* " an ass ". Here the *dh* is not original, but is a contraction of *dah* (Pr. *gaddaha-*); *dhū* " a daughter ". Here, also, the *dh* is a contraction of *duh* (Skt. *duhitṛ-*); *dhain* (or Bid. *daĩ*) " running " (cf. Skt. *dhāvana-*). Biddulph also gives *midhal* " a ram ", the derivation of which is unknown to me.

bh, in *bhā* " a brother ". This word has been specially tested, and is certain. The reason for the retention of the aspiration is unknown to me. There is no *bh* in the other Dardic forms of the word.

The following are examples of the regular disaspiration of sonant aspirates, whether original or derived (as above explained, § 3*d*) from surd aspirates.

gh > *g*, in *gā* (< *ghāsa-*) " grass "; *jig* or *jik* (< *dīrgha-*) " long "; √*gin-* (Lahndā √*ghinn-*) " take "; *gan* (< *ghana-*) " large "; *langī* (< √*laṅgh-*) " they crossed over ".

dh > *d*, in *dīmī* (< *dhūma-*) " smoke ".

kh > *gh* > *g*, in √*lig-* (< √*likh-*) " write "; but √*lek-* " count ".

ṭh > *ḍh* > *ḍ* (*ṛ*, *ṛ*), in *bēḍū* (< *upaviṣṭakaḥ* > *uvaïṭṭhaō*) " seated "; √*kuṭh-* " beat ", but *kuḍē-dū* " he beats "; *pēṛa* (< *pīṭhikā*) " a generation "; *pīḍ* (< *pṛṣṭha-* > *piṭṭha-*) " the back ".

th > *dh* > *d*, in *thū* (< *sthitakaḥ*) " is ". But, between vowels, this becomes *dū* (§ 158).

3*f*. As regards other consonants, we may note two instances of Aphaeresis in *pel* (< *pipīla*) " an ant ", and *buš* (? *buṣ̌*) (< *bubhukṣā* " hunger ". We have a curious instance of Metathesis in *bōgul* " the cheek ". The hypothetical stages of development of this word are *kapōla*- > **kabōla* > **bōkala*- > **bōgala*- > *bōgul*.

4. Turning now to single consonants, we have :—

-*k*- elided, in *niō* (< *nikaṭē*) " near ". But -*k*- is preserved in *bōgul* " above ". Cf. 3*d* for -*k*- > -*g*-.

-*g*- elided in *chal* (< *chagalī*) " a she-goat ". But cf. *bōgul* " above ".

gh- preserved in *ghō* " a horse ", see above, § 3*e*. But it generally becomes *g*, see above, § 3*e*.

-*c* > -*š*, in *ciš* (< *cūci*-) " the breast of a woman " (§ 2). Cf. *š* and *c*, below.

-*c* > -*j*. See above, § 3*d*.

-*j* optionally becomes -*ž*, in *kujū* or *kužū* " a dog " ; *biž* (< *bīja*-) " seed " ; *pāji* or *paiž* " after " ; *jada* or *žet* " on ". But elsewhere initial *j* seems to be preserved, as in *jib* (< *jihvā*) " tongue " ; *jang* (< *jaṅghā*) " leg ". Cf. √*jan*- (√*jñā*-) " know " ; √*ji*- (√*jan*-) " be born ". The *ž* is hardened to *š*, in *mūj* or *mūš* " before ".

-*ṭ*- > -*ḍ*- > -*ṛ*-, and is then treated exactly like *ṛ*. See below.

ḍh- is preserved in *ḍhē* " the belly ". No other example. See § 3*e*.

-*t*- is preserved in *gīt* (*gīta*-) " singing " ; *pattang* (Bid. ? *patang*) (< *pataṅga*-) " a butterfly " ; *žit* (< *rīti*-) " brass " ; *šet* (< *śarat*-) " autumn " ; *ugāt* (< *udgāta*-) " gone away " ; *sabāt* (< *saṁbhārita*-) " arranged ", and other past participles given in § 196.

t > *d*. See above, § 3*d*.

-*t* > -*d* > -*l*, in *ūtal* (? *ūthal*) (< *utthita*-), high (Bid.) ; *balai* (< *vāta*-), wind ; *sigal* (< *sikatā*) " sand " ; *thalū* (< *sthāpitaḥ*) " placed ".

-t- elided in many past participles, such as *gā* (< *gataḥ*) and others in §§ 182 ff., 190 ff. So also in the 3rd sing. Future (Old Present), as in *kuḍī* (< *kuṭṭayati*), he will beat. In other past participles, the *-t-* is retained (see § 196).

-th > *c*, in feminines, by epenthesis due to an original palatal vowel or semi-vowel following. See § 48, and compare the corresponding change in Kāšmīrī.

-d- retained in *ned* (< *nada-*) " a river ".

-d- elided, in *agāš* (< *ēkādaśa*) " eleven " ; *paī* (< *pāda-*) " a foot " ; *hü* (< *hṛd-*) " the heart ".

-d > *-l*, in *talā* (< *tadā*) " then " ; √*til-* (< √*tīd-*) " go ". According to Rāma Tarkavāgīsa's *Prākṛta-Kalpataru*, II, iii, 25, the same change occurs in Ābhīrikā Prakrit.

-d > *-l* > *-ž*, in feminines, by epenthesis due to an original palatal vowel or semivowel following. See § 48, and compare the corresponding change in Kāšmīrī.

d- > *ḍ-*, in *ḍiṭ* (< *dṛṣṭā*) " seen ". This is a solitary case, and the reason is obvious. So Ksh. has *ḍīṭh*[u].

dh preserved. See above (§ 3*e*).

-dh- elided in √ *bū-* (< *bōdhati* " see ".

-dh- > *-h-*, in *lehir* (< *rudhirā*) " red ".

-n- elided in *māš* (< *manuṣya-*) " a man ". This is the only case noted.

-p-, is elided in *kūi* (< *kūpikā*) " a well " ; *thalū* (< *sthāpitaḥ*) " placed ".

p becomes vocalized (through *v*) in *ū* (< *āp-*) " water ".

-f- > *-p-*, in *kufār* or *kupār* " a Kāfir ".

bh preserved. See above (§ 3*e*).

bh- > *h-*, in √*hō-* (< √*bhū-*), " become ".

-m- remains unchanged in *nām* (< *nāma*) (Ts.) " a name " ; but Ksh. *nāv*. Cf. *-v-* > *-m-*, below.

y- remains unchanged, as in *yo* (< *yavaḥ*) " barley " ; *yē* (< *āyāti*) " he will come ".

-aya- > *-e-* in *šen* (< *śayana-*) " a bedstead ".

r- > *l-*, in *lāṭ* (< √ *raṭ-*) " a fight " ; *lehir* (< *rudhirā*) " red " ; *loj* (< *ruci-*) " light ".

r- > *l-* > *ž-*, in *žed* (< *rakta-*) "blood"; *žamung* (Bur. *rabong*), "a bean"; *žon* (< *raṇḍa*) "a widower" *žōš* (> *rōṣa-*) "anger"; *žāt* (< *rātri-*) "night", *žit* (< *rīti-*) "brass". In Ksh. the epenthetic change of *l* to *j* is regular. Cf. *l* > *j*, *ž*, below.

-r is always elided, as in *ūgū* (< *guru-*) "heavy"; *umu* (Psht. *'umr*) "age"; *angā* (< *aṅgāra-*) "fire"; *āngī* (< *aṅguri-*) "a finger"; √*ka-* (< √ *kṛ-*) "do"; *kera* (< *kartari-* > **kaḍari-*) "a knife"; *kū* (< *krūra-*) "hard"; *cai* (Ṣiṇā *char*) "a cliff"; *cau* (Ṣiṇā *cār*) "four"; √*ciā-* (< *cārayati*) "graze"; *cū* (< *chūrikā*) "a dagger"; *cimu* (Bur. *comar*) "iron"; *huša* (Psht. *huṣyār*) "intelligent"; *hwa* (Psht. *χwār*) "destitute"; *Jebēr*, "N. of a place", Obl. Sing. *Jebēya*; *jagō* (Psht. *jigar*) "liver"; *tiā* (Psht. *taiyār*) "ready"; *Tōwāl*, Tōrwāl; *dū* (< *dūra-*) "far"; √*pai-* (< *prērayati*) "send"; *pō* (Munjānī *pūr*) "a boy"; *pay(im)* (< *parē*) "across" (cf. Ksh. *pạ̄rimᵘ*); √*mā-* (< *mārayati*) "kill"; *maiyūsa* (< *mṛ-*) "to die"; *šā* (< *śiraḥ*) "head"; *šet* (< *śarat*) "autumn"; *sabāt* (< *saṁbhārita-*) "arranged"; *sugā* (< *sukarā*) "easy".

-ṛ- (*-ḍ-*) and *-ṛh-* (*-ḍh-*) are elided, exactly following *-r-*. Thus, *ašay* (Psht. *ašāṛai*) "an apricot"; *kugū* (< *kukkuṭa-* > **kukuḍa-*) "a cock"; *kol* (< *kuṭila-* > **kuḍila-*) "crooked"; *ghō* (Hindī *ghōṛā*) "a horse", *dö* (< *dāḍhikā*) "the beard"; *niō* (< *nikaṭē* > **niaṛē*) "near"; *šeš* (< *ṣōḍaśa*) "sixteen".

-ṭ > *-ḍ* > *-r* (? *-ṛ*), in √*por-* (< *sphōṭayati*) "break" (trans.); √*pūr-* (< *sphuṭati*) "break" (intrans.). Both these words come from Biddulph, who does not distinguish between *r* and *ṛ*. We should probably read *poṛ-* and *puṛ-*.

-l- is preserved in *kumul* (< *kōmala-*) "soft".

-l- > *-j-* *-ž-*, in *kujū* or *kužū* (< *kaulēya-*) "a dog". Cf. *r-* > *l-* > *ž-*, above.

v- > *b-*, in *balai* (< *vāta-*) "wind"; √*ban-* (< *varṇayati*) "say"; *basān* (< *vasanta-*) "spring"; so *-v-*, in √*āb-* (Pr. *āvaï*) "come".

ava > *ō*, in *ōš* (< *avaśyāya-*) "ice"; *yo* (< *yavaḥ*) "barley".

-v- > *-m-*, in *nam* (< *nava-*) "new"; *nōm* (< *nava*) "nine". Cf. *-m-* and *ava* > *ō* above.

š and *c* are interchangeable, as in *pašin* or *pacin* "a bird"; so √*cuj-* (< *śudhyatē*) "learn". Cf. *-c* > *-š*, above.

ś- > *š-*, in *šā* (< *śiraḥ*) "the head"; *šidal* (< *śītala-*) "cold".

-ś- > *-š-*, in *daš* (< *daśa*) "ten"; *diš* (< *diś-*) "direction"; *dvāš* (< *dvādaśa*) "twelve", and so other similar numerals.

-ś- > *-h-* or elided, in *bʻhēṭh* or *bēṭh* (< *upaviṣṭa-*) "seated".

ṣ > *š* (? *ṣ̌*), in *šō* (? *ṣ̌ō*) (< *ṣaṣ-*) "six"; *tiš* (? *tiṣ̌*) (< *tṛṣā*) "thirst"; *mūš* (? *mūṣ̌*) (< *mūṣaka-*) "a mouse"; *šeš* (? *ṣ̌eš*) (< *ṣōḍaśa*) "sixteen".

-s- is preserved in √*has-* (< *has-*) "laugh".

-s- is elided in *šū* (< *svasā*) "a sister"; *gā* (< *ghāsa-*) "grass". Cf. *-sy* > *-s* > elided in § 5*d*.

s > *h*, in *hut* (< *supta-*) "slept"; *māh* (< *māsa*) "a month".

-h- is elided in *bʻhēṭh* or *bēṭh* "seated"; *set* or *sed* (< *sahitē* > Ksh. *sütʻ*) "with".

5*a*. As regards conjunct consonants, we can consider them under the following heads :—

A. *Conjuncts of Class Consonants.*—As in Prakrit and Apabhraṁśa, the first consonant of the conjunct is usually dropped; but, as in other Dardic languages, the remaining consonant is not doubled. Thus :—

-kt > *-t* > *-d*, in *žed* (< *rakta-*) "blood"; *tid* (< *tikta-*) "bitter".

-cch > *-ch* > *-š*, in *tuš* (< *tuccha*) "empty"; *pišul* (< *picchala-*) "smooth".

-ṭṭ > *-ṭh*, in √*kuṭh-* (< √*kuṭṭ-*) "beat".

-ṭṭh > *-ṭh* > *-ḍ*, in *pīḍ* (Pr. *piṭṭha-*) "the back".

-ḍḍ > *-ḍ* > *-r* (? *ṛ*), in *har* (? *haṛ*) (< *haḍḍa-*) "a bone" (Bid.).

-tt > *-t*, in *dit* (< *datta-*) "given".

-tth > *-t* (? *-th*), in *ūtal* (? *ūthal*) (< *utthita-*) " high " (Bid.).

-dg > *-g*, in *ugāt* (< *udgāta-*) " arose ".

-pt > *-t*, in *ucit* (< *utkṣipta-*) " arose " ; *wat* (< *avâpta-*) " arrived " ; *sat* (< *sapta-*) " seven " ; *hut* (< *supta-*) " slept ".

5*b*. B. *Nasal Conjuncts.*—(*a*) If the Nasal precedes :—

-ṅk > *-ng*, in *tongū* (? *ṭongū*) (< *ṭaṅkakaḥ*) " a pear " (Bid.).

-ṅgh > *-ng*, in *jang* (< *jaṅghā*) " the leg ".

-ñc > *-nj*, in *panj* (< *pañca*) " five ".

-ṇḍ > *-n*, in *ān* (< *aṇḍa-*) " an egg " ; *tunōl* (< *taṇḍula-*) " rice " ; *dan* (< *daṇḍa-*) " a handle " ; (*žon* < *raṇḍa-*) " a widower ".

-nt > *-n*, in *dan* (< *danta-*) " a tooth " ; *basān* (< *vasanta-*) " spring " ; *himān* (< *himanta-*) " winter ".

-nth > *-nd* or *-n*, in √*gan-* (< √*granth-*) " bind " ; *pand* or *pan* (< *panth-*) " a road ".

-ndh > *-n*, in *an* (< *andha-*) " blind " ; *kan* (< *skandha-*) " the shoulder ".

(*b*) If the Nasal follows :—

-gn > *-g*, in *lagū* (< *lagnakaḥ*) " he went near ".

-tsn > *nh* > *n*, in *yun* (< *jyōtsnā*, Pr. *joṇhā*) " the moon ".

-pn > *n*, in *sen* (< *svapna-*) " a dream ".

-tm > *t*, in *tanū* (< *ātman-*) " own ". Cf. Ksh. *tąn*ᵘ.

-tm > *p*, *-b* in *pāē* " he ", and *āban* " self " ; both < *ātman-*. See §§ 129, 138.

5*c*. C. *Semi-vowel Conjuncts.* (*a*) If the semi-vowel is *y* :—

jy- > *y-*, in *yun* (< *jyōtsnā*) " the moon ".

-ṭy > *-ṭ* > *-ḍ* > *-r* (? *-ṛ*), in *nār* (? *nāṛ*) (< *nāṭya-*) " dancing " (Bid.).

-ḍy > *-r* (? *-ṛ*), in *kur* (? *kuṛ*) (< *kuḍya-*) " a wall ".

-dy > *-j*, in *aj* (< *adya*) " to-day ".

-dhy- > *-j*, in √*buj-* (< *budhyatē*) " hear " ; √*cuj-* (< *śudhyatē*) " learn ".

(*b*) If the semi-vowel is *r*. (1) If the *r* precedes :—

-rṇ > *-n*, in *kan* (< *karṇa*) " the ear " ; *pin* (< *pūrṇa-*) " the full moon ".

-rt > *-r*, in *kera* (< *kartari-*) " a knife ". Here the second *r* has been elided. See above (§ 4).

-rth > *-th*, *-t*, *-d*, in *sāth*, *sāt*, or (before *m*) *sād* (< *sārtha-*) " with ".

-rdabh > *dh*, in *gadhō* (< *gardadhaḥ*) " an ass " (§ 3*e*).

-rdr > *-ž* (? *-ẓ̌*), in *öž* (? *öẓ̌*) (< *ardra-*) " mud " (Bid.).

-rdh > *-r*, in *ar* (< *ardha-*) " half ".

-rm > *-m*, in *kam* (< *karma* " work "; *cam* (< *carma*) " skin ".

-ry > *-r* > elided, in *sī* (< *sūrya-* > **sīre-* > *sī*) " the sun " (§ 2).

-rv > *-r* > elided, in *de* (< *darvī* > **darī* > *de*) " a spoon ".

-ršt > *t*, *d*, in *pat* or *pad* (< Av. *paršti-*) " behind ".

(2) If the *r* follows :—

kr-, *-kr* > *k*, in *kū* (< *krūra-*) " hard "; *cuk* (< *cukra-*) " acid ".

-kr > *š* (? *ṣ̌*), in *ceš* (? *ceṣ̌*) (< *cakra-*) " a circle " (Bid.).

gr- > *g-*, in √*gan-* (> √*granth-*) " bind "; *gām* (< *grāma-*) " a village ".

tr- > *c-* (? *ç-*), in *cā* (? *çā*) (< *tri-* " three "; *ceš* (? *çeš*) (< *trayōdaśa*) " thirteen " (Bid.).

tr- > *tl-* (? *ṭl-*), in *tlūi* (? *ṭlūi*) (< *tṛtīya-*) " third " (Bid.). Cf. G. *pult*, P. *puṭhlē* (< *putra-*) " a son ".

-tr > *-t*, in *kēt* (< *kutra*) " where ? "; *žāt* (< *ratri-*) " night ". This is the ordinary Prakrit change.

-ttr > *-t*, in *pet* (< *pattra-*) " a feather ". This also is the Prakrit change.

-tr > *-c* (? *-ç*), in *pūc* (? *pūç*) (< *putra-*) " a son ". This is the Dardic change.

dr- > *d-*, in *daš* (? *daṣ̌*) (< *drākṣā*) " a grape ". This is the Prakrit change.

dr- > *j-* (? *ẓ̌-*), in *jīg* (? *ẓ̌īg*) (< *dīrgha-* > **drīga-*) " long ". This is the Dardic change.

-dr > *-n*, in *nīn* (< *nidrā* > **niddā* > **nindā*) " sleep ". This is a common Indian change.

pr- > *p-*, in √*pōw-* (< *prâpayati*) " receive " ; √*pai-* (< *prêrayati*) " send".

bhr- > *bh-*, in *bhā* (< *bhrātā*). See § 3*e*, above.

vr- > *b-*, in √*baj-* (< √*vraj-*), " go ".

(*c*) If the semi-vowel is *v* :—

-jjv > *-j*, in *ūjal* (< *ujjvala-*) " white ".

-tv > *-d*, in *bud* (< *bahutva-*) " many ".

dv- > *d-*, in *der* (< *dvar-*) " a door ".

dv- > *b-* and *du-*, in *bī* (< *dvitīya-*) " again " ; *duyi* (< *dvitīya-*) " second ".

-hv > *-b*, in *jib* (< *jihvā*) " the tongue ".

(*d*) If the semi-vowel is *l* :—

-ld > *-l*, in *gal* (< *galda-*) " abuse".

5*d*. D. *Sibilant Conjuncts.*

-śc > *-š*, *-ž*, in *paš* or *paiž* (< *paśca-*) " after " (§ 3*d*).

-śy > *-š*, in √*paš-* (< *paśyati*) " see ".

śv, *šv* > *s*. See Article *sā* in Vocabulary.

-ṣk > *-kh* > *-g*, in *šug*(*il*) (< *śuṣka-* > **sukha-* > *suga-*), " dry " ; *nigālī* (< *niṣkālayati*) " he will extract ".

-ṣṭ > *-ṭ*, in *ḍiṭ* (< *dṛṣṭā*) " seen ".

-ṣṭ > *-d* (? *-ḍ*) in *mid* (? *miḍ*) (< *miṣṭa*) " sweet ".

-ṣṇ > *-šun*, in *kišun* (< *kṛṣṇa-*) " black ".

-ṣp (? *-ṣy*) > *-š*, in *pašū* (< *puṣpa-* or *puṣya-*) " a flower ".

kṣ > *š* (? *ṣ̌*) or *c* (? *ç*), in *daš* (? *daṣ̌*) (< *drākṣā*) " a grape " (Bid.) ; *buš* (? *buṣ̌*) (< *bubhukṣā*) " hunger " (Bid.) ; *pacin* (Bid.) (? *paçin*) or *pašin* (? *paṣ̌in*) (< *pakṣin-*) " a bird " ; *achī* (? *açī*) (< *akṣi-*) " the eye ") ; *kac* (? *kaç*) (< *kakṣē*) " near " ; *ciī* (? *çūī*) (< *kṣīra-*) " milk ".

-tkṣ > *-c*, in *ucit* (< *utkṣipta-*) " arose ".

-kṣṇ > *-n*, in *tīn* (< *tīkṣṇa-*) " sharp ".

-kṣm > *-m*, in *pām* (< *pakṣman-*) " wool ".

sk- > *k-*, in *kan* (< *skandha-*), " the shoulder ".

-st > *-t*, in *nāt* (< *nasta-*) " the nose " ; *hat* (< *hasta-*) " the hand ".

-st > *-s*, in *dōs* (Psht. *dōst*) " a friend ". This is a borrowed word.

str- > *c-* (? *ç-*) in *cī* (? *çī*) (< *strī*) "a woman". Cf. Sh. *cäi*, *çäi*.

sth- > *th-*, in *thalū* (< *sthāpitaḥ*) "placed"; *thū* (< *sthitakaḥ*) "is".

sph- > *p-*, in √*pūr-* (< *sphuṭati*) "break" (intrans.); √*por-* (< *sphōṭayati*) "break" (trans.).

-sm > *-zm*, in *àzmān* (Psht. *āsmān*) "heaven". A deformation of a borrowed word. Cf. *es*, sing. obl. of *ē* "this", sing. loc. *ez-ma*.

-sy > *-s* > elided, in *aĩ* (< *āsya-*) "the mouth". Cf. Ksh. *ạsᵘ*, and (§ 4) *-s-* elided

sv- > *s-*, in *sen* (< *svapna-*) "a dream".

sv- > *šu*, in *šū* (< *svasā*) "a sister". This change of *s* to *š* seems to be abnormal. In *sā* < *śvāsa-*, there is a reverse change. See Article *sā* in the Vocabulary.

-ṁs > *-s*, in *mās* (< *māṁsa-*) "meat".

6. *Summary.*—It will have been observed that, while many of the above phonetic changes are the same as those found in Indian Prakrits, many are of a quite different character, and are peculiar to Tōrwālī and other Dardic languages. It is natural that in Dardic, even if we suppose it to be not of Indian origin, some of its phonetic changes should be the same as those that have occurred in India, and also in other Indo-European languages, such as, for instance, the Romance forms of speech. But there are other cases in which a sound follows Indian analogies in one word, and Dardic analogies in another. For example, *tr* in *rātri-* "night", becomes *t* in the Tōrwālī *žāt*. Here we have an Indian change. On the other hand, when the *tr* in *putra-* "a son", becomes *c* (or *ç*) in Tōrwālī *pūc* (*pūç*), we recognize a Dardic change, unlike anything found in India. Tōrwālī is one of the most southern of the Dardic languages, and lies close to the Indian border. Such facts show that in it there has been a certain admixture of Indian elements, and I here give a list of those sound-changes which seem to me to be non-Indian, and to be purely Dardic. I pay no attention to those cases in which Dardic and Indian

developments coincide, as it is usually impossible to say whether they are independent Dardic forms or are due to borrowing.

7. We must first note such general peculiarities as (1) the alveolar pronunciation of sounds that in India would be cerebral, (2) the fact that intervocalic single occlusives are not necessarily elided,[1] (3) the frequent interchange of surds and sonants,[2] (4) the disaspiration of sonant aspirates, (5) the fact that certain consonants are epenthetically affected by a following palatal vowel or semi-vowel, (6) the frequent interchange of *c* and *š*, and of *j* and *ž*, and (7) the almost certain existence of the cerebralized palatals *ç*, *j̣*, *ṣ̌*, and *ẓ̌*.

For particular consonantal changes, we have *d* > *l*, and *d* > *l* > *ž*; initial *y* remaining unchanged, while initial *v* > *b*; change of initial *r* (through *l*) to *ž*; *l* > *j* > *ž*; intervocalic *š* does not necessarily become *h*, but does so in one recorded instance; *cch* > *š*; *ṇḍ*, *nt*, *nth*, *ndh*, all > *n*; *tm* > both *t* and *p*; *jy* > *y*; *kr* > *š* (? *ṣ̌*); *tr* > *c* (? *ç*) and *tl* (? *ṭl*); *dr* > *j* (? *j̣*, *ẓ̌*); *dv* > both *b* and *d*; *kṣ* > *š* (? *ṣ̌*) and *c* (? *ç*); *kṣm* > *m*; *st* > *t*; *str* > *c* (? *ç*); *sph* > *p*; and, in one case, *sv* > *šu*. Intervocalic *n* is occasionally, and intervocalic *r* and *ṛ* (including *ṛy* and *rv*) are always, elided.

The only prominent Dardic peculiarities that I have not noted in Tōrwālī are the preservation unchanged of *st*, and of other sibilant conjuncts such as *sm*, *sv*, preserved as *sp*; and the regular preservation of initial *r*-compounds, such as *pr-* and the like. In such cases, Tōrwālī has, with modifications, followed the Indian custom.

8. Attention may here be drawn to one prominent feature of Tōrwālī which is of some general interest. It is that Tōrwālī is an absolutely unwritten language. It is known

[1] Here, however, Tōrwālī agrees with Apabhraṁśa Prakrit. As Apabhraṁśa was a North-Western dialect, it may be suggested that it has here fallen under the influence of Dardic.

[2] Here also, so far as concerns intervocalic surds, there is agreement with Apabhraṁśa. The same remarks apply also here.

only as it has come out of the mouths of its speakers, and not from any indigenous document; and, *pace* my friends who might wish, in regard to it, to follow the rules of Indo-European philology, these rules cannot be applied in all their strictness to such a language. The philological rules to which we are accustomed are based everywhere on written documents, whether Sanskrit, Latin, Greek, Gothic, English, or what not. We have such languages in a form that had become petrified by the fact that they were written. The written form represents the language as it was formalized at some definite period, or periods, of time. But a spoken language is never petrified, never formalized. It is always changing, and is never resting. At each particular moment it is actually passing through a process of development on its own lines, and the language as a whole of fifty years ago is not the same as that spoken at the present day. Moreover, on the same day, no two persons speak exactly the same language—one will say, for instance *pata-ge*, while another will say *pade-ge*, for " backwards ".[1] Again, in a spoken language, as distinct from one the standard of which has been fixed by writing, all words do not develop at the same rate. Different causes retard the development of particular words. Such a reason might be religious associations, or old memories that keep the word in its ancient form, or it might be—the most important of all—the demand for intelligibility. As an example, let us take the old Sanskrit word *ghōṭa-* " a horse ". If we followed the rules that, in the case of other similar words, obtain in Tōrwālī, the *ṭ* would become *ṛ* and would then be elided, and the aspirated sonant *gh* would lose its aspiration, so as to become *g*. The resultant Tōrwālī word would thus be *gō*. But, unfortunately, in Tōrwālī, the word *gō* is already taken up for another purpose, and means " bull ".

[1] The same is true, say, for colloquial English. We might take three persons, one of whom will use the literary " are not ", another will say " aren't ", while the third will say " aint ". It is obvious that the phonetic rule that accounts for the literary " are not " will not account for the simultaneous existence of both " aren't " and " aint ".

As the first object of all language is not to oblige phoneticians, but to be intelligible, the normal development of *ghōṭa-* was stopped at an earlier stage, and the word remained as *ghō*—useful and intelligible, but disappointing to framers of phonetic rules. To take a parallel example from Indian colloquial speech :—according to the Prakrit grammarians and the literature standardized by them, the Sanskrit word *kāka-* " a crow ", became the literary Prakrit *kāa-*, the line of development being *kāka-* > *kāga-* > *kāa*. But the colloquial language felt the uncertainty of the word *kāa*. It could, it is true, represent *kāka-* " a crow ", but it could also represent *kāca-* " crystal ", and *kāya-* " the body ". As the speakers looked upon language, not as a machine for concealing thought, but as a machine for expressing it, and felt that *kāa-* in ordinary use would be unintelligible, it stopped its development at the second stage, *kāga-*, and, as we know from Hemacandra IV, 396, kept the word in that form for centuries after the literary language had given its blessing to *kāa*. Thus, *kāg* it has remained in Hindī to the present day. If this could occur in a language which had a written literature to act as a standard for normal pronunciation, what may we not expect from a language like Tōrwālī which has no written literature at all. In such a language, phonetic development in no way progresses so evenly as our comparative philologists would have us believe. Some words progressed along " regular " lines, as the Sanskrit *gāv-* has become the Tōrwālī *gō* ; and others, in the same language, stopped their developments at the point where unintelligibility began. In the history of a language that has never been recorded in writing, and which at every moment of its life—for it, and it only, is really living—is developing on its own lines and at its own speed, halting here, progressing there, at no date is it possible, as some philologists would have us do, to draw a line, and to say that here it will be found that all words have arrived at the same stage of development. Tōrwālī, like all the Dardic languages, gives many examples of this. Some words are in one stage of development, and others are in another. In one word an intervocalic *t* may be elided, in another it may be changed to *d*, and in yet another to *l*. No general law will cover all these cases. Or, again, one man will develop a word in one way, and his neighbour (though speaking the same language) in another ; or the same man, as the spirit moves him, will develop *dv*, into *b*, at one time, and into *d* at another. We cannot say that there are any definitely fixed rules for the development of an unwritten language. We must be content with acknowledging the existence of a general tendency towards one line of development. To attempt to twist such a tendency into a universal law is doing that for which the Indian Prakrit Grammarians have been condemned by every European scholar who has studied them.

The Article

9. The numeral *ē* " one ", serves as an indefinite article. Examples will be found under the head of numerals (§ 51).

As in other connected languages, a demonstrative pronoun is often found where we should employ the definite article. Numerous examples will be found in the sections dealing with pronouns.

Declension

Gender of Nouns

10. The feminine gender certainly exists as a grammatical form, but is most easily observed in the case of adjectives and participles. As regards nouns, there are, as usual, certain cases in which different words are employed to distinguish gender. For human beings, such are :—

Masculine	*Feminine.*
bāp " father " (L. 47).	*yai* " mother " (L. 48).
bhā " brother " (L. 49).	*šū* " sister " (L. 50).
māš " man " (L. 51).	*chī* (I, 51, 53), *cī* (? *çī*) " woman " (L. 57).
pūc " son " (L. 55).	*dhū* " daughter " (L. 56).

For animals, we have :—

ghō " horse " (L. 138).	*ghē* " mare " (L. 139).
gō " bull " (L. 142).	*gā* " cow " (L. 143).
kujū " dog " (L. 146).	*kijī* " bitch " (L. 147).
birāṭ " he-goat " (L. 150).	*chal* " nanny-goat " (L. 151 ; II, 18).
husai " stag " (L. 153).	*husī* " doe " (L. 154).

A few words occurring in the folktales are feminine by meaning. Such are :—

chī (? *çī*) " a wife " (I, 51, 53).
rājgana " a queen " (III, 47 ff.).
saran " a girl " (III, 17 ff.).

11. Other words can be identified as feminine by their terminations, by the corresponding Paṣtō gender, or by words with which they are in agreement. Such are :—

arzī " a request " (III, 5).
χušālī " happiness ", in *χušālī Xudā Pāk dī-cī* " God, the Pure has given happiness " (I, 20).
mubārakī " congratulation " (I, 36).
pādšāhī, *bādšāhī* " rule ", in *pādšāhī hī* " his rule became " (III, 46, so 61).
māliyā " tax " (II, 6).
bāt " a word ", in *mēlī bāt banī* " said the same word " (I, 35).
duwā " a prayer " (II, 42 ff.).
majlas " an entertainment ", as in *majlas ašī* " there was an entertainment " (I, 18).
mukadima " a quarrel " (II, 6).
pan, *pand* " a road ", in *pan na hī* " there was no road " (III, 57) ; *mē aj cir pand kī-jī* " I have walked a long way to-day " (L. 224).
sē " a bridge ", in *sē telī* " he broke the bridge " (II, 13).
yāp " a canal ", in *tē yāp nigālī* " he excavated that canal " (III, 54).
zōg " noise ", in *derē zōg hī* " there was a noise at the door " (III, 20).
žāt " night ", in *ar žāt hī* " it was midnight " (III, 43).

12. As a rule, no means are available for testing the genders of the nouns occurring in the Folktales. Indeed, only of the words given in the above lists is the gender fairly certain. Biddulph, however, in his vocabulary marks the gender of every noun mentioned by him, and this information is taken from it, and recorded again in the vocabulary appended to the present account of the language.

Declension

13. The following may be taken to be the principal forms in the declension of *šir*, a house :—

	Singular.	*Plural.*
Nominative	*šir*	*šir*
Agentive	*širē, šir*	*šir*, (?) *širā*
Accusative	*šir*	*šir*
Instrumental	*širē-dē*	*širā-dē*
Dative	*šir-kē*, (*-gē, -yē*)	*širā-kē*
Ablative	*širā, šir-mā, -kĕjā*	*širā-mā, -kĕjā*
Genitive	*šir-si*	*širā-si*
Locative	*širē, šir-mē*	*širā-mē*

The above paradigm is to be taken only as a general guide. No complete paradigm of any single word can be gathered from the forms given in the Folktales. Details for each case are given below.

14. **Singular Nominative.**—Naturally, no remarks are necessary for this case.

15. **Singular Vocative.**—Two Vocatives occur in the Folktales. In *Sulaimāniga* " O Sulaimānik ! " (III, 40), the Interjection is probably *a*, and the final *k*, coming between two vowels, has been softened to *g* (§ 3*d*). The other vocative is *ē zuwān* " O youth ! " (I, 47), and calls for no remarks.

16. **Singular Accusative.**—The object of a transitive verb takes no special termination. In other words, the Accusative is the same in form as the Nominative. Thus, *ū nīgal* " draw water ! " (L. 237) ; *bayān kō* " recite ! " (II, 35) ; *dērā wadān kō*

"put the house in order!" (I, 25); *dērā janā* "make ye the house clean!" (I, 27); *duwā kō* "grant thou a favour!" (II, 44); *gil diū-šad* "was giving bread" (I, 29); *χānī nimā-dū* "(I) desire Khānship" (II, 38); *lāṭ kuwa* "do ye fighting!" (III, 5, 28); *mubārakī de* "give congratulation!" (I, 36); *pan sabā* "prepare a road!" (III, 37); *saran mē-gē dē* "give the daughter to me" (I, 48); *mē saran ā gina-dū* "I take this girl" (III, 25); *miā šālmī pāyis-ke de* "give this rupee (? these rupees, § 94) to him!" (L. 234); *tanū šū me-gē dū* "give thy sister to me!" (I, 33); *tapōs kōnin* "he may make inquiry" (I, 37).

17. **Singular Oblique Form.**—There are traces of an Oblique Form used before postpositions, the termination being *a* (or *ā*) or *e* (or *ē*). Occasionally, the oblique form in *e* (*ē*) by itself indicates some case. Thus, we shall see that it is employed to indicate the Agentive (§ 21) and the Locative (§ 38). Similarly, we have the Oblique form in *a* in *lāḍa šit* "aware of the fight" (III, 19, 21). With postpositions, the form in *e* occurs in *Sulaimānike sāt* "with Sulaimānik" (III, 3), and in *Mingaore-ye* "(went) to Mingaora" (I, 1), and is also common before the Instrumental postposition *de* (§ 23).

Generally, however, as in Tirāhī, the termination of the Oblique Form is dropped before a postposition, so that it is the same in form as the Nominative. Numerous instances will be found in the following paragraphs.

18. Two feminine words ending in *ū* deserve special mention here. One is *šū* "a sister", which has an Oblique Form *šī*, in *tanū šī-ge* (or *-yē*) "(said) to his sister" (I, 27, 42). No occurrence of the Plural of this word has been noted. The other word is *dhū* "a daughter". For this, we have no example of the Oblique Singular, but the Nominative Plural is *dhī*, with an Oblique Plural *dhia* (? *dhiā*) (L. 115, 116). We may conclude, therefore, that these two words are declined as follows :—Sing. Nom. *šū, dhū*; Obl. *šī, dhī*; Plur. Nom. *šī, dhī*; Obl. *šia* (? *šiā*), *dhia* (*dhiā*). It may be noted that in Wazīrī Ṗaštō *ū* regularly becomes *ī*, and that in Kāšmīrī

ū becomes *ī* in an oblique case, as in *krūr*[u] "a well", sg. dat. *krīris*.

19. As in the last two words, the termination of the Plural Oblique form is *a* or *ā*. This will be considered more particularly under the head of the Plural (§ 45).

20. In Ṣiṇā, the Singular Oblique Form ends in *ă*, and the Plural in *ō*.

21. **Singular Agentive.**—As in cognate languages, the subject of a transitive verb in a tense formed from the past participle is put into the Agentive case. The full form of this case is the same as that of the Oblique Form in *e*, but is rarely used. Examples are :—*pōē* (Nom. *pō*) *tapōs kī* "the boy made inquiry" (I, 24) ; *puē* (Nom. *pō*) *bĕbā kī-dū* "the boy has made a marriage" (L. 225) ; *Sulaimānike hukum kī* "Sulaimānik made an order" (III, 13, so 59).

22. Generally, however, as in Tirāhī, the termination is dropped, so that the Agentive case is the same in form as the Nominative. Thus : *jumāldār bāt banī* "the headman said a word" (I, 35) ; *kufār hažat* "the Kāfir drove (them) away" (II, 15) ; *χušālī Xudā Pāk dī-cī* "God, the Pure, has given happiness" (I, 20) ; *māš mē χān-ma tapōs kī* "the man made inquiry from this Khān" (I, 5), and so elsewhere ; *rājgana gin* "the queen took him" (III, 55) ; *pūc* (or *puē*, see above) *bĕbā kī-dū* "the son has made a marriage" (L. 225). From these examples, it will be seen that the special form for the Agentive case has practically gone out of use, and has been noted only in regard to two words.

23. **Singular Instrumental.**—The postposition of the Instrumental case is *te* (or *tē*). The same postposition is used to form the Conjunctive Participle (§ 202). The meaning of the case is often indefinite, and sometimes approaches that of a Locative. The postposition generally follows the Oblique Form in *e* (*ē*). Examples (without the Oblique Form) are : *jabal hat-te gina-gā* "he took the pick-axe with (i.e. into) his hand" (III, 38) ; *melāštōp-te gā* "he went by (i.e. on) a visit" (III, 48).

24. After a vowel or *n*, *te* becomes *de*, as in *payim diśe-de* "on the opposite side" (III, 56) ; *γame-de* "on account of a trouble" (I, 11, *dē* 55) ; *khē-de gan* "bind with a rope" (L. 236) ; *cir miḍē-dē kūḍū-dū* "(I) have beaten with many stripes (L. 228) ; *sē-dē langī* "crossed by a bridge" (II, 12). In one case—*kan-de did* "struck (her) with an arrow" (III, 30) —the termination of the Oblique Form has been dropped.

25. The postposition *te* is common both in Dardic and in Indian. Cf. Hindī *tẽ*, and my *Piśāca Languages*, p. 34.

26. **Singular Dative.**—The postposition of the Dative is *kē*, *gē*, *yē*, or *ē*, often written *ke*, *ge*, *ye*, *e*. With *kē*, we have : *dād-ke* "(said) to the ancestor" (II, 8, 9) ; *gām-ke* "(went) to the village" (III, 45) ; *kufār-ke* "for the sake of the Kāfir" (II, 11) ; *lāṭ-ke* "(ready) for fighting" (III, 11, 12) ; *māś-ke* "(said) to the man" (III, 12) ; *rabaṛ-ke* "(go) for a fight" (III, 13) ; *Sulaimānik-kē* ("said) to Sulaimānik" (III, 11) ; *Sulaimānik-ke*, id. (III, 58) ; *śir-ke* "(came, went) to the house" (I, 42 ; II, 15 ; entered, III, 29). In *Sulaimānike baidāt kī* "made Sulaimānik defeated" (III, 16), *Sulaimānike* is contracted from *Sulaimānik-ke*, and the word (in the *bhāvē prayōga*) is the object of a transitive verb in the past tense. Similarly, *tē rājgana Sulaimānige gin* "that queen took Sulaimānik" (III, 55), in which the *k* of the contracted *Sulaimānike* has been softened to *g*, as coming between two vowels (§ 3*d*).

27. For *gē*, we have :—*tanū bādśāhī-ge wat* "came to his own rule" (III, 60) ; *Bihū-ge* "(go, etc.) to Bihun" (III, 13, 14, 48, 51) ; *gām-ge* "to the village" (III, 56, 60) ; *Gurnāl-gē* "(came) to G." (III, 10) ; *kām-gē* "(recited) to the tribe" (II, 33) ; *Kanbel-ge* "(took) him to K." (III, 36) ; *pade-ge* "(drove them) backwards" (II, 13, 14, 15) ; *pat-gē āp* "came back" (I, 26) ; *pō-gē* "(said) to the boy" (I, 33) ; *Semū-ge* "(said) to S." (III, 35) ; *śī-ge* "(said) to the sister" (I, 27) ; *watan-gē* "(went, etc.) to the country" (I, 46 ; II, 1, 7) ; *yai-ge* "(said) to the mother" (I, 27).

28. For *yē or ē*, we have :—*Bāba-ye* "(brought him) to

the Bābā " (II, 24) ; *karmā-ye* " (said) to the army " (III, 13) ; *mubāraki-ye āp* " came for congratulation " (I, 40) ; *Mayō-ye* " (said) to Mayō " (III, 34) ; *mē pō-ē bana-dū* " he says to this boy " (I, 25) ; *rājgana-ye* " (said) to the queen " (III, 50) ; *Semū-ye* " (said) to S. " (III, 7, so 33) ; *šī-yē* " (said) to the sister " (I, 42). In *pō-ē*, above, the *y* has been dropped between two vowels.

In *γāra-ye* " (an exile) on the bank (of the Indus " (III, 4), and in *šir-ke* " in the house " (I, 27), the Dative is used in the sense of the Locative. In *Mingaore-ye* " (went) to Mingaora " (I, 1), *Mingaore* is in the Oblique Form.

29. From instances like *gām-ke* and *gām-ge*, *šī-ge* and *šī-yē*, we can conclude that these three postpositions may be used *ad libitum*, one for the other. The original postposition was probably *ke*, of which *ge* and *ye* (*e*) are weakened forms. *Ke* (< *kṛtē*) is a common Dative suffix in Dardic and Indian languages, and in Maiyā̃ it reappears as *gai*. So far as we can see, words ending in vowels seem to prefer *ge* or *ye* (or *e*), or, in other words, the *k* between two vowels tends to become *g*, and then to disappear, a *y* being inserted in compensation. Similarly, in Ṣiṇā, the termination *ägo*, of the past participle, is liable, in the colloquial language, to be sounded as *äyo*.

30. **Singular Ablative.**—The Singular Ablative sometimes ends in *ā* (or *a*). Thus, *širā jāma pewū* " he sent clothes from the house " (I, 50) ; *puχtuā nigāt* " issued (i.e. ceased) from enmity " (I, 52) ; *šira nigāt* " issued from the house " (III, 31) ; *Sulaimānik nīnā ucit* " Sulaimānik arose from sleep " (III, 43) ; *Kalāma-wa* " down from Kalām " (III, 61) ; *Semū watana hažat* " Semū drove (him) from the country " (III, 3).

31. More often, the Ablative is indicated by the postposition *ma* (or *mā*), or *miā* " from in ", or by the postposition *kĕjā* " from ". The former may be compared with the Tirāhī *mā*, the Kāšmīrī *manza*, and the Sanskrit *madhyāt*. *Kĕjā* is a compound of *ke*, the postposition of the Dative, and *jā*. With *jā*, compare the Ṣiṇā *jō*, *žō*. Examples with *mā*, etc.,

are: *kūī-mā* "from the well" (L. 237); *χān-ma* "(asked) from the Khān" (I, 5); *māš-ma* "(asked) from the man" (I, 24); *saran-ma* "(asked) from the girl" (III, 28); *Badaχšān-miā* "(he came) from Badakhshān" (II, 7); *tē Kufār-miā pade-ge šeyat* "they were driven backwards from (i.e. by) that Kāfir" (II, 13); *Gurnāl-miā* "(the army came) from Gurnāl" (III, 14); *Katār-miā* "(he came) from Katār" (II, 1); *Tōwāl-miā* "(he took taxes) from Tōrwāl" (II, 5).

32. For *kĕjā*, we have:—*dukāndār-kĕjā* "(I bought it) from a shopkeeper" (L. 241); *šū-kĕjā* "(taller) than the sister" (L. 231).

33. Postpositions signifying "after" govern the Ablative, as in *telā pāš* "after from then", i.e. after that time (II, 49; III, 47); *pō te-kĕjā piyāj ye-dū* "the boy comes behind thee" (L. 239).

34. **Singular Genitive.**—The Genitive takes the termination *-si* (sometimes written *-se, -sē*). This may be compared with the Tirāhī Genitive termination *-s* or *-si*, with the Kāšmīrī Dative termination *-s*, with the Ṣiṇā termination *-se* [1] of the Agentive, and with the Sanskrit Genitive termination *-sya*. There does not appear to be any difference of function between the termination *-si* and the termination *-se* (*-sē*).[2] Examples are:—*Abā-sīn-si γara-ye* "to the bank of the Indus" (III, 4); *Bāba-si kām-gē* "to the tribe of the Bābā" (II, 33); *χušālī bāp-si* "happiness of the father" (I, 22); *biū-si thām* "a *biū*-tree" (II, 31); *chal-si ciš* "the breast of a she-goat" (II, 18); *dād-si e pō* "a son of the ancestor" (II, 16); *ḍē-si kaman* "a master of the share" (II, 25); *gām-si χalak* "the people of the village" (I, 30); *ghō-si zīn* "the saddle of the horse" (L. 226); *Jebēya-si dād* "the ancestor of the Jabēr (clan)" (II, 7, etc.); *kām-si imām* "the Imām of the tribe" (II, 50); *χān-sē saran* "the

[1] This is really a Dative termination, transferred to the Agentive under the influence of Tibetan.

[2] Phrases such as *māš-se bhā* "the brother of the man" and *māš-si šū* "the sister of the man" (both in L. 231) suggest that *se* is masculine, and *si* feminine; but this is not borne out by the other examples.

daughter of a Khān " (I, 39, 43); *χān-sē malāž* " a guest of the Khān " (I, 46); *χān-sē watan-gē* " to the country of the Khān " (I, 46); *χān-sē chī* (? *çī*) " the wife of the Khān " (I, 53); *χāna-si dād* " the ancestor of Khāna " (II, 34); *māš-si šū* " the man's sister" (L. 225); *māš-se pō* " the man's son " (L. 228); *māš-se bhā* " the man's brother " (L. 231); *Mayō-si māš* " men of Mayo " (III, 22); *Mišku-si cālā-bā* " up to the rock of Mishku " (III, 61); *Nariā-si dād* " the ancestor of the Narēr (clan) " (II, 1); *pō-si šū* " the sister of the boy " (I, 44); *pižī-si pūc* " the son of the uncle " (L. 225); *Semū-se lāṭ-ke* " for a fight of (i.e. with) Semū " (III, 12); *Semū-si karmā* " S.'s army " (III, 14); *Semū-si šir-ke* " to S.'s house " (III, 39); *sitār-sē māš* " the man of the guitar " (I, 5, etc.); *Sulaimānik-si karmā* " S.'s army " (III, 14); *Sulaimānik-si saran* " S.'s daughter " (III, 23); *Sulaimānik-si pādšāhī* " the rule of S. " (III, 46, so 61); *šai-se kīmat* " the price of the thing " (L. 232); *Tōwāl-si Imām* "the Imām of Tōrwāl " (II, 51); *ṭubak-si duwā* " the grant of a rifle " (II, 44, 45); *watan-sē χān-se pušt* " a descendant of the Khān of the country " (I, 12); *watan-si šerīkat* " division of the country " (II, 8); *watan-si wazīr* " the wazīr of the country " (II, 42); *yai-si ciš* " the breast of the mother " (II, 18, 21).

35. The Genitive is sometimes governed by a postposition as in *ghō-se jada* " on a horse " (L. 230); *Ningōlī-se kac-ke* " (went) near N." (I, 2); *saran-si kan-ke* " (went) near the girl " (III, 29); *dadan-si ken-ta* " by the side of the fire-place " (III, 42); *Tōwāl-si muš-ke* " in front of Tōrwāl " (II, 31); *thām-si ṭin* " under a tree " (L. 230).

36. In one instance, the Oblique Form, or Ablative, alone, is used for the Genitive. It is *nedā phēm diše*, on the opposite side of the river " (II, 3).

37. The verb √*di-* " strike " apparently puts the object struck in the Genitive, as in *saran-si kan-de did* " he struck the girl with an arrow " (III, 30); *Semū-si šā-si did* " he struck Semū's head " (III, 44). It is to be noted that in Ṣiṇā verbs

of striking do not take the accusative, but take a special variety of the Oblique Form for the object struck.[1]

38. **Singular Locative.**—The Oblique Form in *e* (*ē*) is commonly used in a locative sense. Thus, *derē* "at the door" (III, 21); *diše* "on the (opposite) side (of the river)" (II, 3; *dišē*, III, 37); *širē* "in the house" (III, 18; L. 223, 226, 233). A Locative in *o* occurs in *panjam kālo* (Nom. *kāl*) "in the fifth year" (III, 9).

39. The postposition *mē* (variants, *mē*, *mi*, *mī*) means "in", as in *hat-mē* "in the hand" (I, 4); *hujrā-mē* "in the guest-room" (I, 18); *kile-mē* "in the village" (II, 19); *manjlas-mē* "in the entertainment" (I, 21); *Tōwāl-mē* "in Tōrwāl" (II, 2); *khanḍ-mē* "on the hill-top" (L. 229).

Bihū-mī "in Bihun" (III, 47); *Kanbel-mī* "in K." (III, 2); *lāṭ-mi* "in the fight" (III, 16); *Mayō-mī* "in M." (III, 4); *Punkā-mī* "in P." (II, 3); *Tōwāl-mī* "in Tōrwāl" (II, 20, 29); *watan-mī* "in the country" (II, 10; III, 8, 46).

40. The postposition *žet* means "over", and also "concerning", "about". Thus, *gām-žet* "(rule) over the village" (III, 1); *rājgana-žet* "(in love) concerning (i.e. with) the queen" (III, 49); *saran-žet pašat* "they quarrelled over the girl" (III, 24).

41. Other Locative postpositions are *bā* "up to"; *pōrē* "up to, till"; *jada* "upon"; *kan-ke* "to near"; and *ken-ta* "beside". Examples are: *Mišku-si cālā-bā* "up to the rock of Mishku" (III, 61); *sattam pēria pōrē* "till the seventh generation" (II, 48); *ghō-se jada* "(seated) on a horse" (L. 230); *te saran-si kan-ke gā* "he went to near that girl" (III, 29); *dadan-si ken-ta* "by the side of the fireplace" (III, 42). It will be observed that *jada, kan-ke,* and *ken-ta* "govern the genitive".

In the phrase *ē dī* "on one day" (I, 18, 32), the locative takes no postposition whatever.

[1] See Dr. Grahame Bailey's *Grammar*, pp. 60, 69. Dr. Bailey calls this form "the 2nd Accusative".

42. Of the above postpositions, *mē* can be compared with the Indian *mẽ*, Kāšmīrī *manz*, Veron *munj*, Maiyā̃ *maz*, Ṣiṇā *mažā*, Paṣ̌tō *miyanj*, Sanskrit *madhyē*, and Avesta *maiδyāna*. The origin of the others is obscure. The word *žet* may be compared with the Ṣiṇā *aže* " on ", and with the Caspian Persian *-ja* (Avesta *haca*). *Pōrē* is borrowed from Paṣ̌tō. *Bā* may be the Persian *bā*. *Jada* is probably merely a by-form of *žet*.

43. **Plural.**—The List of Words shows a few substantives that form the plural by adding *e*, which, when the word ends in a vowel, forms a diphthong. These are *bāpe* (sing. *bāp*) " fathers " (L. 106) ; *ghē* " a mare ", plur. *ghai* (L. 141) ; *gā* " a cow ", plur. *gai* (L. 145). Similarly, in the Folktales, we have *saranē* " girls " (sing. *saran*) (III, 17). The plural of *dhū* " a daughter ", is *dhī* (L. 115), and the word *šū* " a sister ", also has its plural probably *šī* (see § 18).

As in Tirāhī, however, the Nominative Plural in the Folktales and List is, except in the cases given above, always the same as the singular. The word *bhai* " brothers ", " cousins "[1] (I, 15, 31) (singular *bhā*) is the only other exception. Examples are *birāṭ* " he-goats " (L. 152) ; *chal* " she-goats " (id.) ; *gō* " bulls " (L. 144) ; *ghō* " horses " (L. 140) ; *husai* " deer " (L. 155) ; *dō kāl* " two years " (II, 47) ; *kiǰī* " bitches " (L. 149) ; *kufār* (sing. *kufār* or *kupār*) " Kāfirs " (II, 17) ; *kuǰū* " dogs " (L. 148) ; *χalak* " people " (collective noun) (I, 30 ; III, 33) ; *māš* " men " (III, 22) ; *Musulmān* " Musalmāns " (II, 29) ; *dvāš puš* " twelve sons " (II, 4) ; *pūc* " sons " (L. 223) ; *saran* " daughters " (cf. *saranē* " above "), (L. 115) ; *dū šālmī* " two rupees " (L. 232).

44. For the **Accusative Plural,** we have *ǰāma pai* " send clothes ! " (I, 49) ; *māl ciā-dū* " he is grazing cattle " (L. 229) ; *tiyā šālmī gin* " take those rupees ! " (L. 235).

45. The Plural has an **Oblique Form** ending in *a* (or *ā*), used before postpositions, but, as in the Singular, it is often

[1] Cf. Biddulph, p. 76, "cousins are styled 'brother' or 'sister'."

dropped. For the **Plural Dative,** we have *bhayā-gē* (Sing. Nom. *bhā*, Plur. Nom. *bhai*) "to the brothers" (I, 32); *bŏba-ye* (Sing. Nom. *bāp*) "to fathers" (L. 108); *dhia-gē* (Sing. Nom. *dhū*, Plur. Nom. *dhī*) "to daughters" (L. 117); *māš* "a man" (Sing. Dat. *māš-ke*, Plur. Nom. *māš*, Dat. *māža-ge*) (§ 3*d*) (L. 119, 121, 124, 126). With the Oblique termination dropped, we have *malāž-ge* "to the guests" (I, 29); *saran-gē* "to daughters" (L. 117).

46. For the **Plural Ablative,** we have *dhia-mā* or *dhia-kĕjā* "from daughters" (L. 118).

For the **Plural Genitive,** we have *bŏba-sē* "of fathers" (L. 107); *dhia-si* "of daughters" (L. 116); and, with the termination dropped, *saran-si* "of daughters" (L. 116).

ADJECTIVES

47. Some genuine Tōrwālī adjectives, especially those strong forms descended from original words with the *ka*-suffix, change for gender as in the allied languages; but, so far as the Folktales go, there are few clear examples available—I have, indeed, noted only two. One is *tē jumāldār bī mēlī bāt banī* "that headman again said the same word" (I, 35). Here *mēlī* is certainly feminine, but we do not know the form of the masculine. The other is *lehir chal* "a red she-goat" (II, 18). Here *lehir* or *lihīr* is the feminine of *lohūr* "red", given in Biddulph's vocabulary. We shall, however, under the head of verbs (§§ 189, 194, 199), find several instances of feminine Past Participles, in which there has been a change of form on account of gender. On the other hand, many adjectives with a weak termination do not change for gender or number, and the same applies to certain adjectives borrowed from Paṣtō. Thus :—

γŏra (variant *γora*) (Paṣtō *γwara*) "good", in *γŏra māš* "a good man" (L. 119); *γora χušālī* "good happiness" (fem.) (I, 20); *γŏra cī* "a good woman" (L. 128); *γŏra māš* "good men" (L. 124); *γŏra cī* "good women" (L. 130).

nākāra " bad ", in *nākāra pō* " a bad boy " (L. 129); *nākāra saran* " a bad girl " (L. 131).

48. As the materials in the Folktales on this important point are so scanty, I here give a list of adjectives that change for gender, abstracted from Biddulph's English–Torwálák vocabulary. These I have arranged in classes, permitting us to formulate rules that will apply to others not given in the list. It will be observed that in many cases the change is, as in Kāšmīrī, due to old epenthesis, although the original termination that caused the epenthesis has in most cases disappeared. One example will show what I mean. The word *kišun* " black " has a feminine *kišen*. This shows that the masculine had originally some such form as **kišanu* (derived from Skt. *kṛṣṇakaḥ*), with a feminine **kišanī*. In the language as at present spoken **kišanu*, by epenthesis, has become *kišun*, and **kišani* has become *kišen*, just as the corresponding Kāšmīrī word *krĕhon*ᵘ has, by epenthesis, *krĕhüñ*ᶦ for its feminine.

Sometimes the epenthesis is carried further back than the final syllable. Thus, from the Skt. *kōmalakaḥ* " soft ", we have *kumul* (for **kumalu* or **kamalu*), with a feminine *kemel* (for **kumali* or **kamali*). This epenthesis even occurs, by analogy, in words borrowed from other languages, such as Persian or Paṣ̌tō. Such a word is *kamzōr* " weak ", of which the feminine is *kemzer*.

49. The following is the list of Adjectives taken from Biddulph's vocabulary :—

Adjectives ending in *ā* or *āh* change the final *ā* or *āh* to *ä*, as in :—

Masculine.	*Feminine.*
hujā " alert "	*hüjä* (note the double epenthesis)
sugāh " easy "	*sugä*

Those in *o* change *o* to *e*, as in :—

šijo " beautiful "	*šije* (cf. *šijū*, bel.)
ošo " ugly "	*eše* (double epenthesis)

Those in *ū* change *ū* to *i*, as in :—

hukū " brave, generous "	*huki*
šijū " clean "	*šiji* (cf. *šijo*, ab.)
But *cunū* " yellow "	*cene* (double epenthesis)

So, words with the adjectival ending *-hū* change to *i*, as in :—

šidàhū " cold ".	*šidaihi* (from *šidal* " cold ", subst.)
bušauhū " hungry "	*bušaihi* (from *buš* " hunger ")
tišauhū " thirsty "	*tišaihi* (from *tiš* " thirst ")

Others change *ū* to *ü*, as in :—

bū " deaf "	*bü*
kū " hard "	*kü*
ūgū " heavy "	*ügü* (double epenthesis)

Words ending in a consonant preceded by *a* generally change *a* to *e*, as in :—

gan " great "	*gen*
jūbal " thin "	*jūbel*
ūjal " white "	*ūjel*

ūtal " high ", however, has *ūtil*, which may be a mere variation of spelling for *ūtel*.

There are two exceptions :—

laš " bad "	*laž*
an " blind "	*an*, in which the *a* of *an* (masc.) is sounded like the *u* in " gun ", while the *a* of *an* (fem.) is sounded like the *a* in " America ".

When a word ends in a consonant preceded by *ā*, the *ā* becomes *ä*, as in :—

bār " fat, thick "	*bär*

In similar circumstances, *e* also becomes *ä*, as in :—

kamāder " industrious "	*kamādär*

In similar circumstances, *i* becomes *ī*, as in :—

bizin " broad " — *bizīn*
jik " long " — *jīk*
cit " low " — *cīt*

In similar circumstances, *o* usually becomes *e*, as in :—

kol, " crooked " — *kel*
anatol " dirty " — *anatel*
koror " round " — *kerer* } (double epenthesis)
kamzōr " weak " — *kemzer* } (double epenthesis)

An exception is :—

sot " slow " — *söt*

In the following word, *ö* becomes *a* :—

öž (? *öẓ̌*) " wet " — *až* (? *aẓ̌*). The corresponding Ṣiṇā word is *aẓ̌u*.

In similar circmustances, *u* sometimes becomes *i*, as in :—

cuk " acid " — *cik*
cun " narrow " — *cin*
lud (? *luḍ*) " small " — *lid* (? *liḍ*)

and sometimes becomes *e* (probably a matter of spelling), as in :—

kišun " black " — *kišen*
χuš " happy " — *χeš*
pišul " smooth " — *pišel*
kumul " soft " — *kemel* } (double epenthesis)
kurrun " short " — *keren* } (double epenthesis)

Exceptions are :—

kud " lame " — *küd*
ūpur " light " — *ipīr* (? *īpir*)

In similar circumstances, *ū* becomes *ī*, as in :—

lohūr " red " — *lihīr* (double epenthesis)
šūš (? *šūṣ̌*) " straight, upright " — *šīš* (? *šīṣ̌*)

50. As in connected languages, comparison is effected by putting the thing with which comparison is made into the

Ablative case, as in *šū-kĕjā ucat* " taller than the sister " (L. 231). The Superlative is obtained with the help of the Locative of *buḍ* or *būḍ* " all ", as in *būḍa-mē ucat* " high among all, highest " (L. 137); *būḍ māža-mī behtar* " best of all men " (L. 134).

NUMERALS

51. **Cardinals.**—" One " is *ē* (variant *e*) or *ek* (variant *ĕk*).

The word *ē* (*e*) is also regularly used as an indefinite article, as in: *mūšā ē māž āp* " a certain man came before him " (I, 3); *ē dī* " on a day, one day " (I, 18, 32); *e māš ašū* " there was a man " (I, 21); *Punkā-mī e kupār ašū* " there was a Kāfir in Punkā " (II, 3; so III, 2); *e pō paidā hō-dū* " a boy has been born " (II, 20); *e biū-si thām ašū* " there was a *biū*-tree " (II, 31); *tesi e dušman ašū* " he had an enemy " (III, 1); *tesi e saran aši* " he had a daughter " (III, 17); *telā pāš Bihū-mī e rājgana aši* " after that there was a queen in Bihun " (III, 47).

As a numeral, we have :—*mō duyimo e huī* " let us two become one (II, 11); *mē Jebēya-si dād-si e pō paidā hū* " of this ancestor of Jabēr, there was one son born " (II, 16); *e māš andere cir hušā ašū* " one man among them was very intelligent " (III, 27); *ek bana-dū* " *mē saran ā gina-dū* ", " one says, 'I will take this girl,' (another says, etc.) " (III, 25); *ek dui-sāt jōr ne ye-dū* " one does not come to agreement with the other " (III, 26); *ĕk* " one " (L. 1).

A more definite form is *e-ga*, in *tā Xodā e-ga dū na kuwē* " may God not make one two for thee " (II, 48) or *e-gī*, in *e-gī ti-hun jumāldār ašū* " one of them was a head man " (I, 16). In III, 15, we have *diumo ek-dije eṛi huī* which means " the two (armies) halted in front of each other ". Regarding this sentence, see § 56, below.

52. " Two " *dū* (variants *du*, *dō*), as in *ā te-gē du žāt majlis kō-dū* " I am making an entertainment for thee for two nights " (I, 10); *dō kāl gai* " two years passed " (II, 47);

tā Xodā e-ga dū na kuwē (as shown under " one ") (II, 48); *dū šālmī* " two rupees " (L. 232).

53. " Three," *cā* (? *c̣ā*) (L. 3); *ca ḍe* " three parts " (II, 10).

" Four," *cau* (L. 4) (Biddulph, *choh*, i.e. *co*).

" Five," *panj* (L. 5) (Bid. *pān*).

" Six," *šō* (? *ṣō*) (L. 6).

" Seven," *sat* (L. 7).

" Eight," *aṭ* (L. 8).

" Nine," *nōm* (L. 9); *nūm bīš saranē tisi-sāt ašī* " nine times twenty girls were with her " (III, 17).

54. " Ten," *daš* (L. 10); *mī daš bhai ašī* " I had ten cousins " (I, 15); *sē daš bhai āban-gē derī* " those ten cousins remained by themselves " (I, 31).

" Eleven," *agāš* (Biddulph).

" Twelve," *tisi dvāš puš ašī* " he had twelve sons " (II, 4). (Bid. *dūwāš*.)

" Thirteen," *ceš* (? *c̣eš*) (Bid.).

" Fourteen," *cettiš* (Bid.).

" Fifteen," *paṅš* (Bid.).

" Sixteen," *šeš* (? *ṣeš*) (Bid.).

" Seventeen," *satāš* (Bid.).

" Eighteen," *atāš* (? *aṭāš*) (Bid.).

" Nineteeen," *anbīš* (Bid.).

" Twenty," *bīš* (L. 11); *nūm bīš* " nine times twenty ", as in § 53.

21, *ek-o-bīš* (Bid.).

30, *daš-o-bīš* (Bid.).

40, *dū bīš* (Bid.).

50, *daš o dū bīš* (L. 12).

60, *cā bīš* (Bid.).

70, *daš o cā bīš* (Bid.).

80, *co bīš* (Bid.).

90, *daš o co bīš* (Bid.).

100, *panj bīš* (L. 13). Biddulph gives *soh* (i.e. *so*).

1,000, *zer* (Bid.).

It will be observed that the counting is vigesimal.

55. **Ordinals.**—We have :—

"First," *awal* (borrowed from Paṣtō), in *awal-mē Xāna-si dād wat* "at first the ancestor of Khāna arrived" (II, 34). Biddulph gives *mūš*, which also means "before".

"Second," *duyi*, in *pāji tisi duyi bhā āp* "afterwards his second brother came" (II, 39). Biddulph gives *pāš*, which also means "after".

"Third," *cui* (? *ċui*) in *pāji tisi cui bhā wat* "afterwards his third brother arrived" (II, 43); *dō kāl gai, cui kāl hō* "two years passed, (and) the third year happened" (II, 47). Biddulph gives *tlūi*. The real word is probably *ċūi*, with a cerebral *ċ*.

"Fourth," *cōthum*, in *cōthum ḍē mī* "the fourth share (is) mine" (II, 10); *pāji ti-hun cōthum bhā ašū* "afterwards there was their fourth brother" (II, 46).

"Fifth," *panjam* (Bid. *pānjam*), in *Semū-sāt panjam kālo karmā ucit* "in the fifth year the army arose with Semū" (III, 9).

"Sixth" *šowam* (? *ṣowam*) (Biddulph).

"Seventh" *sattam*, in *tā Xodā sattam pērīa pōrē e-ga dū na kuwē* "may God not make one two (i.e. increase) for thee till the seventh generation" (II, 48).

56. Other numeral words are :—

duī "another", in *duī bana-dū, "mē saran ā gina-dū"*; *ek dui-sāt jōr ne ye-dū* "another says, 'I am taking this girl'; one does not come to agreement with another" (III, 25). Compare *ek-dije*, under "one", above (§ 51). The word *dije* is doubtful, not being clear in the original MS. Perhaps we should read *duye*.

diumo [1] or *duyimo* "the two, both", in *diumo ek-dije eṛi huī* "the two armies halted in front of each other" (III, 15), but see above; *mō duyimo te Kufār-ke e huī*; *ā duyimo sē-dē langī* "'let both of us become one for (the sake of) that Kāfir'; they both crossed (the river) by a bridge" (II, 11, 12).

[1] So clearly in the original MS. We should expect *duimo*.

57. *ar* " half ", in *ar žāt hī* " half night became (i.e. it became midnight) " (III, 43) ; *dū šālmī ō ar* " two rupees and a half " (L. 232).

PRONOUNS

58. The **Pronoun of the First Person** is *ā* (variant *a*) " I ". The following forms have been noted :—

Singular,	Nom.	*ā, ai.*
	Ag.	*mē, mẽ, mai, mā.*
	Acc.	*mā,* (Biddulph) *mai.*
	Gen.	*mī* (variant *mẽ*) (*mā o chī* " of me and of thee ").
	Obl.	*mē* (variants *me, mẽ*), (Bid.) *ma.*
Plural,	Nom.	*mō* (variant *mõ*), *mõi* (emph.), (Bid.) *ma.*
	Ag.	*mahī, mōi* (emph.).
	Acc.	(Bid.) *ma.*
	Gen.	*amun, mun.*
	Obl.	(Bid.) *mo.*

When forms are not available in the specimens I have given those shown by Biddulph. I have also given forms shown by him when they differ from mine. Examples of the use of this Pronoun are :—

59. **Singular Nominative.**—*ā sªwāl kō-dū* " I make a request " (I, 9) ; *ā χān-se pušt thū* " I am the descendant of a Khān " (I, 12) ; *ā lūṭ āšū* " I was small " (I, 13) ; *ā ka cal keī* " what device shall I do ? " (I, 24) ; *ā χušāl hō* " I became happy " (I, 40) ; *ā gā* " I went " (I, 43) ; *ā biži* " I shall go " (I, 44) ; *ā abanī baže-dū* " I am going myself " (I, 45) ; *ā te-gē dai* " I will give (her) to thee " (I, 49) ; *ā γamjān hō-thū* " I have become worried " (I, 55) ; *ā nimā-dū* " I wish (for) " (II, 38, 41) ; *ā jōr thū* " I am ready " (III, 12) ; *ā gina-dū* " I am taking " (III, 25) ; *ā kī* " I shall make " (III, 28) ; *ā* (fem.) *ta gina-žī* " I take thee " (III, 51) ; *yāp ā nigālī* " I will excavate a canal " (III, 52) ; *ā ta ginī* " I will take thee " (III, 53) ; *ai nidā kao-dud* " I was making inspection " (I, 19).

60. **Singular Agentive.**—*mē banū* "I said" (I, 20); *mē tanū šū tĕs-kē na dit* "I did not give my sister to him" (I, 34); *mē aj cir pand kī-jī* "to-day I have made a long journey" (L. 224); *mē kūḍū-dū* "I have beaten" (L. 228); *mai kuḍū* "I struck" (L. 185); *mā pan sabat* "I prepared the road" (III, 41).

61. **Singular Accusative.**—*mā gin* "take me!" (III, 50).

62. **Singular Genitive.**—*mī bāp mū, mī dērā šaṭ hū* "my father died, my house became ruined" (I, 13–14); *mī daš bhai ašī* "I had ten cousins" (I, 15); *sē mī tarbūr ašū* "he was my paternal cousin" (I, 17); *mī dērā janā* "clean ye my house" (I, 27); *cōthum ḍē mī* "the fourth share (is) mine" (II, 10); *mī yai ū bāp kāfir thī* "my mother and father are unbelievers" (II, 29); *mī bāp* "my father" (L. 233); *mē piži-si pūc* "the son of my uncle" (L. 225); *watan-si mā o chī šerīkat hī* "let there be division of the country of (i.e. between) me and thee" (II, 8).

63. **Singular Oblique.**—*chī mē-gē ka kam thū* "what business is there of thee for (i.e. with) me?" (I, 7); *tanū šū me-gē dū* "give thy daughter to me!" (I, 33); *ē tanū šū me-gē na dit* "he did not give me his daughter" (I, 35); *tā me-gē ka mubārakī dit* "what congratulations didst thou give to me?" (I, 38); *tanū saran mē-gē dē* "give me thy daughter!" (I, 48); *me-gē jāma pai* "send to me clothes!" (I, 49); *mē-ge ṭubak-si duwā kō* "do to me the benediction of (i.e. present me with) a rifle!" (II, 44); *aban mē-gē lāṭ-ke jōr ku* "make thyself for me ready for a fight!" (III, 11); *mē-tē-gē kam thū* "there is business for me and for thee" (I, 6); *mē-ye kalimā bayān kō* "repeat the creed to me" (II, 35).

mē-kĕjā mūj baž "walk before me!" (L. 238).

mē-sāt lāṭ kuwa "make ye a fight with me" (III, 5).

64. **Plural Nominative.**—*mō bana-dū* "we say" (I, 33); *mō biži* "let us go" (I, 36); *mō banin* "let us say" (I, 39); *mō puχtuā nigāt* "we have gone out (i.e. ceased) from enmity" (I, 52); *mō duyimo e huī* "we two shall become one" (II, 11);

mō tihā musulmān keī "let us make them Moslems" (II, 29); *mō* is recorded only in L. 17; *mōi te-sāt karmā yanin, te watan-mī mōi lāṭ kī, mōi barai kī, besyāt mōi ginin* "we verily will go with thee as an army, we verily did fighting in that country, we verily made victory, we verily shall take loot" (III, 7, 8). This sentence is the only authority for the form *mōi*, which seems to be an emphatic form—"It is we who, etc."

65. **Plural Agentive.**—*mahī kuḍū* "we struck" (L. 188). This is the only authority. Cf. *tahī*, the corresponding form of *tū* "thou" (§ 69). For *mōi*, see *te watan-mī mōi lāṭ kī, mōi barai kī*, at the end of the preceding paragraph.

66. **Plural Genitive.**—The only authority for *amun* and *mun* is L. 18, 19. *Amun* appears to be doubtful. Biddulph also gives *mun*.

67. **Plural Oblique.**—*tē mō-ma tapōs kō-nin* "(if) he make (i.e. ask) a question from us" (I, 37).

68. All the above forms can easily be explained from Indo-Eranian analogies, except the Genitive Plural, *amun* or *mun*. These last can be compared with the Gawar-bati *amō-na*. It is evident that the final *n* is the relic of an old postposition. Compare also the Ḍōḍā dialect of Kāšmīrī *āhmō*, and the Gārwī *mō*, both Genitives Plural.

69. The **Pronoun of the Second Person** is *tū* "thou". The following forms have been noted :—

Singular,	Nom.	*tū* (variant *tu*), *ta*.
	Ag.	*tā* (variant *ta*), *tai*.
	Acc.	*tā*, (Biddulph) *tai*.
	Gen.	*chī* (variant *chi*), (Bid.) *ci*.
	Obl.	*tē* (variant *te*), (Bid.) *tai*.
Plural,	Nom.	*tō* (variant *to*), *thō*.
	Ag.	*tahī*.
	Acc.	(Bid.) *to*.
	Gen.	*tun, thun*.
	Obl.	(Bid.) *to*.

When forms are not available in the specimens, I have given those shown by Biddulph. I have also given forms shown by him when they differ from mine. Examples of the use of this Pronoun are :—

70. **Singular Nominative.**—*tū kēt-si thū* "of where are thou ?" (I, 6) ; *tu ka s^a wāl kō-dū* "what request dost thou make ?" (I, 9) ; *tu ka γame-de γam-jān hō-dū*, "by what trouble art thou troubled ?" (I, 11) ; *tu baž* "go thou !" (I, 25, 44, 45) ; *tu gā-šū* "thou hadst gone" (I, 39) ; *tu kē āp* "why art thou come ?" (I, 47) ; *tu beš-te me-gē jāma pai* "do thou, having gone, send clothes to me !" (I, 49) ; *tu γora māš thū* "thou art a good man" (I, 56) ; *tu ka nimā-dū* "what dost thou desire ?" (II, 37, 40) ; *tu yāp nigāl* "do thou excavate a canal" (III, 51).

71. **Singular Agentive.**—*tā me-gē ka mubārakī dit* "what congratulation didst thou give me ?" (I, 38) ; *saran tā aban-ge lehī* "thou demandest the girl for thyself" (I, 39) ; *tā pan sabat* "didst thou prepare the road ?" (III, 40) ; *ta yāp nigālī* "(if) thou didst excavate the canal" (III, 53) ; *pāē cīz tā kis-kĕjā gin-thū* "from whom hast thou bought that thing ?" (L. 240). The form *tai* occurs only in *tai kuḍū* "thou struckest" (L. 186).

72. **Singular Accusative.**—*tā mānin* "they may kill thee" (I, 44) ; *tā Xodā e-ga dū na kuwē* "may God not make two one (for) thee (i.e. increase thy offspring)" (II, 48) ; *ā ta talā gina-žī* "I (fem.) am then taking thee" (III, 51, similarly 53).

73. **Singular Genitive.**—*ē χušālī chi bāp-si ašī* "this pleasure was of thy father" (i.e. he used to have it) (I, 22) ; *ca ḍe mī watan-mī chī* "three shares in this country (are) thine" (II, 10) ; *chī nām ka thū* "what is thy name ?" (L. 220) ; *chī bāp-si širē* "in thy father's house" (L. 223).

74. **Singular Oblique.**—*mē-tē-ge kam thū* "there is business for me (and) thee" (i.e. I have business with thee) (I, 6) ; *ā te-gē majlis kō-dū* "I (will) make an entertainment for thee" (I, 10) ; *te-gē mubāraki-ye āp* "I came to thee for

congratulation " (I, 40) ; *ā te-gē dai* " I give to thee " (I, 49) ; *ā te-gē s^a wāl kō-dū* " I make a request to thee " (I, 56) ; *hē te-gc kasab kuwē* " he may do work for thee " (III, 35).

ā te-kĕjā s^a wāl kō-dū " I am making a request from thee " (I, 8) ; *ā te-kĕjā χānī nimā-dū* " I desire Khānship from thee " (II, 38) ; *te-kĕjā piyāj* " behind thee " (L. 239).

ā te-sāt šerīkat na kō-dū " I do not do sharing with thee " (II, 9) ; *mōi te-sāt karmā yanin* " we verily will go with thee as an army " (III, 7) ; *te-sād maškulā* " conversation with thee " (I, 56).

75. **Plural Nominative.**—*to baža* " go ye ! " (I, 41) ; *to lāṭ na kuwa* " do not ye fighting ! " (III, 28). The word is written *thō* in L. 160, 166, 183, 199, 209, 215.

76. **Plural Agentive.**—*tahī kuḍū* " ye struck " (L. 189).

77. **Plural Genitive.**—*ē manjlas thun hujrā-mē hō-dut* " this entertainment used to be in your guest-house " (I, 23). L. 24, 25 have *tun*.

78. It will be observed that the above forms are parallel to those of the first person. Most can at once be explained by Indo-Eranian analogies. The aspirated forms *thō* and *thun*, alongside of *tō* and *tun*, may be compared with the Rājasthānī (Mārwāṛī, etc.) *thē*, as well as with the Gārwī *thā* and Ḍōḍā *tuh* (Standard Kāšmīrī, *tŏh^i*), all meaning " you ". Compare, also, the Ṣiṇā (Drās) *thō* " thou ".

DEMONSTRATIVE PRONOUNS

79. The **Proximate Demonstrative Pronoun** is *ē* (written *ēh* in L. 26) " this (near), he ". It also appears under the form *hē* (Biddulph, *he*). Biddulph gives the following declension :—

	Singular.	*Plural.*
Nom.	*he.*	*iya.*
Acc.	*ess* (? *es*).	*iyā.*
Gen.	*issa* (? *isa*).	*iyasa.*
Abl.	*ez-ma.*	*iya-ma.*

80. **Singular Nominative.**—Examples in the specimens are: *hē mē lāḍa šit hī* "she became aware of this fight" (III, 21); *hē kāmē māš gina-šī* "which man does she take?" (III, 28); *hē te-ge kasab kuwē* "he may do work for thee" (III, 35).

81. **Singular Agentive.**—*ē tanū šū me-gē na dit* "he did not give his sister to me" (I, 35).

We have an **Oblique Form** in *ēs paš* "after this" (I, 30). Before a sonant this becomes *ez*, as in Biddulph's *ez-ma*.

82. **Plural Nominative.**—*ē bažē-dī* "they go" (L. 210), and *hē pade-ge nurī* "they turned backwards" (II, 14); *tē Kufār hē hažat* "they were driven away by that Kāfir" (II, 15); *hē gai* "they went" (III, 32). Biddulph, as we have seen, gives *iya*.

83. As a **Pronominal Adjective,** *ē* seems to be immutable, as in:—*ē χušālī chi bāp-si ašī*; *ē manjlas thun hujrā-mē hō-dut* "this pleasure was thy father's; this entertainment used to be in your guest-room" (I, 22, 23); *ē pō pat-gē āp* "this boy came back" (I, 26); *ē pō andare bēṭh* "this boy sat inside" (I, 29); *ē jamāldār bana-dū* "this headman says" (I, 32, 52); *ē χān lewānai hū* "this Khān became mad" (I, 54); *ā beš-te e saran-ma tapōs kī* "having gone, I will make inquiry from this girl" (III, 28).

84. Another immutable **Pronominal Adjective** is *ā* "this, that" (Biddulph *āga*[1] "this"). Examples are: *ā māš mē pō-ē bana-dū* "this man says to this boy" (I, 25); *ā pō* "that boy (says, went, came)" (I, 41, 45, 48, 50; so II, 28); *ā pō na pō-šat* "that boy was not drinking" (II, 18); *ā māš nigāt* "that man went out" (III, 31); *ā Sulaimānik gā* "that Sulaimānik went" (III, 48).

For the Plural, we have:—*ā duyimo sē-dē langī* "these two crossed by a bridge" (II, 12).

In the original manuscript this word is sometimes translated "this", and sometimes "that". The latter seems to be the

[1] Cf. Biddulph's *paga*, in § 122.

correct meaning, although Biddulph gives *he* and *aga* for " this ", and *tiya* and *paga* for " that ".

It will be observed that all the above examples are in the Nominative case. I have no information as to whether *ā* is used in other cases.

85. The **Pronominal Adjective** *mē* (variants *mē*, *mī*) is sometimes translated " this ", and sometimes " that ". An examination of its use shows that it is clearly a Proximate Demonstrative, and should be translated by " this ". In the specimens it is not used with a noun which is the subject of a verb, but is twice used with the object of a transitive verb in a tense formed from the past participle. It is also used in agreement with a noun in the Accusative, but occurs most often in agreement with a noun in some Oblique Case. Its use with the plural is a matter of doubt, and will be separately considered in § 94. Examples are :—

86. **With the Object of a Transitive Verb in a Tense derived from the Past Participle.**—*mē pō ti šēχ nū* " that disciple took away this boy " (II, 23) ; *Sulaimānike mē cai cinū* " Sulaimānik cut this cliff " (III, 59).

87. **With Singular Accusative.**—*mē saran ā gina-dū* " I am taking this girl " (III, 25) ; *mē saran buā* " look ye at this girl ! " (III, 31) ; *mē Sulaimānik na mā* " do not kill this Sulaimānik ! " (III, 35) ; *mē cai cin* " cut this cliff ! " (III, 58).

88. **With Singular Agentive.**—*mē pōē tapōs kī* " this boy made inquiry " (I, 24).

89. **With Singular Oblique Form.**—*mī Sulaimānike sāt rabaṛ kī* " he made a fight with this Sulaimānik " (III, 3).

90. **With Singular Dative.**—*mō bana-dū mē pō-gē* " we say to this boy " (I, 33) ; *dād mē watan-gē āp* " the ancestor came to this country " (II, 1, 7) ; *tu mē Bihū-ge yāp nigāl* " excavate thou a canal to this Bihun " (III, 51).

91. **With Singular Ablative.**—*mē χān-ma tapōs kī* " he made inquiry from this Khān " (I, 5) ; *mē māš-ma tapōs kī*

"he made inquiry from this man" (I, 24); *mē Tōwāl-miā sē māliyā neyu-dut* "he was taking taxes from this Tōrwāl" (II, 5); *ā maš mē šira nigāt* "that man went out from this house" (III, 31).

92. **With Singular Genitive.**—*mē gām-si χalak* "the people of this village" (I, 30); *mē pō-si šū* "the sister of this boy" (I, 44); *mē māš-sē* "of this man" (I, 52); *mē χān-sē chī muī* "the wife of this Khān died" (I, 53); *mī Nariā-si dād mī Jebēya-si dād-ke banū, "mē watan-si mā-o-chī šerīkat hī"* "the ancestor of this Narer said to the ancestor of this Jaber, 'let there be division of (i.e. between) me and thee of this country'" (II, 8); *mī Jabēya-si dād* "the ancestor of this Jaber" (II, 9, cf. 16); *mē pō-si nām* "the name of this boy" (II, 26); *mē kām-si Imām* "the Imām of this tribe" (II, 50); *mē Sulaimānik-si saran* "the daughter of this Sulaimānik" (III, 23); *mē saran-si kan-de did* "shot this girl with an arrow" (§ 37) (III, 30); *mē ghō-si umu* "the age of this horse" (L. 221).

93. **With Singular Locative.**—*mē manjlas-mē* "in this entertainment" (I, 21); *mī watan-mī* (II, 10); *mē watan-mī* (III, 46) "in this country"; *sē mē saran-žet pašat* "they quarrelled over this girl" (III, 24).

94. **With Plural.**—No certain instance occurs, but I believe that with plural nouns *mē* takes the form *miā* or *miyā*, and that it appears in *miā šālmī pāyis-ke de* (L. 234), which is given as a translation of "give this rupee to him". I think that the translator has mistaken "this" for "these" and that *miā šālmī* really means "these rupees". Compare *tiyā*, the plural of *tē* (§ 96).

95. The origin of this pronoun must be sought in the Avesta *ima-* (cf. Waχī *yem*, Sarīkolī *yam* "this"). We may also compare the Veron *m-iš*, and Khōwār *hamu* "his". In the plural there are (beside other more doubtful forms) Gawarbati *eme*, Veron *mū* "they".

96. **From the Aryan Pronominal base** *ta-* " he, she, it, that ", we have the following forms :—

	Singular.	*Plural.*
Nom.	*tē*, (Biddulph) *tiya.*	*tiyā.*
Ag.	*ti*, *te.*	*tihē.*
Acc.	(Bid.) *tes.*	*tihā*, (Bid.) *tiyā̃.*
Obl.	*te*, (? Gen.) *tisi*, (Bid.) *tes.*	(Bid.) *tiya.*
Dat.	*tes-kē* (variant *tĕs-kē*).	(Bid.) *tiya-ke.*
Abl.	*tes-ma*, (Bid.) *tez-ma.*	(Bid.) *tiya-ma.*
Gen.	*tesi* (variants *tesē*, *tisi*, *tisē*, *tasi*) (Bid.) *tissa.*	*ti-hun* (variant *tiyun*), (Bid.) *tiyasa.*

Examples are :—

97. **Singular Nominative.**—*tē mō-ma tapōs kōnin* " he may make inquiry from us " (I, 37). In the Nominative the pronoun *sē* (§ 117) is more usual than *tē.*

Object of a Transitive Verb in a Tense derived from the Past Participle.—*rajgāna tē ḍiṭ* " the queen saw him " (III, 49); *tes Musulmān kī* " (he) made him a Musalmān " (II, 47). In the latter example, *tes* is in the Oblique Form in *Bhāvē prayōga.*

98. **Singular Agentive.**—*ti būda* " he saw " (II, 25); *te si Semū watana hažat* " he drove that Semū from the country " (III, 3).

99. **Singular Oblique Form.**—*te-set mukadima kī* " made a quarrel with him " (II, 6); *saranē tisi-sāt ašī* " girls were with her " (III, 17). In the latter, however, *tisi* is really a Genitive governed by *sāt* (§ 35).

100. **Singular Dative.**—*mē tanū šū tĕs-kē na dit* " I did not give my sister to him " (I, 34); *tes-ki mubārakī dē* " give congratulation to him " (I, 36); *tes-ke bana-dū* " says to him " (II, 10, 37, 40); *tes-ke kalimā bayān kī* " recited the creed to him " (II, 36, 39); *tes-ke Bāba duwā kī* " the Bābā made a benediction (i.e. grant) to him " (II, 42, 45); *tes-ke šulan dit* " gave a curse to him " (i.e. cursed him) (II, 48).

Singular Ablative.—*tes-ma gām ṭin kī* "the village was taken (? subdued) from him" (III, 16).

101. **Singular Genitive.**—*tasi šū gā* "his sister went" (I, 28); *tesē chī ruksat kī* "(he) let his wife depart" (I, 51); *tisē dērā-mī bⁱhī* "let us sit in his house" (I, 52); *tisi dvāš puš ašī* "he had twelve sons" (II, 4); *tesi yai-yū-bāp kufār ašī* "his mother and father were Kāfirs" (II, 17); *tisi ṭin bēḍū šū* "he was seated below it" (§ 35) (II, 32); *tisi duyi bhā āp* "his second brother came" (II, 39); *tisi cui bhā wat* "his third brother arrived" (II, 43); *tisi aulād āχūnzāda thī* "his descendants are Ākhūnzādas (II, 51); *tesi e dušman ašū . . . tesi nām Semū* "he had an enemy . . . his name (was) Semū" (III, 1, 2); *tesi e saran ašī* "he had a daughter" (III, 17).

102. **Plural Nominative.**—*tiyā kuḍī* "they will beat" (L. 200).

103. **Plural Agentive.**—*tihē mē Sulaimānik-si saran ḍiṭ* "they saw the daughter of this Sulaimānik" (III, 23).

104. **Plural Accusative.**—*mō tihā Musulmān keī* "let us make them Musalmāns" (II, 29).

105. **Plural Genitive.**—*egī ti-hun* "one of them" (I, 16); *ti-hun dērā* "their house' (I, 17); *ti-hun hujrā-mē* "in their guest-room" (I, 18); *ti-hun cōthum bhā ašū* "they had a fourth brother" (II, 46). In L. 30, 31, we find *tiyun* instead of *ti-hun*. The Oblique Plural being *tiya*, the full form of the genitive was without doubt *tiya-hun*, of which both *ti-hun* and *tiyun* are contractions.

106. With the termination *hun* of the Genitive Plural, we may compare the Kašmīrī *hond*ᵘ, as in *ti-hond*ᵘ "of them".

107. No instance has been noted of the adjectival use of this pronoun with a noun in the Nominative Singular. With every other singular case it has the immutable form *tē* (variants *te*, *ti*). In the one instance in which it is found in agreement with a plural noun (in the Accusative case), as we might expect, it takes the form *tiyā*. Examples are :—

108. **With the Object of a Transitive Verb in a Tense**

derived from the Past Participle.—*te dērā janū* "(she) cleaned that house" (I, 28); *tē saran māil ḍiṭ* "(they) saw that girl killed" (III, 32); *Sulaimānige tē yāp nigālī* "Sulaimānik excavated that canal" (III, 54); *tē rājgana Purangām-ge wālī* "he brought that queen to Puran-gām" (III, 56).

109. **With Singular Agentive.**—*ti māš hat-mē sitār gin-thū* "that man has taken a guitar in his hand" (I, 4); *tē jumāldār bī mēlī bāt banī* "that headman again said the same word" (I, 35); *tē χān tesē chī ruksat kī* "that Khān let his wife depart" (I, 51); *tē Kufār-miā pade-ge šeyat* "(they) were driven backwards from that Kāfir" (II, 13; similarly 15); *mē pō ti šēχ nū* "that disciple took away this boy" (II, 23); *tē Semū tē χalak-ke arzī kī* "that Semū made request to that people" (III, 5); *te māš mē saran-si kan-de did* "that man shot this girl (§ 37) with an arrow" (III, 30); *tē rājgana tē ḍiṭ* "that queen saw him" (III, 49); *tē rājgana Sulaimānige gin* "that queen took Sulaimānik" (*Bhāvē prayōga*) (III, 55).

110. **With Singular Accusative.**—*Sulaimānik te jabal gin-de Semū-si šā-si did* "Sulaimānik, having taken that pickaxe, hit Semū's head" (§ 37) (III, 44).

111. **With Singular Instrumental.**—*ā te γamē-dē γamjān hō-thū* "I have become worried owing to that trouble" (I, 55).

112. **With Singular Dative.**—*mō duyimo te Kufār-ke e huī* "let us two, for the sake of that Kāfir become one" (II, 11); *tē χalak-ke* "for that people" (III, 5, 6); *Sulaimānike tē māš-ke banū* "Sulaimānik said to that man" (III, 12); *ā Sulaimānik te Bihū-ge gā* "that Sulaimānik went to that Bihun" (III, 48); *tē rājgana-ye bana-dū* "he says to that queen" (III, 50).

113. **With Singular Genitive.**—*ā pō gā te χān-sē watan-gē, tē χān-sē malāž hō* "that boy went to that Khān's country, he became that Khān's guest" (I, 46); *te saran-si kan-ke gā* "he went to the neighbourhood of (i.e. near) that girl" (III, 29).

114. **With Singular Locative.**—*ti Tōwāl-mē* "in that Tōrwal" (II, 2); *tē watan-mī* "in that country" (III, 8); *sē tē rājgana-žet mayin hū* "he became in love on (i.e. with) that queen" (III, 49).

115. **With Singular Oblique.**—*te Kufār-sāth* "with that Kāfir" (II, 12).

116. **With Plural Accusative.**—*tiyā šālmī pāyis-kĕjā gin* "take those rupees from him" (L. 235).

117. The **Aryan pronominal base** *sa-* appears under the immutable form *sē* (sometimes written *si, seh*) "he, she, it, that". As a pronoun, it has been noted only in the Nominative case, Singular and Plural. It therefore serves as an alternative, and more usual, form of the Nominative of the Pronoun *tē* (§ 97). So also, as a Pronominal Adjective, it is used only with a noun in the Nominative Singular or Plural. Under any circumstances it does not change for gender or number. Examples are :—

118. **Singular Nominative.**—*sē mī tarbūr ašū* "he was my paternal cousin" (I, 17); *sē bana-dū* "he says" (I, 22; II, 35, 38, etc.; III, 28, 52); *sē cir zālim ašū* "he was very powerful" (II, 4); *sē māliyā neyu-dut* "he was taking taxes" (II, 5); *sē buzurg ašū* "he was a saint" (II, 17); *sē til šit hū* "he then became aware" (II, 19); *sē tanū yai-si ciš na pō-dū* "he does not drink his mother's breast" (II, 21); *sē Musulmān hū* "he became a Musalmān" (II, 36); *sē watan-si wazīr hū* "he became Wazīr of the country" (II, 42); *sē širē pām dugū-dut, sē mē lāḍa šit na aši* "she was weaving wool in the house, she was not aware of this fight" (III, 18, 19); *sē tē rājgana-žet mayin hū* "he became in love over (i.e. with) that queen" (III, 49); *sē bana-žī* "she says" (III, 51, 53).

119. **Plural Nominative.**—*sē telā ugāt* "they went away from there" (II, 30); *sē ai Gurnāl-gē* "they came to Gurunai" (III, 10); *sē mē saran-žet pašat* "they quarrelled over this girl" (III, 24).

120. As a **Pronominal Adjective** we have :—**with Singular Nominative** : *sē χān bana-dū* "that Khān says" (I, 47) ; *sē pō gani hū* "that boy became big" (II, 27) ; *sē rājgana χušāl hī* "that queen became pleased" (III, 60). **With Object of a Transitive Verb in a tense derived from the Past Participle** : *te si Semū watana hažat* "he drove that Semū from the country" (III, 3).

121. **With Plural Nominative.**—*sē daš bhai āban-gē derī* "those ten cousins remained by themselves" (I, 31) ; *sē χalak jama hī* "those people (singular collective noun) became assembled" (III, 33).

122. One other **Demonstrative Pronoun** is *pāē* "he, that" which appears only in the List of Words. The Singular Nominative is *pāē*, which once occurs with the *ka*-suffix as *paigā* (Biddulph, *paga*),[1] in *paigā thū* "he is" (L. 158). The Singular Oblique Form is *pāyis*, and the Plural Nominative is *paiyē*. Examples are :—

123. **Singular Nominative.**—*pāē tanū māl ciā-dū* "he is grazing his own cattle" (L. 229). **Singular Oblique** : *pāyis γora kuḍ* "beat him well" (L. 236) (we have seen that verbs meaning "to beat" govern the Genitive, § 37). Here the Oblique Case is used, or, possibly, *pāyis* is a corruption of *pāē-si*) ; *miā šālmī pāyis-ke de* "give this rupee" (? these rupees, § 94) to him" (L. 234) ; *tiyā šālmī pāyis-kĕjā gin* "take those rupees from him" (L. 235). **Plural Nominative** : *paiyē thī* "they are" (L. 161) ; *paiyē ašī* "they were" (L. 167) ; *paiyē kuḍē-dī* "they strike" (L. 184).

124. As a **Pronominal Adjective** we have :—**With Singular Nominative** : *pāē māš ghō-se jada thām-si ṭin b'hēṭh thū* "that man is seated on a horse under a tree" (L. 230) ; **With Object of a Transitive Verb in a tense derived from the Past Participle** : *pāē cīz tā kis-kĕjā gin-thū* "from whom did you buy that thing ?" (L. 240).

125. **With Singular Genitive.**—*mē pižī-si pūc bĕbā kī-dū pāē māš-si šū-sed* "the son of my uncle has made a marriage

[1] Cf. Biddulph's *aga* "this", in § 84.

with his sister" (L. 225); *pāē māś-se pūc me cir miḍē-dē kūḍū-dū* "I have beaten that man's son with many stripes" (L. 228); *pāē śai-se kīmat* "the price of that thing" (L. 232).

126. **With Singular Locative.**—*mī bāp pāē liḍe śirē hō-dū* "my father lives in that small house" (L. 233).

127. In L. 231 the word *pātē* occurs twice as an oblique Pronominal Adjective. I am unable to explain the form. The sentence is *pātē māś-se bhā pātē māś-si śū-kĕjā ucat thū* "that man's brother is taller than that man's sister".

128. The nearest Dardic relations to this Pronoun are Drās Ṣ̌iṇā *pe-rō* "he", and Ḍāh-Hanū Ṣ̌iṇā *phō* "he". We may also compare the Syrian Gypsy *pānjī* "he". But the word can be more directly compared with the European Gypsy **pō* "self", Singular Oblique *pes* (compare Tōrwālī *pāē*, Singular Oblique, *pāyis*).

129. The word must be referred to the Skt. *ātman-* "self". This word also survives independently in the word *tanū* "own". In Prakrit *ātmā* becomes either *appā* or *attā*, and, similarly, in several Dardic languages, the *tm* of *(ā)tman-* is changed both to *p* and to *t*, with a slight distinction of meaning in each case. Thus, in Ksh. we have the two suffixes *pą̄n*[u] and *tą̄n*[u] (*pôn*[u], *tôn*[u]), both indicating relationship. The suffix *tą̄n*[u], however, indicates a more intimate relationship than *pą̄n*[u] (see *Kaśmīraśabdâmṛta*, iv, 63), as in *mą̄l*[i]*tą̄n*[u] "fatherhood", but *vĕsapą̄n*[u] "comradeship". On the other hand, the Ksh. for "self" is *pāna*. Similarly, in Tōrwālī, *tanū* is reserved for the reflexive possessive pronoun, and *pāē* for the demonstrative pronoun.

130. There is a **Reflexive Pronoun** *aban* (variant *āban*), meaning "self". It is immutable, but can take the termination *ī* (< *ēva*) for the sake of emphasis, as in *abanī* "(I, my, etc.) very self". Examples are :—

131. **Singular Nominative**, with emphatic *ī*:—*ā abanī baže-dū* "I am myself going" (I, 45). **Singular Dative**: *saran tā āban-gē lehī* "thou demandest the girl for thyself" (I, 39);

Tōwāl-mē aban-gē karwanda kī "he did cultivation for (him)self in Tōrwāl" (II, 2); *aban-mē-gē lāṭ-ke jōr ku* "make (thyself) ready for a fight for (thy)self (and) me" (III, 11). **Plural Dative:** *sē daš bhai āban-gē derī* "those ten cousins remained for (i.e. by) themselves" (I, 31).

132. The origin of the word *aban* must again, like Ksh. *pāna* "self", be referred to the Sanskrit *ātman-*, through the Prakrit *appaṇa-*. In Dardic *appaṇa-* would become **apaṇa-*, and the intervocalic *p* would, in Tōrwālī, regularly become *b* (see § 3*d*).

133. The **Reflexive Possessive Pronoun** is *tanū* "own", immutable, and used like the Hindī *apnā*. Like that word it usually refers to the logical subject of the sentence. The following are examples of its use: *tu baž, tanū dērā wadān kō* "go thou, and set (thine) own house in order" (I, 25); *tanū yai-ge tanū šī-ge banū* "(he) said to (his) own mother and to (his) own sister" (I, 27); *ē jamāldār tanū bhayā-gē bana-dū* "this headman says to (his) own brothers" (I, 32); "*tanū šū me-gē dū*"; *mē tanū šū tĕs-kē na dit* . . ."*ē tanū šū me-gē na dit*" "'give to me (your) own sister'; I did not give (my) own sister to him . . . 'he did not give (his) own sister to me'" (I, 33–5); *ā pō tanū šir-kē āp*; *tanū šī-yē bana-dū* "this boy comes to (his) own house; he says to (his) own sister" (I, 42); *tanū saran mē-gē dē* "give to me (thine) own daughter" (I, 48); *tanū širā jāma pewū* "he sent clothes from (his) own house" (I, 50); *tanū χānī cai gā* "(he) abandoned (his) own Khānship" (I, 54); *pade-ge tanū šir-ke ai* "(they) came backwards to (their) own house" (II, 15); *ā pō tanū yai-si ciš na pō-šat* "this boy was not drinking (his) own mother's breast" (II, 18, so 21); *tē χalak-kē tanū yarak sabāt* "(he) arranged (their) own *jirga* for that people (here, if my translation is right, *tanū* does not refer to the logical subject) (III, 6); *tanū karmā-ye banū* "(he) said to (his) own army" (III, 13); *Purangām-ge tanū bādšāhī-ge wat* "(she) came to Purangām for (her) own rule" (III, 60); *pāē tanū māl khanḍ-mē ciā-dū* "(he) is grazing (his) own cattle on the hill-top" (L. 229).

134. This form is again to be compared with the Sanskrit *(ā)tman-*. For further particulars, see under *pāē* (§ 129).

135. No example of the **Relative Pronoun** has been noted. Probably, as in Ṣiṇā, when needed, the Persian *ki* is used.

136. **Interrogative Pronouns.**—The Animate Interrogative Pronoun is *kām* "who?" (L. 92). When used as a Pronominal Adjective, it has the form *kāmē* or *kāme* in the two instances in which it has been noted. These are *hē kāmē māš gina-žī* "which man does she take?" (III, 28); *kāme māš-se pō te-kĕjā piyāj ye-dū* "the son of what man comes behind thee?" (L. 239).

An Oblique Form of this Pronoun is *kis* (cf. Veron *kese*, Ṣiṇā *kēse*), as in *pāē cīz tā kis-kĕjā gin thū* "from whom didst thou buy that thing?" (L. 240).

137. With *kām*, we may compare the Tirāhī *kāma* and the Gārwī *kum* "who?", the Ksh. Oblique Base *kam-*, and the Wai-alā Sing. Gen. *kuma*.

138. The Inanimate Interrogative Pronoun is *ka* (? *kā*) "what?" (L. 93), used both as a Pronoun and as a Pronominal Adjective. Examples are:—*tu ka s^a^wāl kō-dū* "what request dost thou make?" (I, 9); *tu ka γame-de γam-jān hō-dū* "owing to what trouble art thou worried?" (I, 11); *ā mere ka cal keī* "what device should I now do?" (I, 24); *tā me-gē ka mubārakī* (fem.) *dit* "what congratulation didst thou give me?" (I, 38); *tu ka nimā-dū* "what dost thou wish?" (II, 37, 40); *chī nām ka thū* "what is thy name" (L. 220).

139. We have seen above that *ka* is used with *mubārakī*, a feminine noun. We have *ke*, instead of *ka*, used with a feminine noun in *ke γora χušālī Xudā Pāk dī-cī* "what good happiness has God, the Pure, given!" (I, 20). Here *ke* is used exclamatorily.

140. The origin of *ka* is the Avesta-Sanskrit base *ka-*. It appears under numerous related forms in nearly all the Dardic languages. Thus, Bašgalī *kē, kai*; Wai-alā *kas*; Khōwār *kya*; Kalāšā *kīa*; Gawarbati *ki*; Pašai *kō*; Tirāhī

ki; Gārwī *kai*; Kāšmīrī *kyāh* "what?" Ṣiṇā [has *jēk* "what?", but also has *kē* "why?"

141. An Interrogative Pronoun of Quantity is *kadak* "how much? how many?" Examples are *mē ghō-sī umu kadak cī* (? *chī*) "how much is the age (fem.) of this horse?" (L. 221); *mhēda Kašmīr kadak dū thū* "from here how much (masc.) distant is Kashmīr" (L. 222); *chī bāp-si širē kadak pūc thī* "how many (masc. pl.) sons are in thy father's house?" (L. 223).

142. As related Dardic words, we may quote Wai-alā and Gārwī *kiti*, Gawarbati *kata*, Ṣiṇā of Ḍāh-Hanū *katāk*, Kāšmīrī *kait-*, and Maiyā *katuk*. As usual in Tōrwālī, intervocalic *t* has been softened to *d* (see § 3*d*.).

143. **Indefinite Pronouns.**—The only Indefinite Pronoun noted is the borrowed Arabic-Persian *fulāna*, which appears under the form *filankē* or *filankai* in the following:—*ā filankai watan-sē χān-sē pušt thū* "I am the descendant of the Khān of a certain country" (I, 12); *filankē χān-sē saran* "the daughter of a certain Khān" (I, 39, 43).

144.—**Miscellaneous Pronominal Adverbs.**

mēl "here" (cf. *tel* "there"), in *mēl ti Tōwāl-mē aban-gē karwanda kī* "here, in that Tōrwāl, he did cultivation for himself" (II, 2).

mhēda "from here" (cf. *telā*[1] "from there") in *mhēda Kašmīr kadak dū thū* "how far is Kashmīr from here?" (L. 222).

145. *til* "there", in *ai beš-te til nidā kao-dud* "I, having gone there, was looking on" (I, 19); *sē til šit hū* "he there became aware" (II, 19).

tel "there" (cf. *mēl* "here"), in *tel te Kufār-sāth lāṭ sabat* "there (they) joined fight with that Kāfir" (II, 12).

telā "from there" (cf. *mhēda* "from here"), in *sē telā ugāt* "they went away from there" (II, 30). Compare *telā pāš* "after that" (II, 49; III, 47).

146. *kēt* "where?", in *tū kēt-si thū* "of where art thou?" (I, 6).

[1] Note here, and in *mēl-ti*, the interchange of *t* and *l*.

147. *talā* "then" (? "from then"), in *ā ta talā gina-žī* "I (fem.) shall then take thee (when thou diggest a canal)" (III, 51).

148. *mere,* "now", in *ā mere ka cal keī* "what device should I do now ?" (I, 24); *mere tilai bižī* "now let us go, let us be off !" (I, 52).

149. *miz* "thus", in *Semū-ye miz banū* "to Semū they said thus" (III, 7).

150. *kē* (or, L. 94, *kai*) "why ?" (cf. Ṣiṇā *kē*) in *tu kē āp* "why didst thou come ?" (I, 47).

kiau "why ?", and, hence, by a common Dardic idiom, "therefore," in *kiau te-gē mubāraki-ye āp* "therefore (we) came to thee for congratulation" (I, 40); *ā kiau te-gē s^a^wāl kō-dū* "therefore I make a request to thee" (I, 56).

151. The connection of the above with the corresponding pronouns is obvious.

CONJUGATION

152. **Infinitive.**—No instances of the Infinitive occur in the folktales. Biddulph gives a form ending in *ōsa* or *ūsa*, as in *kuḍūsa* "to strike". I can find no difference in meaning between the two terminations, and possibly the distinction is a mere matter of spelling. For the sake of completeness, I here give a list of these Infinitives taken from Biddulph's English-Torwâlâk Vocabulary. It will be observed that one word, *kowōsa* or *kowūsa* "to eat", appears under both heads.

Infinitives in *ōsa* :—

abōsa "to arrive".
olōsa "to open".
cōsa "to let go".
hōsa "to be, become".
kōsa "to do".
žoš kowōsa (? *žoṣ khowōsa*) "to be angry" (cf. *kowūsa*, below).
lāmōsa "to swim".
porōsa "to break" (trans., cf. *pūrūsa*, below).
wōsa "to dismount".
yōsa "to come".

Infinitives in *ūsa* :—

ucūsa "to take up" (cf. *ušūsa*, 2, below).
amašūsa "to forget".
anūsa "to bring".
ušūsa, 1, "to enter" (Ksh. *atsun*).
ušūsa, 2, "to rise, to stand" (cf. *ucūsa*, above).
biginūsa "to sell".
bàjūsa "to go".
bujūsa "to hear".
bandūsa "to order".
banūsa "to say".
birārūsa "to search for".
pad-ge būsa "to return".
būūsa "to see".
baiyūsa "to sit".
cujūsa "to learn".
cūjūsa "to teach".
dyūsa "to give".
cigān gālūsa "to shout".
ganūsa "to shut".
gašūsa "to take".
hasūsa "to laugh".
kujūsa (? *khujūsa*) "to ask".
kowūsa (? *khowūsa*) "to eat" (cf. *žoš kowōsa*, above).
ligūsa "to write".
lekūsa "to count".
milūsa "to touch".
mowūsa "to kill".
maiyūsa "to die".
ba-ge nikūsa "to go out".
neyūsa "to take away".
pugūsa "to blow".
pergūsa "to move" (trans.).
pūrūsa "to be broken" (cf. *porōsa*, above).
pūsa "to drink".
pašūsa "to look at".
powūsa "to receive".
pyūsa "to send".
šijūsa "to fly" (as a bird).
tàlūsa "to throw".
tašūsa "eto creep".
zucūsa "to grieve".
žigalūsa "to pull".
žujūsa "to overthrow".
žingūsa "to weep".

153. **Verb Substantive. Present.** The Present tense of the Verb Substantive does not change for person, but does change for gender and number. The Masculine Singular is *thū*, and the Masculine Plural is *thī*. The Feminine in both numbers is noted as *cī*, which we should probably correct to *chī*. When employed as an Auxiliary Verb, it changes its form, and will be dealt with separately in §§ 157 ff. For the First and Second Persons Plural, there are no examples in the Folktales, but the List of Words gives *thī* for each.

The following examples are available for the other persons :—

Sing. Masc. 1 :—*ā filankai watan-sē χān-sē pušt thū* " I am the descendant of the Khān of a certain country " (I, 12) ; *ā Semū-se lāṭ-ke jōr thū* " I am ready for a fight of (i.e. with) Semū " (III, 12).

Sing. Masc. 2 :—*tū kēt-si thū* " of where art thou ? " (I, 6) ; *tu γora māš thū* " thou art a good man " (I, 56).

Sing. Masc. 3 :—*mē-tē-gē kam thū* " there is business for me and thee " (I, 6, similarly 7) ; *chī nām ka thū* " what is thy name " (L. 220) ; *ujil ghō-si zīn širē thū* " the saddle of the white horse is in the house " (L. 226) ; *pāē māš ghō-se jada thām-si ṭin b'hēṭh thū* " that man is seated on a horse under that tree " (L. 230) ; *bhā šū-kējā ucat thū* " the brother is taller than the sister " (L. 231).

Plur. Masc. 1 :—*mō thī* " we are " (L. 159).

Plur. Masc. 2 :—*thō thī* " you are " (L. 160).

Plur. Masc 3 :—*mī yai ū bāp kāfir thī* " my mother and father are unbelievers " (II, 29) ; *tisi aulād āχūnzāda thī* " his descendants are Ākhūnzādas " (II, 51) ; *chī bāp-si širē kadak pūc thī* " how many sons are there in thy father's house ? " (L. 223) ; *pāē šai-se kīmat dū šālmī ō ar thī* " two and a half rupees are the price of that thing " (L. 232).

Sing. Fem 3 :—*mē ghō-sī umu kadak cī* (? *chī*) " how much is the age of this horse ? " (L. 221).

154. The fact that this tense does not change for person, and does change for gender and number, shows that it is of participial origin. It can therefore be compared with the Avesta *stāta-*, Sanskrit *sthita-*. The change of *th* to *c* (? *ch*) in the Feminine is, as in Kāšmīrī, due to epenthesis, **thya* becoming *cī* (? *chī*). In Ksh. *ty* regularly becomes *ts*. *Thū* is universal through all the Kōhistānī dialects, and reappears in the Kaṣṭawāṛī dialect of Kāšmīrī.

155. The **Past Tense of the Verb Substantive** is, Masculine *ašū* (occasional variant, *āšū*), Plural, *aši*. The Feminine is *ašī*, for both Singular and Plural. When used as an Auxiliary

Verb, to form an Imperfect (§ 177) or Pluperfect. (§ 200), the initial *a* (or *ā*) is omitted, and the word is also liable to undergo other changes which will be discussed in §§ 160 ff. Examples of the use of this word as a Verb Substantive are :—

Sing. Masc. 1 :—*ā lūṭ āšū* " I was small " (I, 13).

Sing. Masc. 2 :—*tū ašū* " thou wast " (L. 162).

Sing. Masc. 3 :—*egī ti-hun jumāldār ašū, sē mī tarbūr ašū, ti-hun dērā wadān ašū* " one of them was a head man, he was my cousin, their house was in order " (I, 16, 17) ; *mē manjlas-mē e māš ašū* " there was a man in this assembly " (I, 21) ; *Punkā-mī e Kupār ašū* " there was a Kāfir in Punkā " (II, 3, similarly III, 2) ; *sē cir zālim ašū* " he was very powerful " (II, 4) ; *sē buzurg ašū* " he was a saint " (II, 17) ; *Pīr kile-mē ašū* " he was in the village of Pīr " (II, 19) ; *ā pō ḍē-si kaman ašū* " that boy was a master of the share " (II, 25) ; *Tōwāl-si muš-ke e biū-si thām ašū* " in front of Tōrwāl there was a *biū*-tree (II, 31) ; *pāji ti-hun cōthum bhā ašū* " afterwards there was their fourth brother " (II, 46) ; *tesi e dušman ašū* " of him there was an enemy " (III, 1) ; *tesi nām Semū ašū* " his name was Semū " (III, 2) ; *e māš andere cir hušā ašū* " one man among (them) was very intelligent " (III, 27).

Sing. Fem. 3 :—*ti-hun hujrā-mē majlas ašī* " there was an entertainment in their guest-room " (I, 18) ; *ē χušālī chi bāp-si ašī* " this pleasure was of thy father " (I, 22) ; *tesi e saran ašī* " there was a daughter of him " (III, 17) ; *sē mē lāḍa šit na ašī* " she was not aware of this fight " (III, 19) ; *telā pāš Bihū-mī e rājgana ašī* " after that there was a queen in Bihun " (III, 47).

Plur. Masc. 1 :—*mō ašī* " we were " (L. 165).

Plur. Masc. 2 :—*thō ašī* " you were " (L. 166).

Plur. Masc. 3 :—*mī daš bhai ašī* " of me there were ten cousins (I, 15) ; *tisi dvāš puš ašī* " of him there were twelve sons " (II, 4) ; *tesi yai-yū-bāp Kufār ašī* " his mother and father were Kāfirs (II, 17).

Plur. Fem. 3 :—*nūm-bīš saranē tisi-sāt ašī* " nine times twenty girls were with her " (III, 17).

156. The fact that this tense (like *thū*) does not change for person, but does change for number and gender, shows that it is participial in origin. It must be referred to the Avesta *šuta-*, past participle of √*šav-*, *šavaitē*, cf. Persian *šudan*. The initial *a*, which is dropped when the tense is used as an auxiliary, is perhaps a relic of the Old Persian, Avesta, and Sanskrit augment,[1] here improperly prefixed to a participle. The final *ū* of *šū* shows that it is a strong form, derived from **šutaka-*, not from the bare *šuta-*.

157. **Auxiliary Verbs.**—In most related languages, the unaltered Verb Substantive is employed as an Auxiliary Verb. In such cases, the Present of the Verb Substantive is used with the Present Participle, or with the Old Present, of the main verb to form a Periphrastic Present, as in the Hindī *caltā-hai* or *calē-hai* "he goes". It is also used with the Past Participle of the main verb to form a Perfect, as in the Hindī *calā-hai* "he has gone". Similarly, the Past of the Verb Substantive forms an Imperfect and a Pluperfect, as in the Hindī *caltā-thā* "he was going", and *calā-thā* "he had gone".

158. In Tōrwālī the case is different. The Present and Past of the Verb Substantive nearly always undergo certain changes when used as Auxiliary Verbs to make periphrastic tenses. The various forms employed are *dū* —with a Past, *dut* (variant, *dud*) ; *šū* or *šat* (variant *šad*) ; and *nin* or *in*. Of these *dū* means "is", and is the same word as *thū*, the change of *th* to *d* being due to the fact that nearly all the verbal forms to which it is appended end in vowels. The *th* accordingly becomes intervocalic, and, as explained in § 3*d*, is changed to *d*. Its Plural is *dī*, and its Feminine, Singular and Plural, is *žī* (variants *jī* and, under special circumstances, *cī*). Examples are *bana-dū* "he says" ; *bažē-dī* "they go" ; *gina-žī* "she takes" ; *hō-dū* "he has become" ; *kī-jī*

[1] The survival of the augment in Dardic was first pointed out by Dr. G. Morgenstierne on p. 71 of his *Report on a Linguistic Mission to Afghanistan*, and the subject is further developed by Professor Turner on pp. 538 ff. of vol. iv of the *Bulletin of the School of Oriental Studies*.

" she has been made " ; and *dī-cī* (contracted from *dit-žī*) " she has been given ". In the case of the Perfect tense, it sometimes happens that the Past Participle of the main verb ends in a consonant, and in such instances, the *th* is *thū* not intervocalic, and remains unaltered. An example is *gin-thū* " he has been taken ". Very rarely, *thū* remains unchanged even after a vowel. The only examples that I have noted are *ā kuḍē-dū* " I beat ", but *tū kuḍē-thū* " thou beatest " *sē kuḍē-thū* " he beats " (L. 179–181) and *hō-thū* " I have become " (I, 55), but *hō-dū* (II, 20). The plural forms given in the list have, however, *dī*, as in *mō kuḍē-dī* " we beat ".

The Past form of *dū*—*dut* (*dud*)—is used to make an Imperfect, as in *kō-dut* or *kao-dud* " (I, etc.) was doing ". I have not noted any certain case of *dut* making a Pluperfect (see § 178), but this tense is of rare occurrence, and nothing can be assumed from the fact that I have not found this form in the specimens.

Alongside of *dut*, we find *šū* very often used to make an Imperfect or a Pluperfect, as in *mē kuḍē-šū* " I was beating " ; *mē kuḍū-šū* " I had beaten ". It is, of course, only *ašū*, the Past tense of the Verb Substantive, with the initial *a* omitted. Instead of *šū*, we sometimes find *šat*, regarding which, see below (§ 160).

The Auxiliary Verb, or termination, *nin* or *in*, will be discussed in §§ 170–1. It is used to make a Present, or Future.

159. Of the above Auxiliary Verbs, the origin of *dū* has been explained above. I think that there can be no doubt about *dut* being, at least in meaning, a Past form of *dū*. Its origin is, however, obscure. To me it seems probable that it has been formed from *dū* by false analogy. As we shall see (§ 196) many Past Participles end in *t*, and *dut* has been formed from *dū*, just as we have *dit* " given ", beside *dai*, " he will give ". The pair (*a*)*šū* and *šat* " to be considered immediately, probably helped the adoption of the false analogy.

160. The word *šat* (variant, *šad*) is equivalent in meaning to (*a*)*šū*, and is used alongside of *šū* and *dut* to form an

Imperfect, as in *pō-šat,* he was drinking (II, 18). It also appears once as forming a Pluperfect, in *banu-šat* " had been said " (II, 27). I would suggest that this *šat* is a corruption of **šut,* on the analogy of Past Participles such as *hažat* " driven out ", *pašat* " quarrelled ", *sabat* " arranged ", *šeyat* " driven back ", and others in *-at* given in § 196. In this case it would, like *šū* be derived from the Avesta *šuta-* " gone " (§ 156), Persian, *šud.* Thus *šū* and *šat* would both be forms of the same word, one of which had originally the *ka-* suffix, with consequent elision of the *t,* while the other had no *ka-* suffix and has preserved the *t.* An alternative origin has been suggested to me by a friend. He would derive *šat* from the Sanskrit *aśayat* " he was lying ". Phonetically, this is quite possible, but it would necessitate denial of the connection between *šat* and *šū,* that seems to me to be almost certain.

161. It may be added here that Biddulph, in his account of " Torwâlâk " grammar, gives a short list of conjugational forms. Among these, he gives a Present Participle ending in *dūt,* as in *kùdùdoot* " striking ". There is nothing like this in Sir Aurel Stein's specimens. In his List, Sir Aurel gives *kuḍunki* " striking ", which is evidently based on the Paṣ̌tō Present Participle ending in *ūnkai.* In the Folktales, *dut* appears only as an Auxiliary Verb making the Imperfect tense (§ 178).

162. **Future (Old Present).**—As in the case of other Dardic languages, and as in the case of the Eranian Ghalchah Languages immediately to their North, the Old Present has lost its original force, and is now used as a Future, or, occasionally, where we should use the Present Subjunctive. The first and third persons sometimes, also, are used in an Imperative sense. Every person of both numbers ends in *ī,* but there are also variant forms. From the √*ka-* " do ", we have *keī* or *kī* for the first person singular and for the first person plural. Similarly, for the first person plural of the √*til-* " go ", we have *tilai* or *tili.* The √*ka-* also has

kuwē for its third person singular, and the √*di-* "give", has its first person singular *dai*, and its first person plural *dē*. If the sense of the future has to be emphasized, the syllable *yā* can be added to any form. The following are examples of the use of this tense :—

163. Sing. 1 :—*biži*, in *ā biži*, "I will go" (I, 44).

dai, in *ā te-gē dai* "I will give (her) to thee" (I, 49).

ginī, in *ā ta ginī* "I will take thee" (III, 53).

keī, in *ā mere ka cal keī* "what device shall I now do ?" (I, 24).

kī, in *ā beš-te e saran-ma tapōs kī* "I, having gone, will make enquiry from this girl" (III, 28).

kuḍī-yā, in *ā kuḍī-yā* "I shall beat" (L. 195).

nigālī, in *yāp ā nigālī* "I will cut a canal" (III, 52).

Sing. 2 :—*kuḍī-yā*, in *tu kuḍī-yā* "thou wilt beat" (L. 196).

Sing. 3 :—*hī*, in *mē watan-si mā-o-chī šerīkat hī* "let there be partition of this country of (i.e. between) me and thee" (II, 8).

kuḍī-yā, in *sē kuḍī-yā* "he will beat" (L. 197).

kuwē, in *tā Xodā e-ga dū na kuwē* "may God not make one two for thee" (II, 48) ; *hē te-ge kasab kuwē* "let him do work for thee" (III, 35).

Plur. 1 :—*biži*, in *yā, mō biži* "come ye, let us go" (I, 36) ; *mere tilai, biži* "let us now go, let us be off" (I, 52) ; *tili, biži* "let us go, let us be off" (II, 28).

dē, in *tes-ki mubārakī dē* "let us give congratulation to him" (I, 36).

huī, in *mō duyimo te Kufār-ke e huī* "we two will become one for (the sake of) that Kāfir" (II, 11).

keī, in *mō tihā Musulmān keī* "let us make them Moslems" (II, 29).

kuḍī-yā, in *mō kuḍī-yā* "we shall beat" (L. 198).

tilai or *tili*, see *biži* above.

bⁱhi, in *tisē dērā-mī bⁱhī* "let us sit in his house" (I, 52).

Plur. 2 :—*kuḍī-yā*, in *thō kuḍī-yā* "you will beat" (L. 199).

Plur. 3 :—*kuḍī-yā*, in *tiyā kuḍī-yā* "they will beat" (L. 200).

164. As regards the forms ending in *ī* (including those in *ē*) it is evident that the third person singular has usurped the functions of both the other persons. The origin, of course, is the Avesta, *-aiti*, Sanskrit *-ati*. We may compare the Kāšmīrī *māri*, and the Munjānī *dehi*, both meaning "he will beat". The form *kuwē* is formed from a base *kō* or *ku*, which we shall notice in the Imperative (§ 167) and in the Periphrastic Present (§ 173). *Tilai* and *dai* are, I suppose, merely older forms of *tili* and *dē* respectively (*-ati* > *-ai* > *-ē* > *-ī*).

165. **Imperative.**—For the first and third persons of the Imperative, we have just seen that the corresponding persons of the Future (Old Present) are employed.

166. The second person singular of the Imperative is, as usual, the bare base. As in other Dardic languages, including Ṣiṇā and Tirāhī, the second person plural is formed by adding *a* or *ā*. Examples of this tense are :—

167. Sing. 2 :—*baž*, in *tu baž tanū dērā* "go thou to thine own house" (I, 25); *ne baž* "do not go" (I, 44, masc.; 45, fem.); *mē kĕjā mūj baž* "walk before me" (L. 238).

bⁱhai "sit thou" (L. 79).

cin, in *mē cai cin* "cut thou this cliff" (III, 58).

dē, or (?) *dū*, in *tanū šū me-gē dū* "give thine own sister to me" (I, 33). Here *dū* is perhaps a slip for *dē* due to the presence of *bana-dū* immediately preceding in the passage); *tanū saran mē-gē dē* "give thine own daughter to me" (I, 48); *miā šālmī pāyis-ke de* "give this rupee (? these rupees, § 94) to him" (L. 234).

gan, in *khē-de gan* "bind (him) with a rope" (L. 236).

gin, in *mā gin* "take me" (III, 50); *tiyā šālmī pāyis-kĕjā gin* "take those rupees from him" (L. 235).

hō, in *iṛi hō* "stand" (i.e. become standing) (L. 82).

khō "eat" (L. 78).

kō or *ku*, in *tanū dērā wadān kō* "make thine own house

in order" (I, 25); *mē-ye kalimā bayān kō* "recite the creed to me" (II, 35); *mē-ge ṭubak-si duwā kō* "make to me the favour (i.e. the gift) of a rifle" (II, 44); *aban-mē-gē lāṭ-ke jōr ku* "for yourself and me make ready for a fight" (III, 11).

kuḍ, in *pāyis γora kuḍ* "beat him well" (L. 236). A variant of this word is *kuṭh* (L. 81, 175). See § 3*e*.

mā, in *mē Sulaimānik na mā* "do not kill this Sulaimānik" (III, 35).

mō "die" (L. 83).

nigāl or *nīgal*, in *tu mē Bihū-ge yāp nigāl* "excavate a canal to this Bihun" (III, 51); *kūī-mā ū nīgal* "draw water from the well" (L. 237).

pai, in *tu beš-te me-gē jāma pai* "do thou, having gone, send clothes to me" (I, 49).

sabā, in *payim dišē pan sabā* "prepare thou a road on the other side" (III, 37). Here the final *ā* is part of the base.

thā, in *ghō-si pīḍ-jada zīn thā* "put thou the saddle on the horse's back" (L. 227). Here also the *ā* is part of the base.

til "go thou" (L. 77).

yē "come thou" (L. 80).

Plur. 2:—*baža*, *buža*, or *boža*, in *buža* "go ye" (I, 27); *to baža* "go ye" (I, 41); *Bihū-ge boža* "go ye to Bihun" (III, 13).

buā, in *mē saran buā* "inspect ye this girl" (III, 31).

janā, in *mī dērā janā* "clean ye my house" (I, 27).

kuwa, in *mē-sāt lāṭ kuwa* "together with me make a fight" (III, 5); *to lāṭ na kuwa* "do not ye make a fight" (III, 28).

tila, in *tila rabaṛ-ke* "go ye to the fight" (III, 13).

yā, in *yā, mō bana-dū* "come ye, we say" (I, 33); *yā, mō bižī* "come ye, we will go" (I, 36).

168. **Periphrastic Present.**—This is formed by adding a present form of the Auxiliary Verb to an abraded form of the Future (Old Present). The same procedure is followed in Ṣiṇā where *ṣidēn* "he strikes", is a contraction of the Future (Old Present) *ṣidè* with *han* "he is". In Tōrwālī, the Future (Old Present), for all persons ends in *ī*, as in *kuḍī*

"I, thou, he, etc. will strike". In the Periphrastic Present, this *ī* is weakened to *ē* or *a*, and to this the Auxiliary *dū* (see § 158) is added as the Auxiliary. Sometimes *nin* or *in* (see below, §§ 169, 170, 176) is used instead of *dū*. When the more usual form with *dū* is employed, we get forms such as *kuḍē-dū* "I, thou, or he strike, strikest, or strikes"; *gina-dū* "I, thou, or he take, takest, or takes". The plural masculine of *dū* is *dī*, so that we get *kuḍē-dī* "we, you, or they strike." The feminine in both numbers of *dū* is *žī* so that we get *kuḍē-žī* "I, thou, she, we, you, or they (all feminine) strike, etc."

Properly speaking, this tense has a present force, but in cases like *bana-dū* "he says", it is used as a Historical Present, and may be translated "he said", as was frequently done in the original manuscript supplied by Sir Aurel Stein. As the tense is certainly a Present, I have not scrupled in each case to alter this to "he says". Sometimes this tense may even have the power of an immediate Future, as we say "I am going", when we mean "I shall go immediately".

169. Besides the usual Present made with *dū*, we occasionally find another Present made with the Auxiliary *nin* or *in*. As we shall see, the latter form seems to be used only when the verbal base ends itself in *n*, so that we are justified in assuming that the real form of the auxiliary is *nin*. Thus, we have *mā-nin* "they will kill", but *gin-in* "we shall take". Although, for the reasons given in the next section, I provisionally class this tense as a Present, in the few examples available (§ 176) it seems to be mainly used with a Future force, and Biddulph, in his grammatical sketch of Torwâlâk, gives "*kùdnin*", as the regular Future, making no mention of the Future (Old Present) described above in §§ 162 ff.[1]

[1] I may here mention that Biddulph distinguishes between a masculine, *kùdnin*, and a feminine *küdnin*. He makes a similar distinction in regard to the ordinary Present with *dū*. He gives a masculine *kùdádoo* (i.e. *kuḍa-dū*), and a feminine *küdüdji* (i.e. *küḍü-žī*), but I have failed to find any trace of such a distinction in the present texts. Moreover, as the verbal base, *kuḍē* or *kuḍa*, is almost certainly derived from the Old Present, and is not participial, I do not see how it can possibly change for gender.

170. The origin of this auxiliary form, *nin*, is to me a matter of doubt. I am inclined to suggest that the termination may originally have been that of the third person plural, and we can then connect forms such as Biddulph's *kuḍnin*, with the Ṣiṇā forms, such as the 3rd person plural *ṣidènen* "they beat", which is a compound of the Future (Old Present) of that language (Plur. 3, *ṣidèn*), with the auxiliary verb *han* "they are". If this is correct, *kuḍnin* should be a compound of a lost **kuḍen* "they will beat", with a Tōrwālī form corresponding to the Ṣiṇā *han*, which has now fallen out of use as a separate word.

171. Examples of the Present with *dū* are :—

Sing. Masc. 1 :—*baže-dū*, in *ā abanī baže-dū* "I am going" (i.e. will go) myself" (I, 45).

gina-dū, in *mē saran ā gina-dū* "I take (i.e. will take) this girl" (III, 25).

kō-dū,[1] in *ā te-kĕjā s^{a}wāl kō-dū* "I am making a request from thee" (I, 8, 56) ; *ā te-gē du žāt majlis kō-dū* "I make (i.e. will make) an entertainment for thee for two nights" (I, 10) ; *te-sād maškulā kō-dū* "I am making business (i.e. talk) with thee "(I, 56) ; *ā te-sāt šerīkat na kō-dū* "I am not making sharing with thee" (II, 9).

kuḍē-dū, in *ā kuḍē-dū* "I beat" (L. 179).

mā-dū, in *ā mē Sulaimānik mā-dū*, "I will kill this Sulaimānik" (III, 34).

nimā-dū, in *ā te-kĕjā χānī nimā-dū* "I wish for a Khānship from thee" (II, 38) ; *ā wazīrī nimā-dū* "I wish for Wazīrship" (II, 41).

Sing. Fem. 1 :—*gina-žī*, in *ā ta talā gina-žī* "I will then take thee" (III, 51).

[1] This is irregular, here, and also elsewhere in this tense. The Future (Old Present) is *keī* or *kī* (§ 163), and the Imperative is *kō* or *ku* (§ 167). The Future (Old Present) Sing. 3 is *kuwē* (§ 163), and is an exceptional form used as an Imperative. Cf. Imperative Plur. 2 *kuwa* (§ 167). See also § 164.

172. Sing. Masc. 2 :—*bažē-dū*, in *tū bažē-dū* " thou goest " (L. 206).

hō-dū, in *tu ka γame-de γamjān hō-dū* " by what trouble art thou becoming troubled ? " (I, 11).

kō-dū, in *tu ka s^{a}wāl kō-dū* " what request dost thou make ? " (I, 9).

nimā-dū, in *tu ka nimā-dū* " what dost thou wish ? " (II, 37, 40).

According to L. 180, " thou beatest " is *tū kuḍē-thū*, in which *thū* is used instead of *dū*. This is exceptional, see § 158.

173. Sing. Masc. 3 :—*bana-dū* " he says " (I, 7, 8, 9, 10, et passim). As stated above, this is throughout used as a Historical Present.

baže-dū, in *Šāh Zamān Xān Mingaore-ye baže-dū* " Shāh Zamān Khān goes (i.e. went) to Mingaora " (I, 1) ; *sē bažē-dū* " he goes " (L. 207).

ciā-dū, in *pāē tanū māl khanḍ-mē ciā-dū* " he is grazing cattle on the hill-top " (L. 229).

hō-dū, in *mī bāp pāē liḍe širē hō-dū* " my father is being (i.e. lives) in that small house " (L. 233).

kuḍē-thū, in *sē kuḍē-thū* " he beats " (L. 181). See above, under " thou beatest ", and § 158,

pō-dū, in *sē tanū yai-si ciš na pō-dū* " he does not drink (from) his mother's breast " (II, 21).

ye-dū, in *ek dui-sāt jōr ne ye-dū* " one does not come (to) agreement with the other " (III, 26) ; *kāme māš-se pō te-kĕjā piyāj ye-dū* " the son of what man comes behind thee ? " (L. 239).

174. Sing. Fem. 3 :—*bane-žī*, in *mē pō-si šū bane-žī* " this boy's sister says " (Historical Present) (I, 44) ; *sē bana-žī* " she says " (id.) (III, 51, 53) ; *rājgana Sulaimānik-ke bana-žī* " the queen says (id.) to Sulaimānik " (III, 58).

gina-žī, in *hē kāmē māš gina-žī* " which man does she take ? " (III, 28).

175. Plur. Masc. 1 :—*bana-dū* (? *bana-dī*), in *yā, mō bana-dū* (? *bana-dī*) *mē pō-gē* "come ye, we (shall) say to that boy" (I, 33).

bažē-dī, in *mō bažē-dī* "we go" (L. 208).

kuḍē-dī, in *mō kuḍē-dī* "we beat" (L. 182).

Plur. Masc. 2 :—*bažē-dī*, in *thō bažē-dī* "you go" (L. 209).

kuḍē-dī, in *thō kuḍē-dī* "you beat" (L. 183).

Plur. Masc. 3 :—*bažē-dī*, in *ē bažē-dī* "they go" (L. 210).

kuḍē-dī, in *paiyē kuḍē-dī* "they beat" (L. 184).

176. Examples of the Present with *nin* or *in* are :—

Sing. Masc. 1 :—*hō-nin*, in *mē hō-nin* "I may be" (L. 172)

Sing. Masc. 3 :—*ban-in*, in *ban-in*, "*tā me-gē ka mubārakī dit*" "(if) he may say, 'what congratulations are given by thee to me ?'" (I, 38).

kō-nin, in *tē mō-ma tapōs kō-nin* "he may make a question from (i.e. inquire from) us" (I, 37).

Plur. Masc. 1 :—*ban-in*, in *mō ban-in* "we may say" (I, 39).

gin-in, in *besyāt mōi gin-in* "it is we who shall take loot" (III, 8).

ya-nin (? *yā-nin*) in *mōi te-sāt karmā ya-nin* (? *yā-nin*) "it is we who shall come with thee as an army" (III, 7).

Plur. Masc. 3 :—*mā-nin*, in *tu ne baž, tā mā-nin* "do not thou go, they may kill thee" (I, 44).

177. **Imperfect.**—This is formed on the same lines as the Periphrastic Present, the Past tense, *(a)šū*, of the Verb Substantive, or the Past Auxiliary *dut* (*dud*) or *šat* (*šad*) (§ 158), being substituted for *dū*. As stated in § 155, the initial *a* of *ašū* has been omitted, so that, in the Imperfect, *ašū* becomes *šū*. Only one example of the Imperfect with *šū* has been noted. It is *mē kuḍē-šū* "I was beating" (L. 192).[1]

[1] Biddulph gives an Imperfect *kùdoosáshoo* (i.e. *kuḍūsa-šū*), with a feminine *kūdùsáshi* (i.e. *kūḍusa-ši*). These are not borne out by the present texts, but may belong to the dialect of some Tōrwāl village other than those visited by Sir Aurel Stein. The form *kùdoosá* is also given by him as the Infinitive, see § 152.

178. Imperfects formed with *dut* (*dud*) are :—

dugū-dut, in *sē širē pūm dugū-dut* "she was weaving wool in the house" (III, 18).

hō-dut, in *ē manjlas thun hujrā-mē hō-dut* "this entertainment was becoming (i.e. used to be) in your house" (I, 23).

kō-dut, *kao-dud*, in *Sulaimānik Purangām-žet bādšāhī kō-dut* "Sulaimānik was doing rule over Purangām" (III, 1) ; *ai beš-te til nidā kao-dud* "I, having gone there, was making inspection" (I, 19).

neyu-dut, in *sē māliyā neyu-dut* "he was taking taxes" (II, 5). This is doubtful. It may perhaps be a pluperfect (§§ 191, 201).

179. Imperfects formed with *šat* (*šad*) are :—

diū-šad, in *malāž-ge gil diū-šad* "he was giving (i.e. continued to give) bread to guests" (I, 29).

pō-šat, in *ā pō tanū yai-si ciš na pō-šat* ; *lehir chal-si ciš pō-šat* "this boy was not drinking (i.e. used not to drink) his mother's breast ; he was drinking the breast of a red goat" (II, 18).

180. **Past Tense.**—The Past Participle, without any addition, is used for the Past tense. Past Participles appear under two forms, a strong (with original *ka*-suffix) and a weak. The strong forms end in a long vowel (*ā*, *ū*, or *ō*), and change for gender and number. Weak forms end in a consonant and do not change for gender or for number. It will be convenient to divide the examples into the two groups of Intransitive and Transitive verbs.

181. **Intransitive Past Tense.**—Here the Past Participle does not change for person. Only in the case of strong participles, does it change for gender and number. Thus :—

182. Sing. Masc. 1 :—*gā* (strong form), in *ā gā filankē χān-sē saran paš* "I went (i.e. I'm off) after the daughter of a certain Khān" (I, 43 ; so L. 211).

hō (strong form), in *ā šid hō*, *χušāl hō* "I became aware, I became (i.e. I am) happy" (I, 40).

183. Sing. Masc. 2:—*āp*, in *tu kē āp* "why didst thou come?" (I, 47).

gā (strong form), in *tū gā* "thou wentest" (L. 212).

184. Sing. Masc. 3:—*āp*, in *ē māž āp* "a man arrived" (I, 3); *ē pō pat-gē āp* "this boy came back" (I, 26); *ā pō tanū šir-kē āp* "the boy came to his own house" (I, 42); *dād mē watan-gē āp* "the ancestor came to this country" (II, 1, 7); *pāji tisi duyi bhā āp* "afterwards his second brother came" (II, 39); *mūš-ke cai āp* "a cliff came (i.e. appeared) in front" (III, 57).

bēṭh or *bⁱhēṭh*, or (strong form, cf. § 3*e*) *bēḍū*, in *ē pō andare bēṭh* "this boy sat inside" (I, 29); *tisi ṭin bēḍū* "he sat under it (sc. a tree)" (II, 32). Cf. *pāē māš thām-si ṭin bⁱhēṭh thū* "that man is seated under a tree" (L. 230).

diū (strong form), in *pata-ge diū* "he fled back" (III, 16); *Sulaimānik diū* "Sulaimānik escaped" (III, 45).

gā (strong form), in *Ningōlī-se kac-ke gā* "he went to the neighbourhood of Ningōlī" (I, 2); *ā pō gā* "that boy went" (I, 46); *tanū χānī cai gā* "he abandoned his Khānship" (I, 54); *māš gā . . . te saran-si kan-ke gā* "the man went . . . he went to the vicinity of that girl" (III, 29); *Sulaimānik jabal hat-te ginu gā* "Sulaimānik, taking a pickaxe in his hand, went" (III, 38); *pata-g Semū-sie šir-ke gā* "he went back to Srmū's house" (III, 39, so 45); *melāštōp-te gā* "he went for a visit" (III, 48).

gya (a variant of *gā*), in *Sulaimānik-si karmā gya Bihū-ge* "Sulaimānik's army went to Bihun" (III, 14).

hū or *hō* (both strong forms), in *mī dērā kūtsā šaṭ hū* "my house (and) lane became ruined" (I, 14); *ē χān lewānai hū* "this Khān became mad" (I, 54); *e pō paidā hū* "a son became born" (II, 16); *sē til šit hū* "he there became aware" (II, 19); *sē pō gani hū* "that boy became big" (II, 27); *sē Musulmān hū* "he became a Musalmān" (II, 36, so 43, 49); *se watan-si wazīr hū* "he became Wazīr of the country" (II, 42); *šerunke hū . . . Mayō-mī dērā hū* "he became an exile (§ 203) . . . his home became in Mayō" (III, 4);

Semū cir χušāl hū " Semū became very glad " (III, 42); *sē tē rājgana-žet mayin hū* " he became in love with that queen " (III, 49).

tē χān-sē malāž hō " he became a guest of that Khān " (I, 46); *cui kāl hō* " the third year became " (II, 47).

It will be observed that the usual form is *hū*.

hut, in *Sulaimānik hut* " Sulaimānik slept " (III, 43).

lagū (strong form), in *šir-ke lagū* " he entered the house " (III, 29).

mū or *mau* (both strong forms), in *mī bāp mū* " my father died " (I, 13); *Semū mau* " Semū died " (III, 45).

nigāt, in *ā māš mē šira nigāt* " that man went out from this house " (III, 31).

ucit, in *karmā ucit* " the army arose " (III, 9).

wat, in *awal-mē Xāna-si dād wat* " First Khāna's ancestor arrived " (II, 34); *pāji tisi cui bhā wat* " afterwards his third brother arrived " (II, 43); *Gurnāl-miā Semū-si karmā wat* " Semū's army arrived from Gurnāl " (III, 14); *payim diše-de wat* " he arrived at the opposite side " (III, 56).

185. Sing Fem. 3:—*gā* (strong form. We should expect *gī* or *gai*), in *tasi šū gā* " his sister went " (I, 28).

hī (strong form), in *na-tsāba derē zōg hī* " there became an unexpected noise at the door " (III, 20); *hē mē lāḍa šit hī* " she became aware of this fight " (III, 21); *ar žāt hī* " it became half night (i.e. midnight) " (III, 43); *mē watan-mī Sulaimānik-si bī pādšāhī hī* " Sulaimānik's rule became again in this country " (III, 46, so 61); *pan na hī* " there was no road " (III, 57); *sē rājgana χušāl hī* " that queen became pleased " (III, 60).

muī or *maī* (both strong forms), in *mē χān-sē chī muī* " the wife of this Khān died " (I, 53); *mē saran maī* " this girl died " (III, 30). Cf. *māil* in *tē saran māil ḍiṭ* " they saw (that) this girl (had been) killed " (III, 32).

wat, in *sē rājgana . . . Purangām-ge tanū bādšāhī-ge wat* " that queen . . . came to Purangām for her own rule " (III, 60).

186. Plur. Masc. 1:—*āp*, in *kiau te-gē mubāraki-ye āp* "therefore we came to thee for congratulation" (I, 40).

gai (strong form), in *mō gai* "we went" (L. 214).

nigāt, in *mō mē māš-sē puχtuā nigāt* "we are gone out from enmity of (i.e. with) this man" (I, 52).

187. Plur. Masc. 2:—*gai* (strong form), in *thō gai* "you went" (L. 215).

188. Plur. Masc. 3:—*ai* (strong form), in *pade-ge tanū šir-ke ai* "they came back to their own house" (II, 15); *sē ai Gurnāl-gē* "they came to Gurnāl" (III, 10); *Mayō-si gan gan māš ai* "a number of big men of Mayō came" (III, 22).

āp, in *mē gām-si χalak bud ēs paš āp* "after this many people of this village came" (I, 30).

derī (strong form), in *sē daš bhai āban-gē derī* "those ten cousins remained by themselves" (I, 31).

gai (strong form), in *dō kāl gai* "two years went (i.e. passed)" (II, 47); *hē gai* "these (men) went" (III, 32); *tiyā gai* "they went" (L. 216).

huī, *hōi*, or *hī* (all strong forms), in *diumo* (? *duimo*, § 56) *ek-dije* (§ 56) *eṛi huī* "both, one with the other, became halted" (III, 15); *derē eṛī hōi* "they became halted at the door" (III, 22); *sē χalak jama hī* "those people became assembled" (III, 33).

langī (strong form), in *sē-dē langī* "they crossed by a bridge" (II, 12).

nurī (strong form), in *hē pade-ge nurī* "they returned back" (II, 14).

pašat, in *sē mē saran-žet pašat* "they quarrelled over this girl" (III, 24).

ugāt, in *sē telā ugāt* "they went away from there" (II, 30).

189. It is hardly necessary to point out that the strong forms in the above examples are derived from original participles, to which the *ka*-suffix has been added. So far as can be gathered from the above examples, the following changes for gender and number occur in the case of these strong forms:—

Sing. Masc.	*Sing. Fem.*	*Plur. Masc.*	*Plur. Fem.*
—	—	*ai*	—
—	—	*derī*	—
diū	—	—	—
gā, gya	*gā* (? *gī* or *gai*)	*gai*	—
hū, hō	*hī*	*huī, hōi, hī*	—
lagū	—	—	—
—	—	*langī*	—
mū, mau	*muī, maī*	—	—
—	—	*nurī*	—

For weak forms, we have *āp*, Masc. Sing., and Masc. Plur., and *wat*, Masc. and Fem. Sing.

190. **Transitive Past Tense.**—The following examples of the Transitive Past are not arranged according to the gender, number, and person of the subject. The arrangement must depend upon the gender and number of the object, as the construction is Passive, and the subject is necessarily in the Agentive case. Unfortunately, the gender, in the case of weak participles, cannot always be ascertained with certainty. So far as I could ascertain this, I have put the verbs with a feminine object separately, but, for want of my knowledge of their genders, some feminine forms may appear in the masculine lists.

191. Masc. Sing. Obj.—*banū* (strong form), in *mē banū* "I said" (I, 20); *tanū yai-ge tanū šī-ge banū* "he said to his own mother and to his own sister" (I, 27); *dād-ke banū* "he said to the ancestor" (II, 8, 9); *Semū-ye miz banū* "they said thus to Semū" (III, 7); *Sulaimānik-kē banū* "he said to Sulaimānik" (III, 11); *Sulaimānike tē māš-ke banū* "Sulaimānik said to that man" (III, 12); *tanū karmā-ye banū* "he said to his own army" (III, 13).

būda or *būdā* (strong form), in *ti būda ā pō-si ḍē-si kaman ašū* "he saw (that) that boy was a master of the share" (II, 25); *būdā Semū hubil thū* "he saw (that) Semū is asleep" (III, 43).

cinū (strong form), in *te cai cinū* "he cut the cliff" (III, 38); *Sulaimānike mē cai cinū* "Sulaimānik cut this cliff" (III, 59).

did, in *Semū-si šā-si did* " he hit Semū on the head " (III, 44).

dit, in *tes-ke šulan dit* " he gave a curse to him (i.e. he cursed him) " (II, 48); *Sulaimānik gaš-te Semū-ye dit* " having captured Sulaimānik, they gave him to Semū " (III, 33).

ḍiṭ in *tē rājgana tē ḍiṭ* " that queen saw him " (III, 49).

gin, in *tē rājgana Sulaimānige gin* " that queen took Sulaimānik (*bhāvē prayōga*) " (III, 55).

hažat, in *te si Semū watana hažat* " he drove that Semū from the country " (III, 3); *tē Kufār hē hažat* " they were driven away by that Kāfir " (II, 15).

janū (strong form), in *te dērā janū* " she cleaned the house " (I, 28).

kī (strong form), in *sitār-sē māš mē χān-ma tapōs kī* " the man of the guitar made inquiry from this Khān " (I, 5); *Tōwāl-mē aban-gē karwanda kī* " he did cultivation for himself in Tōrwāl " (II, 2); *laṭ kī* " they did fighting " (II, 14); *kalimā bayān kī* " he recited the creed " (II, 33, 36, 39); *tes Musulmān kī* " he made him a Moslem " (*bhāvē prayōga*) " (II, 47); *mē kām-si Imām kī* " (he) made him Imām of this tribe " (II, 50); *mī Sulaimānike sāt rabaṛ kī* " he made a fight with this Sulaimānik " (III, 3); *tē watan-mī mōi lāṭ kī, mōi barai kī* " we verily did fighting in that country, we verily made victory " (III, 8); *Sulaimānike hukum kī* " Sulaimānik made an order " (III, 13); *lāṭ šuru kī* " they began to do fighting " (III, 15); *lāṭ-mi Sulaimānike baidāt kī . . . tes-ma gām ṭin kī* " in the fight he made Sulaimānik defeated (*bhāvē prayōga*) . . . the village was captured from him " (III, 16); *dadan-si ken-ta baṭhā kī* " (he) made him seated by the side of the fireplace " (III, 42).

kuḍū (strong form), in *mai kuḍū* " I struck " (L. 185, and so on through the tense).

nū (strong form), in *mē pō ti šēχ nū* " that Shekh took away this boy " (II, 23); *Sulaimānik gaš-te nū* " having captured Sulaimānik, they took him away " (III, 36). Perhaps *neyu* in *neyu-dut* (§ 178) is a variant of *nū*.

pewū, *peyū*, or *piyū* (all strong forms), in *tanū širā jāma pewū* " he sent a garment from his own house " (I, 50) ; *Miā Kāsim Bāba tanū šēχ peyū* " Miyān Kāsim Bābā sent his own Shēkh (= disciple) " (II, 22) ; *Semū māš piyū* " Semū sent a man " (III, 10).

sabāt, in *tē χalak-kē tanū yarak sabāt* " for those people their own tribal council was arranged " (III, 6) ; *tel te Kufār-sāth lāṭ sabat* " there they joined battle with that Kāfir " (II, 12).

thāu or *thalū* (both strong forms), in *Miā Kāsim Bāba mē pō-si nām thāu* " Miyān Kāsim Bābā put a name of (i.e. to) this boy " (II, 26) ; *šen thalū* " she placed a bed " (apparently an *l*-participle, § 195) (I, 28).

192. Masc. Plur. Obj. :—*hažat*, in *tē Kufār hē hažat* " that Kāfir drove them away " (II, 15).

kī (strong form), in *lēb bāliχ barābar kī* " she made right a cover (and) pillow " (I, 28).

šeyat, in *tē Kufār-miā pade-ge šeyat* " they were driven backwards from that Kāfir " (II, 13). Here the construction is purely passive.

193. Fem. Sing. Obj. :—*banī* (strong form), in *tē jumāldār bī mēlī bāt banī* " that head man again said the same word " (I, 35).

did, in *tē māš mē saran-si kan-de did* " that man struck this girl with an arrow " (III, 30). This is a doubtful case, as the feminine object is in the genitive (§ 37).

dit, in *mē tanū šū tēs-kē na dit* " I did not give my own sister to him " (I, 34) ; *ē tanū šū me-gē na dit* " he did not give his own sister to me " (I, 35) ; *tā me-gē ka mubārakī dit* " what congratulation did you give me " (I, 38).

ḍiṭ, in *tihē mē Sulaimānik-si saran ḍiṭ* " they saw the daughter of this Sulaimānik " (III, 23) ; *saran māil ḍiṭ* " they saw the girl (that she was) killed " (III, 32).

kambai (? strong form), in *māliyā ne kambai* " they did not (?) pay the tax " (II, 6). Sir Aurel Stein translates the word *kambai* by " stopped ", but with a query. If the word is correct, it seems to mean " paid ".

kī (strong form), in *tē χān tesē chī ruksat kī* "that Khān allowed his wife to go" (I, 51); *Nariā-si dād te-set mukadima kī* "the ancestor of Narēr made a quarrel with him" (II, 6); *tes-ke Bāba duwā kī* "to him the Bābā made a prayer (i.e. grant)" (II, 42, so 45); *tē Semū tē χalak-kē arzī kī* "that Semū made a request to those people" (III, 5).

lehī (strong form), in *filankē χān-sē saran tā aban-gē lehī* "thou askedst for thyself the daughter of a certain Khān" (I, 39).

nigālī (strong form), in *Sulaimānige tē yāp nigālī* "Sulaimānik excavated that canal" (III, 54).

sabat, in *pan sabat* "(he) prepared a road" (III, 38, 40, 41).

telī (strong form), in *mī Jebēya-si dād sē telī* "this ancestor of Jabēr broke the bridge" (II, 13).

wālī (strong form), in *tē rājgana Purangām-ge wālī* "(he) brought that queen to Purangām" (III, 56).

194. The following are the strong forms of Participles occurring in the above examples :—

Masc. Sing.	*Fem. Sing.*	*Plur. Masc.*
banū	—	—
būda, būdā	—	—
cinū	—	—
janū	—	—
kī	*kī*	*kī*
kuḍū	—	—
—	*lehī*	—
—	*nigālī*	—
nū, (? *neyu*)	—	—
pewū, peyū, piyū	—	—
thāu, thalū	—	—

The rest are all weak forms, and do not change for gender or number. See §§ 180, 189.

195. If I am right in looking upon *thalū* as a variant of *thāu*, we have here an example of the Dardic *l*-participle, which is also found in Ṣiṇā and other Dardic languages. The original

sthāpitakaḥ, would in the one case become **thāpiu*, and then *thāvu*, *thāu*. In the other case it would become **thāpidu*, **thāvilu* and then *thalū* (? *thālū*). The *l* is not the *illa*-suffix common in India, for, in Ṣiṇā, we find several pairs of participles such as *uthīdo* or *uthīlo* " risen " ; *cādī* or *cālī* " delivered of a child "; *sīçīdo* or *sīçīlo* " learnt ", and so on, which show that we have here the change of *d* to *l* that is common in many Eranian languages. Another example of the *l*-participle is *māil* " killed " (III, 32). See *-t* > *-d* > *-l*, and *-d* > *-l*, in § 4.

196. The existence of this *l*-participle raises the question whether the original *t* of the Past Participle has been preserved in the case of any other verbs. This has certainly been the case in some verbs quoted in the foregoing lists, viz. *hut* < *supta-* ; *wat* < *avâpta-* (cf. Ksh. √*wāt-* " arrive ") ; *ucit* < *utkṣipta-* ; and *dit* < *datta-*. The participle *ḍiṭ* (? *ḍiṭh*) is derived from *dṛṣṭa-*, and *bēṭh* from *upaviṣṭa-*. The √*di-* " give ", in many Dardic languages also means " strike ", and we are thus justified in looking upon *did* " struck ", as a variant of *datta-* (cf. § 3*d*). In all these the final *t* originally formed part of a conjunct consonant, and its preservation offers no difficulties.

There are other Past Participles ending in *t*, of which the origin is not so manifest. These are *ābāt* (< *āpita-*) " brought " ; *hažat* " driven out " ; *nigāt* (< *nikāsita-*) " gone out " ; *pašat* " they quarrelled " ; *sabat* or *sabāt* (< *saṁbhārita-*) " arranged " ; *šeyat* " driven back " ; and *ugāt* (< *udgāta-*) " arose ". In some of these, at least—*ābāt*, *nigāt*, *sabāt*, and *ugāt*—the single intervocalic *t* of the original has been preserved. Regarding the others, I must reserve my opinion till their derivations are established.

One word more. Three pure Past Participles must be added to the above. One is *baidāt* " defeated ", and is used as a participle, and not as a Past tense in *lāṭ-mi Sulaimānike baidāt kī* " in the fight he made Sulaimānik defeated " (III, 16). Another is *baṭhā* " caused to be seated ", in *dadan-si ken-ta baṭhā kī* " he made him seated near the fireplace "

(III, 42). The third is *māil* (< *māritā*) " killed ", in *saran māil ḍiṭ* " they saw the girl (that she was) killed " (III, 32).

197. **Perfect Tense.**—The Perfect is obtained by conjugating the Present tense of the Auxiliary Verb with the Past Participle of the principal verb. The Auxiliary Verb is *thū*, or, between vowels, usually *dū* (§ 158). The following are examples :—

198. **Intransitive Perfect.**—Sing Masc. 1 :—*hō-thū*, in *ā te γamē-dē γamjān hō-thū* " I have become worried from that trouble " (I, 55).

Sing. Masc. 3 :—*hō-dū*, in *Tōwāl-mī e pō paidā hō-dū* " a boy has been born in Tōrwāl " (II, 20).

199. **Transitive Perfect.**—Masc. Sing. Obj. :—*gin-thū*, in *ti māš hat-mē sitār gin-thū* " that man has taken (i.e. held) a guitar in his hand " (I, 4) ; *pāē cīz tā kis-kĕjā gin-thū ? gām-se dukāndār-kĕjā gin-thū* " from whom hast thou taken (i.e. bought) that thing ? (I) have bought (it) from a shop-keeper of the village " (L. 240–1).

kī-dū, in *mē piži-si pūc bĕbā kī-dū* " the son of my uncle has made a marriage " (L. 225).

kūḍū-dū, in *pāē māš-se pūc mē cir miḍē-dē kūḍū-dū* " I have beaten that man's son with many stripes " (L. 228).

Fem. Sing. Obj. :—*dī-cī* (for *dit-žī*, § 158), in *ke γora χušālī Xudā Pāk dī-cī* " what good happiness has the Almighty given ! " (I, 20).

Similarly (§ 158) the feminine of *dū* is *žī*, which appears as *jī*, in :—

kī-jī, in *mē aj cir pand kī-jī* " to-day I have made much travelling " (L. 224).

200. **Pluperfect.**—The Pluperfect is obtained by conjugating the Past tense of the Auxiliary Verb—*(a)šū* or *šat* (§ 158)—with the Past Participle of the principal verb. As in Indian and other Dardic dialects, the Pluperfect is often employed to indicate a Remote Past. Examples are :—

201. Masc. Sing. *bēḍū-šū* (§ 3e), in *tisi ṭin Miā Kāsim Bāba bēḍū-šū* "under it Miyān Kāsim Bābā was seated" (II, 32).

gā-šū, in *tu gā-šū filankē χān-sē saran tā āban-gē lehī* "thou hadst gone and asked for the daughter of a certain Khān for thyself" (I, 39).

kuḍū-šū, in *mē kuḍū-šū* "I had beaten" (L. 193).

banu-šat, in *sē pō sabak banu-šat* "that boy said (i.e. studied) (his) lesson" (II, 27).

neyu-dut (II, 5) is perhaps also a pluperfect (see § 178).

202. **Conjunctive Participle.**—A form corresponding to the Conjunctive Participle of Indian languages is formed by adding *te*, the postposition of the Instrumental, to a verbal noun similar to the present base. As in the Instrumental, after a vowel or nasal this *te* becomes *de*. Examples are :—

beš-te, in *ai beš-te til nidā kao-dud* "I having gone there was doing looking on" (I, 19) ; *tu beš-te me-gē jāma pai* "do thou, having gone, send to me a garment" (I, 49) ; *ā beš-te e saran-ma tapōs kī* "I, having gone, will make inquiry from this girl" (III, 28) ; *beš-te mē saran buā* "having gone, look ye at this girl" (III, 31).

gaš-te, in *Sulaimānik gaš-te Semū-ye dit* "having captured Sulaimānik, they gave him to Semū" (III, 33) ; *Sulaimānik gaš-te nū Kanbel-ge* "having captured Sulaimānik, he took him away to Kanbel" (III, 36).

gin-de, in *Sulaimānik te jabal gin-de Semū-si šā-si did* "Sulaimānik, having taken that pickaxe, struck Semū's head" (§ 37) (III, 44).

203. **Present Participle.**—Two forms are given in the List of Words for the Present Participle. These are *kuḍunki* "beating" (L. 177), and *bažunge* "going" (L. 218). Both are evidently corruptions of the Paṣ̌tō Noun of Agency in *-ūnkai*, and need not detain us further. In other Dard languages (e.g. Kāšmīrī), the Noun of Agency is frequently used as a Present Participle, and is so translated into Sanskrit by Paṇḍits.

INDECLINABLES

204. It will be convenient to consider together Adverbs and Postpositions, as the border line between the two classes is ill-defined. Omitting the Postpositions used to form cases, and described in §§ 23 ff., the following Adverbs and Postpositions have been noted :—

aj " to-day ", in *mē aj cir pand kī-jī* " I have walked a long way to-day " (L. 224).

andare, andere " inside, among ", in *ē pō andare bēṭh* " this boy sat inside (the house) " (I, 29) ; *e māš andere cir hušā ašū* " one man among (them) was very intelligent " (III, 27).

bā (L. 86) " up ", in *Kalāma wa Mišku-si cālā-bā* " down from Kalām up to the rock of Mishku " (III, 61).

bī " again ", in *tē jumāldār bī mēlī bāt banī* " that head man again said the same word " (I, 35) ; *mē watan-mī Sulaimānik-si bī pādšāhī hī* " Sulaimānik's rule of this country again took place " (III, 46).

kac (? *kaç*) " near ", in *Ningōlī-se kac-ke gā* " he went to near Ningōlī " (I, 2).

kan, ken " near ", in *te saran-si kan-ke gā* " he went to near that girl " (III, 29) ; *dadan-si ken-ta baṭhā kī* " he made him seated near the fireplace " (III, 42).

niō " near " (L. 87).

mūj, muš, mūš, mūšā " before ", in *mē kĕjā mūj baž* " walk before me " (L. 238) ; *Tōwāl-si muš-ke* " in front of Tōrwāl (there is a tree) " (II, 31) ; *mūš-ke cai āp* " a cliff came in front " (III, 57) ; *mūšā ē māš āp* " a man came before him " (I, 3). Cf. *mū̃š* " first ", § 55.

pāji " afterwards ", *piyāj* (L. 91), *paiž* " behind ", in *pāji tisi duyi bhā āp* " afterwards his second brother came " (II, 39, so 43, 46) ; *kāme māš-se pō te-kĕjā piyāj ye-dū* " the boy of what man comes behind you ? " (L. 239). Cf. *pāš.*

pāš, paš " afterwards, later, after ", in *telā pāš buḍ kām Musulmān hū* " after then the whole tribe became Moslem " (II, 49) ; *telā pāš Bihū-mī e rājgana ašī* " after that time there was a queen in Bihun " (III, 47) ; *mē gām-si χalak bud ēs paš āp* " after this many people of this village came " (I, 30) ; *ā gā filankē χān-sē saran paš* " I am gone after (i.e. for) the daughter of a certain Khān " (I, 43). Cf. *pāji*.

pat-gē, pata-gē, pade-gē " backwards, back ", in *ē pō pat-gē āp* " that boy went back (i.e. returned home) " (I, 26 ; so I, 50, but *pade-gē*) ; *tē kufār-miā pade-ge šeyat* " they were driven back from that Kāfir " (II, 13 ; similarly 14, 15) ; *pata-ge diū* " he fled backwards " (III, 16) ; *Sulaimānik pata-ge Semū-si šir-ke gā* " Sulaimānik went back to Semū's house " (III, 39).

paiž, see *pāji*.

pōrē " till, until ", in *sattam pērīa pōrē* " till the seventh generation " (II, 48).

sāt, sād, sāth " with ", in *te sād maškulā kō-dū* " I am doing business (i.e. talk) with thee " (I, 56). Here the final *t* has apparently been softened to *d* before the following *m*. *ā te-sāt šerīkat na kō-dū* " I do not make sharing with thee " (II, 9) ; *tel te Kufār-sāth (? sāt) lāṭ sabat* " there they joined fight with that Kāfir " (II, 12) ; *mī Sulaimānike sāt rabaṛ kī* " he made a fight with this Sulaimānik " (III, 3) ; *mē-sāt lāṭ kuwa* " make ye fighting with me (i.e. on my side) " (III, 5) ; *mōi te-sāt karmā yanin* " we verily are going with thee (as) an army " (III, 7) ; *Semū sāt panjam kālo karmā ucit* " in the fifth year the army arose with Semū " (III, 9) ; *nūm bīš saranē tisi sāt ašī* " nine (times) twenty girls were with her " (III, 17) ; *ek dui sāt jōr ne ye-dū* " one does not come to agreement with the other " (III, 26).

set " with ", in *Nariā-si dād te set mukadima kī* " the ancestor of Narēr made a quarrel with him " (II, 6). This is not the same word as *sāt* (< *sârtha-*). It is the same as the Kāšmīrī *sŭty* (< *sahitē*).

ṭin " down " (L. 88), " below," in *tisi ṭin Miā Kāsim Bāba bēḍū šū* " under it Miyān Kāsim Bābā was seated " (II, 32) ; *thām-si ṭin* " under a tree " (L. 230). Cf. *tes-ma gām ṭin kī*

" the village was made captured (? was made subject) from him " (III, 16).

wa, wā (L. 88) " down ", in *Kalāma-wa Miśku-si cālā-bā* " down from Kalām to the rock of Mishku " (III, 61).

In addition to the above, see also the list of Pronominal Adverbs in §§ 144 ff.

205. **Negative.**—The Negative is generally *na.* Examples are :—*mē tanū śū tĕs-kē na dit* " I did not give my sister to him " (I, 34, so 35) ; *ā te-sāt śerīkat na kō-dū* " I do not make sharing with thee " (II, 9) ; *yai-si ciś na pō-śat* " he was not drinking (from) the mother's breast " (II, 18, so 21) ; *sē kalimā na banadū* " he does not repeat the creed " (II, 46) ; *Xodā na kuwē* " may God not make " (II, 48) ; *sē mē lāḍa śit na aśī* " she was not aware of this fight " (III, 19) ; *pan na hī* " there was no road " (III, 57).

As a Prohibitive, we have :—*to lāṭ na kuwa* " do not ye fight " (III, 28) ; *mē Sulaimānik na mā* " do not thou kill this Sulaimānik " (III, 35).

Instead of *na,* we have *ne* in : *māliyā ne kambai* " he does not (?) pay taxes " (II, 6) ; *ek dui sāt jōr ne ye-dū* " one does not come to agreement with another " (III, 26). As a Prohibitive, we have *tu ne baž* " do not thou go " (I, 44, 45).

206. **Conjunctions** :—

" And," *ō, ū, (yū),* in *dū śālmī ō ar* " two rupees and a half " (L. 232) ; *mī yai ū bāp Kāfir thī* " my mother and father are unbelievers " (II, 29) ; *tesi yai yū bāp Kufār aśī* " his mother and father were Kāfirs " (II, 17). In the last, the *y* of *yū* is a *ya-śruti,* due to the preceding *ai.*

The Paṣṭō *hum* " also ", is used to mean " and " (L. 95).

" But " is the Paṣṭō *lēkin* (L. 96).

" If " is *kala* (L. 97). Cf. Paṣṭō *kala* " when ? "

207. **Interjections.**—The usual Interjection is *ē* " O ", as in *ē ! tū kēt-si thū* " O ! of where art thou ? " (I, 6) ; *ē zuwān ! tu kē āp* " O youth ! why art thou come ? " (I, 47) ; *ē ! mere tilai* " O ! now let us go " (I, 52).

The word *ga* is translated as an interjection in *Sulaimāni-ga* " O Sulaimānik " (III, 40), but the word should probably be divided *Sulaimānig-a*, the final *k* being softened to *g*, as explained in § 15.

" Yes " and " no " are *ah* and *na*, respectively (L. 98, 99).

" Alas " is the Paṣ̌ṭō *armān* (L. 100).

INDEX TO THE GRAMMATICAL SKETCH

Numbers refer to sections. The order of words is that followed in the Vocabulary.

PART III

The Folktales

After the above account of the language, I give the folk-tales and the list of sentences as recorded by Sir Aurel Stein. To each of the former I have added a free translation. These tales abound in local names, some of which are explained in footnotes ; but, before giving the text, I here supply a list of them, with their identification as given by Sir Aurel.

List of Local Names in the Folktales

Asrēt	Nullah and hamlet on right bank of Swāt River a quarter of a mile beyond Shigā Pattī, and about 5 miles above Chōḍgrām and Mankiāl.
Basharai	Name of a cliff on the left bank of the Swāt River, opposite Asrēt.
Bihun	Name of the locality now occupied by Braniāl village, the chief place of Tōrwāl.
Braniāl	Present chief place of Tōrwāl, on right bank of Swāt River at the mouth of Darāl-dara.
Buḍur	Name of a subsection of Tōrwālī tribes.
Chamōr	Name of a subsection of Tōrwālī tribes.
Darāl-dara	Large side valley debouching towards Swāt River at Braniāl.
Gurunai	Valley debouching on the left (eastern) bank of the Swāt River, opposite to the village of Tōrwāl.
Jabēr	A tribe.
Kalām	Name of a large village and of the surrounding open valley plain where the rivers of the Utrōt and Ushu Nullahs meet to form the head of the Swāt River. Kalām is considered distinct from Tōrwāl, and the Miāngul of Swāt's present territory stops about 2 miles short of Kalām village.

Kanbēl or *Kambēl*	Where Semū lived : a part of Braniāl, and about four chains west of it.
Katār	(Uncertain locality.)
Khāna	Name of a subsection of Tōrwālī tribes.
Lailōt	Name of a subsection of Tōrwālī tribes.
Masulo-bat	A precipice in Darāl-dara valley, over which old people were thrown.
Mayō	Tract of the Indus Kohistān.
Mingaora	Market town near left bank of Swāt River close to where the important side valleys of Saidu and Janbil meet.
Mishkū	N. of a rock between Satāl and Shāhgrām, supposed to mark boundary between Tōrwāl and Upper Swāt.
Narēr	A tribe.
Pīr	It is here that Miyā̃ Kāsim lived. Locality uncertain. (For several reasons it is very improbable that Pīrsar can be meant.)
Punkā	A small village on the left bank of the Swāt River, and half a mile from Kadam towards Tōrwāl.
Purangām	Tōrwālī name of " Old Braniāl " village, known also by the Pashtō designation of Zōṛ-Braniāl. On hill above Braniāl.
Satāl	Small village situated at a distance of ¾ of a mile from Kharisha, towards Shāhgrām, on the right bank of the Swāt River.
Shāhgrām	Village on right bank of Swāt River, nearly opposite to Churṛai.
Tōrwāl	Name of a group of hamlets counting about 120 homesteads at the mouth of a side valley debouching on the right bank of the Swāt River about 4 miles above Braniāl. The name is applied also to the whole of the Swāt Kohistān from above Churṛai to below Kalām.

Tōrwālī Stories

I. Story of Shāh Zumān Khān. *Told by Muqadar of Braniāl, Tōrwāl.* 10*th April*, 1926.

1. *Šāh Zumān Xān Mingaore-ye baže-dū.*
1. Shāh Zumān Khān Mingaora-to goes (i.e. went).

2. *Ningōlī-se kac-ke gā.* 3. *Mūšā ē māž*
2. Ningōlī-of near-to he-went. 3. In-front a man

āp. 4. *Ti-māś hat-mē sitār gin-thū.*
arrived. 4. By-that-man hand-in guitar held-is.

5. *Sitār-sē māš mē-Xān-ma tapōs kī.*
5. Guitar-of by-the-man this-Khān-from question was-made.

6. "*E! tū kēt-si thū? Mē-tē-gē kam thū.*"
6. "O! thou where-of art? Me-thee-for business is."

7. *Xān bana-dū* "*chī mē-gē ka kam thū?*"
7. The-Khān says, "Of-thee me-for what business is?"

8. *Sitār-se māš bana-dū,* "*Ā te-kĕjā s*[a]*wāl kō-dū.*"
8. Guitar-of man says, "I thee-from request make."

9. *Xān bana-dū,* "*Tu ka s*[a]*wāl kō-dū?*"
9. The - Khān says, "Thou what request makest?"

10. *Sitār-se māš bana-dū,* "*Ā te-gē du žāt*
10. Guitar-of man says, "I thee-for two nights

majlis kō-dū." 11. *Xān bana-dū,* "*tu*
entertainment (will-) make." 11. The-Khān says, "Thou

ka-γame-de γam-jān hō-dū?" 12. *Sitār-se*
what-trouble-by worried art-becoming?" 12. Guitar-of

māš bana-dū, "*Ā filankai-watan-sē Xān-se pušt*
man says, "I a-certain-country-of Khān-of descendant

thū. 13. *Ā lūṭ āšū, mī bāp mū* 14. *Mī dērā*
am. 13. I small was, my father died. 14. My house

kūtsā šaṭ hū. 15. *Mī daš bhai āšī.*
lane ruined became. 15. Of-me ten cousins were.

16. *E-gī ti-hun jumāldār āšū.* 17. *Sē mī*
16. One them-of head-man was. 17. He my

tarbūr ašū. Ti-hun dērā wadān ašū.
paternal-cousin was. Them-of house in-good-order was.

18. *Ē dī ti-hun-hujrā-mē majlas ašī.*
18. One day their-guest-room-in an-entertainment was.

19. *Ai beš-te til nidā kao-dud.* 20. *Mē*
19. I gone-having there view making-was. 20. By-me

banū, 'Ke γora χušālī Xudā-Pāk
it-was-said, 'What good happiness by-God-the-Pure

dī-cī!' 21. *Mē-manjlas-mē e māš ašū.*
given-is!' 21. This-entertainment-in a man was.

22. *Sē bana-dū, 'Ē χušālī chi-bāp-si ašī.*
22. He says, 'This happiness thy-father-of was.

23. *Ē manjlas thun-hujrā-mē hō-dut.'*
23. This entertainment your-guest-room-in being-was.'

24. *Mē-pōē mē-māš-ma tapōs*
24. By-this-lad (i.e. by me) this-man-from inquiry

kī, 'Ā mere ka cal keī?' 25. *Ā*
was-made, 'I now what artifice may-do?' 25. That

māš mē-pō-ē bana-dū, 'Tu baž tanū dērā
man this-lad-to says, 'Thou go, thine-own house

wadān kō.' 26. *Ē pō pat-gē*
in-good-order make.' 26. This lad back-to (i.e. home)

āp. 27. *Šir-kē tanū-yai-ge tanū-šī-ge*
came. 27. House-to his-own-mother-to his-own-sister-to

banū, 'buža, mī dērā janā.' 28. *Tasi šū*
it-was-said, 'Go-ye, my house clean-ye.' 28. His sister

gā, te dērā janū, šen thalū, lēb
went, that house was-cleaned, bedstead was-placed, cover

bāliχ barābar kī. 29. *Ē pō andare bēṭh,*
pillow right were-made. 29. This lad inside sat,

malāž-ge gil diū-šad. 30. *Mē-gām-si χalak*
guests-to bread giving-was. 30. This-village-of people

bud ēs-paš āp. 31. *Sē daš bhai āban-gē*
many this-after came. 31. Those ten cousins themselves-to

derī. 32. *Ē dī ē jamāldār tanū-bhayā-gē*
remained. 32. One day this head-man his-own-brothers-to

bana-dū, 33. *'Yā, mō bana-dū mē-pō-gē,*
says, 33. 'Come-ye, we say this-lad-to,

"Tanū šū me-gē dū? (? dē)."' 34. *Mē*
"Thine-own sister me-to give."' 34. By-me

tanū šū tĕs-kē na dit. 35. *Tē-jumāldār*
my-own sister him-to not was-given. 35. By-that-head-man

bī mēlī bāt banī, 'Ē tanū šū
again the same word was-said, 'By-him his-own sister

me-gē na dit. 36. *Yā, mō-bižī, tes-ki*
me-to not was-given. 36. Come-ye, let-us-go him-to

mubārakī dē. 37. *Tē mō-ma tapōs*
congratulation let-us-give. 37. He us-from inquiry

kō-nin. 38. *Banin, "Tā me-gē ka*
may-make. 38. He-may-say, "By-thee me-to what

mubārakī dit?" 39. *Mō banin, "Tu*
congratulation was-given?" 39. We may-say, "Thou

gā-šū filankē-Xān-sē saran tā āban-gē
gone-wast, a-certain-Khān-of daughter by-thee thyself-for

lehī. 40. *Ā šid hō, χušāl hō,*
was-asked-for. 40. I aware became, happy became,

kiau *te-gē* *mubāraki-ye* *āp."'*
why (i.e. therefore) thee-to congratulation-for came."'

41. *Ā* *pō* *bana-dū,* *'To* *baža.'* 42. *Ā* *pō*
41. That lad says, 'You go.' 42. That lad

tanū-šir-kē *āp,* *tanū-šī-yē* *bana-dū,* 43. *'Ā*
his-own-house-to came, his-own-sister-to says, 43. 'I

gā, *filankē-Xān-sē* *saran* *paš.'* 44. *Mē-pō-si*
am-gone, a-certain-Khān-of daughter after.' 44. This-lad-of

šū *bane-žī,* *'Tu* *ne* *baž.* *Tā* *mā-nin.*
sister says, 'Thou not go. Thee they-may-kill.

Ā *bižī.'* 45. *Ā* *pō* *bana-dū,* *'Tu* *ne* *baž,*
I will-go.' 45. That lad says, 'Thou not go,

Ā *aban-ī* *baže-dū.'* 46. *Ā* *pō* *gā*
I myself-even going-am.' 46. That lad went

tē-Xān-sē *watan-gē.* *Tē-Xān-sē* *malāž*
that-Khān-of country-to. That-Khān-of guest

hō. 47. *Sē* *Xān* *bana-dū,* *'Ē* *zuwān!* *tu*
he-became. 47. That Khān says, 'O youth! thou

kē *āp?'* 48. *Ā* *pō* *bana-dū,* *'Tanū*
why camest?' 48. That lad says, 'Thine-own

saran *mē-gē* *dē.'* 49. *Xān* *bana-dū,* *'Ā*
daughter me-to give.' 49. The-Khān says, 'I

te-gē *dai.* *Tu* *beš-te* *me-gē* *jāma*
thee-to will-give. Thou gone-having me-to a-garment

pai.' 50. *Ā* *pō* *pade-gē* *āp.*
send.' 50. That lad back-to (i.e. home) came.

Tanū-širā *jāma* *pewū.* 51. *Tē-Xān*
From-his-own-house a-garment was-sent. 51. By-that-Khān

tesē *chī* *ruksat* *kī.* 52. *Ē*
of-him the-wife discharged was-made. 52. This

jumāldār bana-dū, ' Mō mē-māš-se puχtuā
head-man says, 'We this-man-of from-enmity

nigāt. Ē! mere tilai, bižī.
(are) gone-out. O! now let-us-go, let-us-be-off.

Tisē-dērā-mī b^{i}*hī.' 53. Mē-Xān-sē chī muī.*
His-house-in let-us-sit.' 53. This-Khan-of wife died.

54. *Ē Xān lewānai hū. Tanū χānī*
54. This Khān mad became. His-own Khānship

cai-gā. 55. Ā te-γamē-dē γam-jān hō-thū.
abandoned. 55. I that-trouble-by worried become-am.

56. *Ā kiau te-gē* s^{a}*wāl kō-dū. Tu*
56. I why (i.e. therefore) thee-to request make. Thou

γora māš thū, te-sād maškulā kō-dū."
good man art, thee-with business (i.e. talk) (I-) make."

FREE TRANSLATION

A Story of Shāh Zumān Khān

Shāh Zumān Khān was once going to Mingaora and, as he approached Ningōlī, there came before him a man carrying in his hand a guitar.[1] This man asked the Khān where he came from, and stated that he had some business with him. The Khān asked what this business might be, and the guitar-player replied that he had a request to make. " What request? " said the Khān, and the man then offered to amuse him for two nights with his playing. The Khān asked him what his trouble was, and he told the following story :—

" I belong to the family of the Khān of such and such a country. My father died when I was but a child and my home fell into ruin. I had ten cousins, one of whom,—my

[1] Sir Aurel Stein tells me that, among Paṭhāns of the Yūsufzai tribe (and probably in other tribes also), life as a guitar-player means either that the person has become deranged through the use of *hashish* or some other drug, or else has lost his senses through some overwhelming misfortune. In the present instance we shall see that the latter was the case.

paternal cousin,—was a head man of the village. They were well-to-do people, and one day I attended an entertainment given in their guest-house.[1] As I looked on, I expressed wonder at the happy prosperity that had been vouchsafed by God, the Pure. A man who chanced to be there said to me, 'This very happy prosperity was once the lot of your father. Entertainments such as this used to be held in your guest-house.' I was but a lad, and asked him what I had best do now, and he advised me to set my home in good order. So home the lad [2] hastened and told his mother and his sister to go and clean up his (old) family house, His sister went and cleaned the house, putting in it a bedstead arranged with a pillow and coverlet. The lad then entered the house, sat there, and invited guests to eat with him. After this many people of the village began to pay visits to him, but the cousins remained apart (and did not come near him).[3]

" One day the head man said to his brothers, 'Come, let us ask this lad to give me his sister to wife.' I refused to give her. Then reported the head man to his brothers, 'He refused to give me his sister. Come, let us go and offer him congratulations. If he ask why, we can tell him that we are pleased to hear that he has been making overtures for his marriage with the daughter of such and such a Khān,[4] and that for this reason we have come to offer our congratulations.' (They carried out this proposal), but the lad sent them away, and returning to his own house told his

[1] Among Yūsufzais, every Khān or man of position has his own *hujra*, or guest-house.

[2] I.e. the narrator, who from now on up to near the end of the story, speaks of himself in the third person, here and there reverting to the first.

[3] They do not wish to recognize their poor relation's claim to his father's position.

[4] The head man first made an ironical sham offer to marry the boy's sister, and, when this was rejected, they offered him ironical congratulations, intimating that if he could secure a wealthy Khān's daughter to be his wife, he might be entitled to assert a claim to his father's position, but not otherwise. The boy sends them away but takes the hint, and, as soon as they are gone, does secure such a wife, and through her secures his position in the village, becoming a Khān himself.

sister that he was off after the daughter of such and such a Khān. The sister advised him not to go, as he would probably be killed if he did so, and offered to go herself in his stead, but the lad (insisted, and) went off himself to the Khān's place of residence.

"The Khān received him as a guest, and asked the purpose of his visit. Thereupon the lad asked the Khān to give him his daughter in marriage. He consented to this, and told the lad to go home and send the present of clothes customary on such occasions. The lad, returning home, dispatched the clothes, and in due course the Khān sent off the bride to her husband's house.

"When the cousin,—the head man,—learnt this, he advised his brothers to abandon their hostile attitude and to visit the lad on a formal (and, this time, real) visit of congratulation.

"(The lad was now a Khān), but his young wife died, and (in grief at this overwhelming misfortune) he went mad and abandoned his Khānship.

"That is the origin of my[1] trouble and the cause for the request that I make to you. I know you to be a good man, and it is for this reason that I address you."

II. Story of Tōrwāl's Conversion to Islām. *Told by Muqadar Ākhunzāda, 11th April,* 1926

1. *Katār-miā Nariā-si dād mē-watan-gē*
1. Katār-from Narēr-of ancestor this-country-to

āp. 2. *Mēl ti - Tōwāl-mē aban-gē karwanda*
came. 2. Here that - Tōrwāl-in himself-for cultivation

kī. 3. *Nedā phēm-diše Punkā-mī e Kupār*
was-made. 3. River on-opposite-side Punkā-in a Kāfir

ašū. 4. *Tisi dvāš puš aši. Sē cir zālim*
was. 4. Of-him twelve sons were. He very powerful

[1] Here the narrator reverts to the first person.

ašū. 5. *Mē-Tōwāl-miā sē māliyā neyu-dut.*
was. 5. This-Tōrwāl-from he taxes taking-was.

6. *Nariā-si dād te-set mukadima kī.*
6. Narēr-of by-the-ancestor him-with quarrel was-made.

Māliyā ne kambai. 7. *Jebēya-si dād*
Taxes not (?) were-paid. 7. Jabēr-of ancestor

Badaχšān-miā mē-watan-gē āp.
Badakhshān-from this-country-to came.

8. *Mī-Nariā-si-dād mī-Jebēya-si-dād-ke*
8. By-this-Narēr-of-ancestor this-Jabēr-of-ancestor-to

banū, " Mē-watan-si mā-o-chī
it-was-said, " This-country-of of-me-and-of-thee

šerīkat hī." 9. *Mī-Jebēya-si-dād*
division let-there-be." 9. By-this-Jabēr-of-ancestor

mī-Nariā-si-dād-ke banū, " Ā te-sāt
this-Narēr-of-ancestor-to it-was-said, " I thee-with

šerīkat na kō-dū." 10. *Nariā-si dād*
division not making-am." 10. Narēr-of ancestor

tes-ke bana-dū, " Ca ḍe mī-watan-mī chī,
him-to says, " Three shares this-country-in thine,

cōthum ḍe mī. 11. *Mō duyimo te-Kufār-ke*
fourth share mine. 11. We two that-Kāfir-for

e huī." 12. *Ā duyimo sē-dē langī.*
one will-become." 12. They two bridge-by crossed.

Tel te-Kufār-sāth lāṭ sabat.
There that-Kāfir-with battle was-joined.

13. *Tē-Kufār-miā pade-ge šeyat.*
13. That-Kāfir-from back-wards they-were-driven.

Mī-Jebēya-si-dād sē telī.
By-this-Jabēr-of-ancestor the-bridge was-broken.

14. *Hē pade-ge nurī, lāṭ kī.*
14. They back-wards turned, fight was-made.

15. *Tē-Kufār hē hažat, pade-ge*
15. By-that-Kāfir they were-driven-away, back-wards

tanū- šir-ke ai.
their-own-house-to they-came.

16. *Mē-Jebēya-si-dād-si e pō paida hū.*
16. This-Jabēr-of-ancestor-of a son born became.

17. *Sē buzurg ašū. Tesi yai-yū-bāp Kufār*
17. He a-holy-man was. His mother-and-father Kāfirs

aši. 18. *Ā pō tanū-yai-si ciš na*
were. 18. That boy his-own-mother's breast not

pō-šat. Lehir-chal-si ciš pō-šat.
drinking-was. Red-goat-of breast drinking-was.

19. *Miā Kāsim Bāba Pīr-kile-mē ašū. Sē*
19. Miyā̃ Kāsim Bābā Pīr-village-in was. He

til šit hū. 20. "*Tōwāl-mī e pō paidā*
there aware became. 20. "Tōrwāl-in a boy born

hō-dū. 21. *Sē tanū-yai-si ciš na*
become-is. 21. He his-own-mother's breast not

pō-dū." 22. *Miā-Kāsim-Bāba tanū šēχ*
drinks." 22. By-Miyā̃-Kāsim-Bābā his-own disciple

peyū. 23. *Mē pō ti-šēχ*
was-sent. 23. This boy by-that-disciple

nū. 24. *Miā-Kāsim-Bāba-ye*
was-taken (-away). 24. Miyā̃-Kāsim-Bābā-to

ābāt. 25. *Ti būda ā pō*
he-was-brought. 25. By-him it-was-seen that boy

ḍē-si kaman ašū.
share-of (i.e. saintship-of) master was.

26. *Miā-Kāsim-Bāba* *mē-pō-si* *nām* *thāu*
26. By-Miyā̃-Kāsim-Bābā this-boy-of name was-put

"*Āχūn Ibrāhim*". 27. *Sē-pō* *sabak* *banu-šat,*
"Ākhūnd Ibrāhīm". 27. By-that-boy lesson said-was

gani *hū.* 28. *Miā-Kāsim* *Bāba-ye* *ā* *pō*
big he-became. 28. To-Miyā̃-Kāsim-Bābā that boy

bana-du, "*Tili,* *biži.* 29. *Tōwāl-mī* *mī*
says, "Let-us-go, let-us-be-off. 29. Tōrwāl-in my

yai-ū-bāp *kāfir* *thī.* *Mō* *tihā*
mother-and-father unbelievers are. We them

Musulmān *keī.*" 30. *Sē* *telā*
Musalmāns let-make." 30. They from-there

ugāt. 31. *Tōwāl-si* *muš-ke* *e* *biū-si*
went-away (? arose). 31. Tōrwāl-of front-to a *biū*-of

thām *ašū.* 32. *Tisi* *ṭin* *Miā* *Kāsim* *Bāba*
tree was. 32. Of-it below Miyā̃ Kāsim Bābā

bēḍū *šū.* 33. *Kalimā* *bayān-kī*
seated was. 33. The-creed was-recited

Āχūn-Ibrāhim-Bāba-si *kām-gē.* 34. *Awal* *mē* *Xāna-si*
Ākhūnd-Ibrāhīm-Bābā's tribe-to. 34. First this Khāna's

dād *wat.* 35. *Sē* *bana-dū,* "*Mē-ye* *kalimā*
ancestor came-in. 35. He says, "Me-to the-creed

bayān-kō." 36. *Miā-Kāsim-Bāba* *tes-ke* *kalimā*
recite." 36. By-Miyā̃-Kāsim-Bābā him-to the-creed

bayān-kī. *Sē* *Musulmān* *hū.* 37. *Miā*
was-recited. He Musulmān became. 37. Miyā̃

Kāsim *Bāba* *tes-ke* *bana-dū,* "*Tu* *ka* *nimā-dū?*"
Kāsim Bābā him-to says, "Thou what wishest?"

38. *Sē bana-dū,* "*Ā* *te-kĕjā* *χānī* *nimā-dū.*"
38. He says, "I thee-from Khānship wish."

39. *Pāji tisi duyi bhā āp.*
39. Afterwards his second brother came.

Tes-ke kalimā bayān-kī. 40. *Bāba*
Him-to the-creed was-recited. 40. The Babā

tes-ke bana-dū, "Tu ka nimā-dū?"
him-to says, "Thou what wishest?"

41. *Sē bana-dū, "Ā wazīrī nimā-du."*
41. He says, "I Wazīrship wish."

42. *Tes-ke Bāba duwā*
42. Him-to by-the-Bābā benediction (i.e. granting)

kī. Sē watan-si wazīr hū.
was-made. He country's Wazīr became.

43. *Pāji tisi cui bhā wat. Tē*
43. Afterwards his third brother came. He

Musulmān hū. Bāba tes-ke bana-dū
Musalmān became. The-Bābā him-to says,

"Tu ka nimā-dū?" 44. *Sē bana-dū, "Mē-ge*
"Thou what wishest?" 44. He says, "Me-to

ṭubak-si duwā kō." 45. *Tes-ke Bāba*
rifle-of benediction make." 45. Him-to by-the-Bābā

ṭubak-si duwā kī. 46. *Pāji ti-hun*
rifle-of benediction was-made. 46. Afterwards their

cōthum bhā ašū. Sē kalimā na bana-dū.
fourth brother was. He the-creed not says.

47. *Dō kāl gai, cui kāl hō.*
47. Two years went, the-third year became.

Tes Musulmān kī. 48. *Tes-ke*
As-for-him Musalmān he-was-made. 48. Him-to

šulan dit. "Tā Xodā sattam
a-curse was-given. "For-thee God seventh

pēria	*pōrē*	*e-ga*	*dū*	*na*	*kuwē.*
generation	till	one	two	not	may-make.

49. *Telā*	*pāš*	*buḍ*	*kām*	*Musulmān*
49. From-then	after	the-whole	tribe	Musalmān

hū.	50. *Āχūn*	*Ibrāhim*	*Bāba*
became.	50. Ākhūnd	Ibrāhīm	Bābā

Miā-Kāsim-Bāba	*mē-kām-si*	*Imām*	*kī.*
by-Miyā̃-Kāsim-Bābā	this-tribe-of	Imām	was-made.

51. *Tisi*	*aulād*	*Āχūnzāda*	*thī.*	*Buḍ*
51. His	descendants	Ākhūndzādas	are.	The-whole

Tōwāl-si	*Imām*	*thī.*
Tōrwāl-of	Imāms	they-are.

Free Translation

The Story of Tōrwāl's Conversion to Islām

The ancestor of Narēr [1] came to this country from Katār, and settled as a cultivator here, in Tōrwāl. On the opposite side of the river (Swāt) in Punkā there was a Kāfir who had twelve sons and was very powerful. He took taxes from Tōrwāl, but he quarrelled with the ancestor of Narēr, who refused to pay them. The ancestor of Jabēr [2] came hither from Badakhshān, and the ancestor of Narēr proposed to him to divide the country in equal parts between them. The ancestor of Jabēr refused to have the division. Then the ancestor of Narēr offered to take one-fourth of the country and to give him the remaining three-fourths, on condition that they should unite in attacking the Kāfir. They crossed the river by a bridge and joined battle with him, but he repulsed them. The ancestor of Jabēr broke the bridge (to prevent pursuit). They returned and fought (again), but they were driven back by the Kāfir, and returned home.

The ancestor of Jabēr had a son born to him who was a

[1] The Narēr section of the Tōrwāl tribe.

[2] The Jabēr section of the Tōrwāl tribe.

saint. His father and mother were Kāfirs. The boy did not drink his mother's milk, but was suckled by a red goat. At that time Miyā Kāsim Bābā was in the village of Pīr, and heard that a boy had been born in Tōrwāl who did not drink his mother's milk. So he sent one of his disciples who brought the child to him. Miyā Kāsim Bābā recognized that he was destined to become a saint, gave him the name of Ākhūnd Ibrāhīm, and educated him. When he grew up, the boy explained to him that his father and mother were unbelievers, and proposed that they should convert them to Islām. So they set out for (the village of) Tōrwāl. In front of Tōrwāl was a *Biū*-tree, and Miyā-Kāsim Bābā, taking his seat beneath it, recited the creed to Ākhūnd Ibrāhīm's tribe. The first to come to him was the ancestor of Khāna.[1] He asked Miyā Kāsim Bābā to recite the creed to him. Miyā Kāsim Bābā did so, and he became a Moslem. Miyā Kāsim Bābā then told him to ask a boon, and he asked to be made a Khān.

Next his second brother [2] came, and the creed was recited to him too. When told to ask a boon, he begged to be made a Wazīr. The boon was granted, and he became Wazīr of the country. Then the third brother [3] arrived and he too became a Moslem. When told to ask a boon, he prayed for the boon of a rifle, and the boon was granted. There was besides a fourth brother,[4] but he refused to repeat the creed. Two years passed by and, when the third year came, he also accepted Islām; but a curse was laid upon him that his family should not increase till the seventh generation. After that, the whole tribe turned Moslem. Miyā Kāsim Bābā appointed Ākhūnd Ibrāhīm to be its Imām, and his descendants, the Ākhūndzādas, are the Imāms of the whole tribe to this day.

[1] His family is now represented by Najīm Khān, Māsum Khān, and Katōr Khān.

[2] The founder of the Chāmōr family.

[3] The founder of the Lailōt family.

[4] The founder of the Buḍur family.

Sir Aurel Stein adds to this story :—Muqadar [the narrator] declares the above conversion to date back eight generations from his own. He says that before Tōrwāl's conversion it was the custom to carry sick or aged people in a *kajāwa* [a kind of camel-litter] to a precipice in Darāl-darra, called Masulo-bat, with two *kajāwas*, one full of meat and the other of bread, and to throw them over the cliff in succession.

III. Story of Sulaimānik. *Told by Muqadar of Braniāl, 16th April,* 1924.

1. *Sulaimānik Purangām-žet bādšāhī kō-dut.*
1. Sulaimānik Purangām-on ruling making-was.

Tesi e dušman ašū. 2. *Kanbel-mī e Kupār*
Of-him an enemy was. 2. Kanbēl-in a Kāfir

ašū. Tesi nām Semū ašū. 3. *Mī-Sulaimānike-sāt*
was. His name Semū was. 3. This-Sulaimānik-with

rabaṛ kī. Te si Semū watana
fight was-made. By-him that Semū from-the-country

hažat 4. *Šerunke hū, Abā-sīn-si*
was-driven-out. 4. Exiled he-became, Indus-of

γāra-ye, Mayō-mī dērā hū. 5. *Tē-Semū*
bank-to, Mayō-in abode became. 5. By-that-Semū

tē-χalak-ke arzī kī, "Mē-sāt lāṭ
those-people-to request was-made, "Me-with fight

kuwa." 6. *Tē-χalak-kē tanū yarak*
do-ye." 6. Those-people-for their-own tribal-council (*jīrga*)

sabāt. 7. *Semū-ye miz banū, "Mōi*
was-arranged. 7. Semū-to thus it-was-said, "We-verily

te-sāt karmā ya-nin. 8. *Tē-watan-mī*
thee-with army will-go. 8. That-country-in

mōi *lāṭ* *kī,* *mōi* *barai*
by-us-verily fight was-made, by-us-verily victory

kī, *besyāt* *mōi* *ginin."* 9. *Semū-sāt*
was-made, loot we-verily will-take." 9. Semū-with

panjam-kālo *karmā* *ucit.* 10. *Sē* *ai*
in-the-fifth-year the-army got-up. 10. They came

Gurnāl-gē. *Semū* *māś* *piyū.*
Gurunai-to. By-Semū a-man was-sent.

11. *Sulaimānik-kē* *banū,* "*Aban* *mē-gē*
11. Sulaimānik-to it-was-said, "Thyself me-for

lāṭ-ke *jōr* *ku.*" 12. *Sulaimānike* *tē-māś-ke*
fight-for ready make." 12. By-Sulaimānik that-man-to

banū, "*Ā* *Semū-se* *lāṭ-ke* *jōr* *thū.*"
it-was-said, "I Semū's fight-for ready am."

13. *Sulaimānike* *hukum* *kī,* *tanū-karmā-ye*
13. By-Sulaimānik order was-made, his-own-army-to

banū, "*Tila* *rabaṛ-ke,* *Bihū-ge* *boža.*"
it-was-said, "Go-ye fight-for, Bihun-to go-ye."

14. *Sulaimānik-si* *karmā* *gya* *Bihū-ge* *Gurnāl-miā*
14. Sulaimānik's army went Bihun-to. Gurnāl-from

Semū-si *karmā* *wat.* 15. *Diumo* (? *Duimo*)
Semū's army arrived. 15. Both

ek-dije (?) *eṛi* *huī.* *Lāṭ* *śuru*
one-with-another halted became. Fight beginning

kī. 16. *Lāṭ-mi* *Sulaimānike* *baidāt*
was-made. 16. The-fight-in as-for-Sulaimānik defeated

kī. *Pata-ge* *diū.* *Tes-ma*
he-was-made. Back-wards he-fled. Him-from

gām *ṭin* *kī.*
village taken (? under) was-made.

17. *Tesi e saran ašī. Nūm-bīš*
17. Of-him a daughter was. Nine-(times-)twenty

saranē tisi-sāt ašī. 18. Sē širē pām
girls her-with were. 18. She in-the-house wool

dugū-dut. 19. Sē mē-lāḍa šit na ašī.
weaving-was. 19. She of-this-fight aware not was.

20. *Na-tsāba derē zōg hī.*
20. Unexpectedly at-the-door a-noise became

21. *Hē mē-lāḍa šit hī. 22. Mayō-si*
21. She of-this-fight aware became. 22. Mayō-of

gan gan māš ai, derē eṛī hōi.
big big men came, at-the-door halted they-became,

23. *Tihē mē-Sulaimānik-si saran ḍiṭ.*
23. By-them this-Sulaimānik-of daughter was-seen.

24. *Sē mē-saran-žet pašat. 25. Ek bana-dūs*
24. They this-girl-over quarrelled. 25. One says,

"*Mē saran ā gina-dū.*" *Duī bana-dū,* "*Mē*
"This girl I taking-am." Another says, "This

aran ā gina-dū." 26. *Ek dui-sāt*
girl I taking-am." 26. One the-other-with

jōr ne ye-dū. 27. *E māš*
agreement not reaching-is 27. One man

andere cir hušā. ašū. 28. *Sē bana-dū,*
among (them) very intelligent was. 28. He says,

"*To lāṭ na kuwa. Ā beš-te e-saran-ma*
"Ye fight not make. I gone-having this-girl-from

tapōs kī, hē kāmē māš gina-žī."
question will-make, she which man taking-is."

29. *Māš gā. Šɪr-ke lagū.*
29. The-man went. The-house to he-entered.

Te-saran-si kan-ke gā. 30. *Te-māš*
That-girl-of near-to he-went. 30. By-that-man

mē-saran-si kan-de did. Mē saran maī
this-girl-of arrow-by she-was-hit. This girl died.

31. *Ā māš mē-šira nigāt. Bana-dū,*
31. That man from-this-house emerged. He-says,

" *Beš-te mē saran buā.*" 32. *Hē gai.*
" Gone-having this girl look-at." 32. They went

Tē saran māil ḍiṭ. 33. *Sē χalak.*
That girl killed was-seen. 33. Those people

jama hī. Sulaimānik gaš-te,
collected became. Sulaimānik (been-) captured-having,

Semū-ye dit. 34. *Semū bana-dū Mayō-ye,* " *Ā*
Semū-to was-given. 34. Semū says Mayō-to, " I

mē Sulaimānik mā-dū." 35. *Mayō Semū-ge*
this Sulaimānik killing-am." 35. Mayō Semū-to

bana-dū, " *Mē Sulaimānik na mā. Hē te-ge*
says, " This Sulaimānik not kill. He thee-to

kasab kuwē." 36. *Sulaimānik gaš-te*
service may-do." 36. Sulaimānik captured-having

nū Kanbel-ge. 37. *Semū bana-dū,*
was-taken-away Kanbēl-to. 37. Semū says,

" *Payim-dišē pan sabā.*" 38. *Sulaimānik*
" On-the-other-side a-road prepare." 38. Sulaimānik

jabal hat-te ginu-gā. Te cai
a-pickaxe hand-with taking-went. That cliff

cinū, pan sabat. 39. *Sulaimānik*
was-cut (by-him), road was-prepared. 39. Sulaimānik

pata-ge Semū-si šir-ke gā. 40. *Semū*
back-wards Semū's house-to went. 40. Semū

bana-dū, "*Sulaimāniga!* *tā* *pan* *sabat?*"
says, "O-Sulaimānik! by-thee the-road prepared?"

41. *Sulaimānik* *bana-dū,* "*Mā* *pan* *sabat.*"
41. Sulaimānik says, "By-me the-road prepared."

42. *Semū* *cir* *χušāl* *hū.* *Dadan-si* *ken-ta*
42. Semu very happy became. Fireplace-of near-to

baṭhā *kī.* 43. *Sulaimānik* *hut.*
seated (Sulaimānik) was-made. 43. Sulaimānik slept.

Ar *žāt* *hī.* *Sulaimānik* *nīnā* *ucit.*
Half night became. Sulaimānik from-sleep arose.

Būdā *Semū* *hubil* *thū.* 44. *Sulaimānik* *te*
Seen Semū asleep is. 44. By-Sulaimānik that

jabal *gin-de* *Semū-si* *šā-si* *did.*
pickaxe taken-having Semū's head-of was-struck.

45. *Semū* *mau.* *Sulaimānik* *diū,* *Purangām-ke*
45. Semū died. Sulaimānik escaped, Purangām-to

gā. 46. *Me-watan-mī* *Sulaimānik-si* *bī* *pādšāhī*
went. 46. This-country-in Sulaimānik-of again rule

hī.
became.

47. *Telā* *pāš* *Bihū-mī* *e* *rājgana* *aśī.*
47. From-then after Bihun-in a queen was.

48. *Ā* *Sulaimānik* *te-Bihū-ge* *melāštōp-te* *gā.*
48. This Sulaimānik that-Bihun-to visit-for went.

49. *Tē* *rājgana* *tē* *ḍiṭ.* *Sē* *tē-rājgana-žet*
49. That queen by-him was-seen. He that-queen-on

mayin *hū.* 50. *Tē-rājgana-ye* *bana-dū,*
in-love became. 50. That-queen-to he-says,

"*Mā* *gin.*" 51. *Sē* *bana-žī,* "*Ā* *ta* *talā*
"Me take." 51. She says, "I thee then

gina-žī, tu mē-Bihū-ge yāp nigāl."
taking-am, thou this-Bihun-to a-canal excavate!"

52. *Sē bana-dū,* "*Yāp ā nigālī.*" 53. *Sē*
52. He says, "A-canal I will-excavate." 53. She

bana-žī, "*Ta yāp nigālī, ā ta ginī.*"
says, "By-thee a-canal excavated, I thee will-take."

54. *Sulaimānige tē yāp nigālī.*
54. By-Sulaimānik that canal was-excavated.

55. *Tē-rājgana Sulaimānige gin.*
55. By-that-queen as-for-Sulaimānik he-was-taken.

56. *Tē rājgana Purangām-ge wālī.*
56. That queen Purangām-to was-brought (by him).

Payim-diše-de wat. 57. *Mūš-ke cai āp.*
The-far-side-by she-came. 57. Front-on a-cliff came.

Pan na hī. 58. *Rājgana Sulaimānik-ke bana-žī,*
Road not was. 58. The-queen Sulaimānik-to says,

"*Mē cai cin.*" 59. *Sulaimānike mē cai*
"This cliff cut!" 59. By-Sulaimānik this cliff

cinū. 60. *Sē rājgana χušāl hī.*
was-cut. 60. That queen happy became.

Purangām-ge tanū-badšāhī-ge wat.
Purangām-to her-own-rule-for she-came.

61. *Kalāma-wa Mišku-si cālā-bā Sulaimānik-si*
61. From-Kalām-down Mishkū-of the-rock-to Sulaimānik's

bādšāhī hī.
rule became.

Free Translation

The Story of Sulaimānik

Sulaimānik ruled formerly in Purangām.[1] He had an enemy named Semū, a Kāfir of Kanbēl. This man fought with

[1] "The Old Village," i.e. the Paṣhtō Zōṛ Braniāl, or Old Braniāl. It is on a hill above the present village.

Sulaimānik, and was driven by him from the country. He became an exile, and took up his abode in Mayō,[1] on the bank of the Indus. Semū asked these people to fight on his side. They called a tribal council, and agreed to go with him as his army. "We have," said they, "in former days fought in that land and been victorious. Now we will (attack and) plunder it." So, in the fifth year, the army arose and came with Semū to Gurunai.[2] Semū sent a man to Sulaimānik, challenging him to make ready for the combat. Sulaimānik told the man that he was ready, and ordered his army to advance to Bihun[3] for the battle. To Bihun his army went, and Semū's army arrived from Gurunai. The two armies halted and joined battle. Sulaimānik's was defeated. He retreated, and his village was captured.

Sulaimānik had a daughter, with whom there were nine times twenty (serving-) girls. She was weaving wool in her house, and knew nothing of the fight till she was made aware of it by the unexpected sound of commotion at her door. A number of big fellows from Mayō had halted there, and they saw this daughter of Sulaimānik. They began to dispute over her. One said, "I will take this girl," and another said, "I will take her," and they could not come to any agreement. One of them was a very intelligent man, and he said to the others, "Don't quarrel, I will go and ask the girl which man she will take." So he entered the house, and, going up to the girl, shot her dead with an arrow. Then he came out and told his companions to look at the girl. They went in and saw that she had been killed.

These people assembled, and took Sulaimānik captive. They made him over to Semū, who told the Mayō people that he intended to kill him. But said they, "Don't kill him. He can work for you as your slave." So Semū bound Sulaimānik

[1] In the Indus Kōhistān.

[2] A valley debouching on the left (eastern) bank of the Swāt River opposite to the village of Tōrwāl and above Braniāl. Access to it can be gained over a high pass from the side of the Dubēr part of the Indus Kōhistān.

[3] The locality now occupied by Braniāl, the chief place of Tōrwāl.

and took him away to Kanbēl. There he ordered him to make a road on the other side of the river. Sulaimānik took a pickaxe in his hand and went off. He cut the cliff and made a road. He came back to Semū's house, and Semū asked him if he had made the road. Sulaimānik replied that he had, and Semū was much pleased. He made Sulaimānik sit by the fireplace. Sulaimānik went to sleep, but at midnight he rose from his slumber, and, seeing that Semū was asleep, he took up the pickaxe and smote him such a blow on the head that he died. Sulaimānik then escaped to Purangām, and again began to rule over this country.

After those days, there was a queen in Bihun. Sulaimānik had occasion to go there on a visit, and fell in love with her at first sight. He asked her to take him, and she replied that she would do so if he would excavate a canal (from the Swāt river) to Bihun. He agreed to do this, and she answered, "When you have dug the canal, I will take you." So he dug the canal, and she took him for her husband. He brought her to Purangām. They arrived at the opposite side of the river, and the way was barred by a cliff.[1] She asked Sulaimānik to cut the cliff, and he did so. She was pleased, and came to Purangām to exercise her own rule. In this way Sulaimānik's authority became established from Kalām to the rock of Mishkū.[2]

IV. Sentences in Tōrwālī

In addition to the above three folk-tales, Sir Aurel Stein also sent to me a translation into Tōrwālī of the Standard List of Words and Sentences used in the Linguistic Survey of India. The words in this List have been distributed

[1] This is the cliff called Basharai, on the left bank of the Swāt River, opposite Asrēt.

[2] This is a rock between Sātāl and Shāhgrām. The latter village, like the large village of Churṛai on the opposite (left) bank of the Swāt River, marks the limit of the Pāṭhān conquest from the Swāt side. Above Shāhgrām and Churṛai the valley of the Swāt River rapidly contracts, and is from here onwards reckoned as belonging to Tōrwāl.

through the Vocabulary appended to this work. The numerals will also be found in §§ 51 ff., and the Personal Pronouns in §§ 58 ff. above. Wherever such a word occurs, its source is indicated in the Vocabulary by the letter L, accompanied by the number in the original, and I therefore do not reproduce that portion of the List.

Numbers 220–41 at the end of the List are, on the other hand, sentences designed to illustrate particular features of Tōrwālī idiom, and are not given elsewhere. They are as follows :—

220. What is your name ?	*chī nām ka thū ?*
221. How old is this horse ?	*mē ghō-sī umu kadak cī* (? *chī*) ?
222. How far is it from here to Kashmir ?	*mhēda Kashmīr kadak dū thū ?*
223. How many sons are there in your father's house ?	*chī bāp-si širē kadak pūc thī ?*
224. I have walked a long way to-day.	*mē aj cir pand kī-jī.*
225. The son of my uncle is married to his sister.	*mē pižī-si puē* (or *pūc*) *bĕbā kī-dū pāē māš-si šū sed.*
226. In the house is the saddle of the white horse.	*ujil ghō-si zīn širē thū.*
227. Put the saddle upon his back.	*ghō-si pīḍ jada zīn thā.*
228. I have beaten his son with many stripes.	*pāē māš-se pō* (or *pūc*) *mē cir miḍē-dē kuḍū-dū.*
229. He is grazing cattle on the top of the hill.	*pāē tanū māl khanḍ-mē ciā-dū.*
230. He is sitting on a horse under that tree.	*pāē* (*māš*) *ghō-se jada thām-si ṭin bʰhēṭh thū.*
231. His brother is taller than his sister.	*pātē māš-se bhā pātē māš-si šū-kĕjā ucat thū.*
232. The price of that is two rupees and a half.	*pāē šai-se kīmat dū šālmī ō ar thī.*

233. My father lives in that small house.	*mī bāp pāē liḍe širē hō-dū.*
234. Give this rupee to him.	*miā šālmī pāyis-ke de.*
235. Take those rupees from him.	*tiyā šālmī pāyis-kĕjā gin.*
236. Beat him well and bind him with ropes.	*pāyis γora kuḍ khē-de gan.*
237. Draw water from the well.	*kūī-mā ū nīgal.*
238. Walk before me.	*mē-kĕjā mūj baž.*
239. Whose boy comes behind you ?	*kāme māš-se pō te-kĕjā piyāj ye-dū ?*
240. From whom did you buy that ?	*pāē cīz tā kis-kĕjā gin-thū ?*
241. From a shopkeeper of the village.	*gām-se dukāndār-* (or *haṭhīwāl-*) *kĕjā gin-thū.*

PART IV

Vocabulary and Indexes

Tōrwālī-English Vocabulary

In the following Vocabulary, besides the words found in Sir Aurel Stein's materials, I have also included all the words in the English-Torwâlâk vocabulary forming Appendix D to Biddulph's *Tribes of the Hindoo Ḳoosh.* The latter words are indicated by the syllable " Bid."

The letter L refers to a List of Words and Sentences provided by Sir Aurel Stein. As all the words contained in it are included in the vocabulary, I have not considered it necessary to print this List in its entirety, but have contented myself with giving some sentences found at the end of the List that illustrate certain common idioms. These will be found on pp. 132 ff.

Roman numerals refer to the three folk-tales recorded by Sir Aurel Stein, and the Arabic figures following them to the numbers of the sentences in each. The mark § indicates a section of the Grammatical Sketch.

The order of words is based on the alphabetical order of the consonants only, without any regard to the vowels. The latter come into consideration only in cases in which the same consonant is, or the same consonants are, followed or separated by different vowels. Thus, the different words containing the consonants *kl* will be found in the succession *kal, kala, kalā, kāl, kilē,* and *kol.* All words beginning with vowels are arranged together at the head of the Vocabulary, their mutual order being determined by their consonants. The letter *ḍ* follows *d, ṭ* follows *t, š* follows *s*, and *ž* follows *z.* In other respects the alphabetical order of the consonants is that of the English alphabet.

So far as was possible, verbs have been quoted under the infinitive form ending in *ōsa* or *ūsa* ; but for several I have had no means of finding that form. In such cases I have not trusted to my imagination, and have contented myself with taking the shortest form actually noted by me as the leading word of the article.

In quoting Kāšmīrī words I have several times departed from the spelling given in my Kāšmīrī Dictionary. In the latter the numerous epenthetic vowel-changes are represented by the spelling. This, while convenient to the student of that particular language, often obscures derivation and hides the connection of a Kāšmīrī word with the corresponding words in other Dardic languages. In the present Vocabulary, I have therefore given each Kašmīrī word as it appears before it is affected by epenthetic change, at the same time indicating that such a change does occur by putting a dot under the affected letter. Thus, the Kāšmīrī word for " ewe " is written *güb*$^{\ddot{u}}$ in the Dictionary, but is here written *gạb*$^{\ddot{u}}$ in order to show that this is the real word, the *ạ* being marked with a dot, in order to show that, in the language of the present day, it is epenthetically affected by the following $^{\ddot{u}}$, and is therefore to be pronounced *güb*$^{\ddot{u}}$. Similarly, the word for " brother " is given as *bôy*^{u} in the Dictionary, but is here spelt *bạ̄y*^{u}.

It has been necessary to alter Biddulph's spelling in order to make it agree with that used elsewhere in these pages. I have transliterated his spelling as follows :—

Biddulph's *a* (as in " have ") > *ȧ*.

á or *ah* > *a*.
â > *ā*.
e > *ĕ*.
é, *eh* > *e*.
è > *ä*.
ê, *ey* > *ē*.
o = *o*.
ò (as in " knot ") > *ŏ*.
ō > *å*.
ô > *ō*.
ö = *ö*.

u (as in " gun ") > *a*.
ù > *u*.
oo > *ū*.
ü = *ü*.
ai > *ay*.
ch > *c*.
ṇ > ~.
g̣ > *ṅ*.
j̣ > *ž*.
sh > *š*.

Biddulph does not distinguish between aspirated and unaspirated, or between cerebral and dental letters, and I have had to follow him in these particulars with regard to words depending on his authority alone. Such words should be adopted with caution. Thus, his *kōwūsa*, " to eat ", should certainly be *khōwūsa*, and his *dē*, " the belly ", should certainly be *ḍhē*.

Attention should also be paid to the remarks on p. 9 above, in which it is explained that the cerebral sounds represented by *ç*, *j̣*, *ṣ̌*, and *ẓ̌* are probably heard in Tōrwālī, but were not noted by Sir Aurel Stein. Allowance should therefore also be made for this. Compare, for instance, the articles *cā* and *pūc* in this vocabulary.

The following abbreviations are used :—

Ar. = Arabic.
Av. = Avesta.
B. = Bašgalī.
Bal. = Balōcī.
Bid. = Biddulph.
Bur. = Burušaskī.
ELA. = W. Geiger, *Etymologie und Lautlehre des Afghānischen.*
EVP. = G. Morgenstierne, *An Etymological Vocabulary of Pashto.*
G. = Gawarbati.
Gār = Gārwī.
GIP. = W. Geiger and E. Kuhn, *Grundriss der iranischen Philologie.*
GNPE. = P. Horn, *Grundriss der neupersischen Etymologie.*
H. = Hindōstānī.
Ish. = Iškāšmī.
K. = Kalāšā.
Kh. = Khōwār.
Ksh. = Kāšmīrī.
L. = List of Words (see above).
Lnd. = Lahndā.
M. = Maiyā̃.
Mj. = Munjānī.
O. Prs. = Old Persian.
Ōr. = Ōrmuṛī.
P. = Pašai.
Phl. = Pahlavī.
Pr. = Prakrit.
Prs. = Persian.
Psht. = Paṣ̌tō.
Sh. = Ṣiṇā.
Shg. = Šiγnī.
Sk. = Sarīkolī.
Skt. = Sanskrit.
T. = Tirāhī.
V. = Veron.
W. = Wai-alā.
Wkh. = Waχī.
Yd. = Yūdγā.
Z. = Zēbakī.

Arabic and Persian words introduced into Tōrwālī through Paṣ̌tō, are classed as Paṣ̌tō, and not according to original source.

---

a, interj., O! *Sulaimānig-a*, O Sulaimānik! (III, 40), addressed by a master to a servant (§§ 10, 207).

ā 1, m., a peach (Bid.).

ā 2, Pers. Pron., I. Sing. Nom. *ā*, *ai*; other forms sing. *mā*, *mē*, *mē*, *mai*, *mī*; plur. *mō*, *mōi*, *mahī*, *amun*, *mun*. For all these, see §§ 58 ff. [Cf. Av. *az*, Skt. *aham*; Ish. *az*; K.G.P. *ā*, T. *au*, Kh. *awa*, V. *yē*, Ksh. (dial.) *aũ*, Gār. *ya*. With sing. gen. *mī*, cf. Psht. *me*, K.Sh. *mai*, Sh. (dial.) *mī*. With plur. nom. *mō*, cf. Prs. Bal. *mā*, Ish. *mōχ*; B. *ima*, W. *yema*, P. *hamā*, Gār. *mā*. With plur. gen. *amun*, cf. G. *amōna*; T. *myāna*, my, our; Ksh. *myạnu*, my.]

ā 3, (Bid.) *aga*, Demonstr. Pron., this, see § 84. [Cf. Av. *an-(a)*, Skt. *an-(ayā)*; Prs. *ān*. See GNPE. § 52; Bal. *ā*.]

ā̃, see *aī*.

a-ā̃, see *ah*.

ai, see *yōsa*.

aī (L. 36) (Bid.) *ā̃*, m., the mouth. [Cf. Skt. *ās-*, *āsya-*; B.K. *aši*, V. *iš*, W. *āš*, M. Gār. *aī*, Sh. *ā̃ī*, Sh. (dial.) *āzī*, T. *azi*, Ksh. *ạsu*.]

e, see *ek*.

ē, 1, f., a ewe (Bid.) Cf. *bogho* and *midhal*. [? Cf. Av. *maẹša-*, Skt. *mēṣa-*, a sheep; Prs. *mēš*, Wkh. *mai*; Psht. *mēγ*, a ewe; B. *wē*, a sheep; Sh. *ež*, a ewe.]

ē 2, interj., O! See § 207.

ē 3, *ēh*, *hē*, Demonstr. Pron. this (near). Other forms are *ēs*, *ess*, *isa*, *issa*, *ez*, *iya*, *iyā*, *iyasa*. See §§ 79 ff. [Cf. Skt. *ēna-*; Sh. *ō*, fem. *ē*, gen. *äsai*, and also Bid. *es-sam* so much.]

o, *ō*, *au*, *ū* 1, *yū*, Conj. and. See § 206. [Cf. Av. Skt. *uta*, Prs. *ū*; Bal. Wkh. Shg. *ō*; P. *au*, Kh. *o-ce*.]

ū 2, m., water (L. 66, 237). [Cf. Av. *āp-*, Skt. *ap-*; Wkh. *vī-k*, Mj. *yau-γā*, Psht. *ōba*; B. *ōv*, *åo*, V. *āv-eh*, W. *ao*, K. *u-k*, G. *aũ*, T. *uwā*, Kh. *ū-γ*, Gār. *ū*, Sh. *waii*.]

abā-sīn-si, sing. gen. of the Indus (III, 4).

aban 1, in *aban hāt*, the left hand (Bid.). Cf. *suban*.

aban 2, Reflex. Pron. (your)self (III, 11); *aban-ī* (emph.) (I my) very self (I, 45); *tā-āban-gē* for yourself (I, 39); *āban-gē*, by (them)selves (i.e. apart) (I, 31); *aban-gē*, for (him)self (II, 2). [Cf. Ksh. *pāna*, self. See § 132.]

Ibrāhim, N.P. (II, 33).

abōsa, to arrive (Bid.); *āp*, I came (I, 40); thou camest (I, 47); he arrived, he came (I, 3, 26, 42; II, 1, 7, 39; III, 57); they (masc.) came (I, 30). [? Cf. Ved. Skt. √*āp*-, arrive at; H. *ā-nā*, *āv-nā*, to come. Gypsy (Europ.) √*ăv*-. The derivation of this modern root has long been a matter of discussion. For the change of class from *āpnōti* to Pr. **āvaï*, cf. Pr. *pāvaï* < *prâpnōti*.]

abāt, Past Part. (Past tense), he brought (II, 24). [Causal of *abōsa*, q.v. Cf. Skt. *āpita*-.]

achī, (? *açī*) (Bid.) *aši*. f., the eye. [Cf. Skt. *akṣi*-; Sh. *açi*, Ksh. *ạch*ⁱ, and so other Dardic languages.]

ucūsa, to take up (Bid.). Cf. *ušūsa*. [? Cf. Skt. *utkṣipati* or *ucchrayati*.]

ucat, high, tall (L. 135, 231). [Psht. *ūcat*.]

ud (? *uḍ*), f. *üd* (? *üḍ*), a camel (Bid.). [Cf. Av. *uštra*-, Skt. *uṣṭra*-; K. Kh. *uṭ*, Sh. *ữṭ*, Ksh. *wữṭh*, and so most other Dardic languages. Cf. *ūχ*.]

āded, accustomed (Bid.). [Psht. ‘*ādat*, a custom.]

aga (Bid.), see *ā* 3.

agā, a cloud (Bid.). [Cf. B. *agal*, rain; Sh. *aẓu*, a cloud, rain. The connection of Sh. *aẓu* with Av. *awra*-, Skt. *abhra*-, is evident, but the forms *agā* and *agal* are more difficult to explain.]

ūgū, f. *ügü*, heavy (Bid.). [Cf. Av. *gouru*-, Skt. *guru*-; Sh. *aguru*. In Tōrwālī there has been elision of intervocalic *r*.]

agarki, although (Bid.). [Psht. *agarci*.]

agāš, eleven (Bid.). [Cf. Skt. *ēkādaśa*; Sh. *akāi*. Dardic languages differ in regard to this number. Cf. B. *yanits*, Kh. *jŏš-ī*.]

ugāt, Past tense, he went away, he got away (II, 30). [Cf. Skt. √*gā*-, pp. **udgāta*-, imperf. *udagāt*.]

ah (L. 99), *a-ā̃* (Bid.), yes.

aj, to-day (L. 224). Cf. *ayū-di*. [Cf. Skt. *adya*; Sh. *aš*, Ksh. *az*.]

ūjul, f. *ūjel*, white (Bid.); *ujil* (m.) (L. 226); *ujil zar*, silver (L. 46); *ūzel zer*, silver (Bid.). [Cf. Skt. *ujjvala*-.]

ek, *e* (Bid. *ek*), Card. one; *ĕk* (L. 1); *ek* (III, 15, 25, 26); *ek o bīš*, twenty-one (Bid.); *ek gona*, once (Bid.); *ē* (I, 18, 32); *e* (I, 48; II, 16; III, 27); *e huī*, we shall become one (II, 11); *e pot*, together (Bid.); *e-gī ti-hun*, one of them (I, 16) (§ 51); *e-ga dū na kuwē*, may he not make one two (II, 48) (§ 51).

As an Indefinite Article, *ē* (I, 3); *e* (I, 21; II, 3, 20, 31; III, 1, 2, 17, 47).

ūχ, a camel (L. 75). [Psht. *ūχ́*.] Cf. *ud*.

āχūn, a religious master (II, 33). *āχūnzāda*, a descendant of an *āχūn* (II, 51). [Psht. *āχūn*.]

aχir, if (Bid.). [Psht. *āχir* finally, with conflation with *agar*.]

aulād, progeny, offspring (II, 51). [Psht.]

olōsa, to open (Bid.). [With √*ol*-, cf. Skt. *apâvṛta*-.]

ama, postpos. from (Bid.). [Cf. *ma*. The word is probably *ma*, with the termination *a* of the oblique case erroneously prefixed.]

umu, f., age, lifetime (L. 221). [Psht. '*umr*, with elision of post-vocalic *r*.]

imām, the chief man of a mosque (II, 51). [Psht.].

amōš, m., forgetfulness (Bid.). [Cf. the next.]

amašūsa, to forget (Bid.). [Cf. Skt. *mṛṣyatē*; Sh. √*amuš*- (with *ā* prefixed), Ksh. √*maš*-; B. √*p'mišt*- (with *pra* prefixed). Cf. Prs. *farāmōš*.]

umēt, f., hope (Bid.). [Psht. *umēd*.]

an, blind (Bid.). [Cf. Skt. *andha*-; Ksh. *ạn*ᵘ.]

ān, m., an egg (Bid.). [Cf. Skt. *aṇḍa*-; Sh. *haṇē*.]

unbiš, Card. nineteen (Bid.).

ancik, f., darkness (Bid.). [? Cf. *an*.]

andarē, inside (a house) (I, 29); *andere* (one) among (a number of persons) (III, 27). [Prs. *andar*.]

angā, (Bid.) *angāh*, m., fire (L. 65) [Cf. Skt. *aṅgāra-*; K.G.P.Kh. *angār*, Sh. *agār*.]

āngī, (Bid.) *angī*, a finger, toe (Bid.). [Cf. Skt. *aṅguri-*, *aṅguli-*; B. *angur*, Sh. *agui*, Ksh. *ąng*[u]*j*[ü]. In Tōrwalī, there has been elision of intervocalic *r*.]

àngut, (? *àngut̩*), m., the thumb (Bid.). [Cf. Av. *añgušta-*, toe, Skt. *aṅguṣṭha-*, thumb; Sh. *aguṭo*, Ksh. *nyŏṭh*.]

inhān, m., a rainbow (Bid.). [Cf. Skt. *indradhanus-*; B. *inḍrōn*, Kh. *drŏnanū*; Ksh. *dọ̄ñ*[ü], a bow.]

anūsa, to bring (Bid.). [Cf. Skt. *ānayati*; Ksh. *anun*.]

anatōl, f. *anatel*, dirty (Bid.).

āp, see *abōsa*.

ep, f., a fault (Bid.). [Psht. *'aib*.]

ūpur, f., *ipīr*, light, not heavy (Bid.).

ar, half (L. 232, and Bid.); *ar žāt*, m., midnight (III, 43, and Bid.). [Cf. Skt. *ardha-*; Ksh. *aḍ*.]

ār, a duck (L. 73). [Cf. B. *ar*, W.K.Kh. *āri*, G. *aṛi*, Gār. *ār*.]

eṛī, (III, 22), *eṛi* (III, 15), or *iṛī* (L. 82) *hōsa*, to stand, to halt. [Cf. Skt. *adhi* + √*sthā-*, *adhiṣṭhita-*, through **ahiṭṭhia-*, **ahiḍia-*. Cf. M. *ōli ha-*, to stand.]

armān, interj. alas! (L. 100). [Psht.]

arzī, f., a request (III, 5). [Psht. *'arẓī*.]

ēs, etc., *es-sam*, see *e* 3.

aši, see *achī*.

ašū, Verb Subst. Past, was (I, 16, 17 (bis)). Sing. Masc. *ašū*, fem. *ašī*; Plur. Masc. and Fem. *ašī*, see §§ 155 ff.; *āšū* (I, 13). For *šū*, *šat* (*šad*), see §§ 157 ff.

ōš, m., ice (Bid.). [Cf. Skt. *avaśyāya-*; B. *šī*, K. *yōz*.]

ošo, f. *eše*, ugly (Bid.). [? Cf. Skt. *yakṣa-*; Ksh. *yĕch*, ugly.]

ašur, a little (Bid.).

ušūsa, to rise, to stand up; to enter (Bid.); Past, *ucit*, got up, arose (III, 9, 43). Cf. *ucūsa*. [With *ucit*, ? cf. Skt. *utkṣipta-*. With √*uš-*, ? cf. Skt. *uttiṣṭhati*, Śr. Pr. *utthadi*, p.p. *utthida-*; W. √*ōšt-*, V. √*išt-*, K.G. √*ušṭ-*, Sh. √*uth-*, Ksh. √*wŏth-*, Gypsy √*ušti-*. The Tōrwālī change of *ṣṭh* or *tth* to *š*, however, presents difficulties.]

ištàman, rich (Bid.).

ašay, f., an apricot (Bid.). [Cf. Psht. *ašāṛai*.]

aṭ (L. 8), *at* (Bid.), Card. eight. [Cf. Av. *ašta*, Skt. *aṣṭa-*; Ksh. *öṭh*, other Dardic *ašṭ*, etc. Cf. Psht. *at*ᵃ, Wkh. *hȧt*, Ish. *ōt*.]

ūtal (? *ūthal*) f. *ūtil* (? *ūthil*), high (Bid.); *ūtel*, up (Bid.). [Cf. Skt. *utthita-*; Sh. *uthalu* (Bid. *utallo*) (*t* > *l*), Ksh. *thạd*ᵘ (*t* > *d*).]

atāš (? *aṭāš*), Card. eighteen (Bid.). [Cf. Skt. *aṣṭādaśa*; B. *aštits*, Sh. *aṣṭāī*.]

awū, m., a touch (Bid.).

awal, adv., first (II, 34). [Psht. *awwal*.]

awās, m., a sound (Bid.). [Psht. *āwāz*.]

ayu-di, adv., to-day (Bid.). Cf. *aj* and *dī*.

ūzel, see *ūjul*.

àzmān, m., the heavens (Bid.). [Psht. *āsmān*.]

öž, m., mud (Bid.); *öž*, f. *až*, wet (Bid.). [Cf. Skt. *ardra-*; Sh. *aẓu*, Ksh. *ạdur*ᵘ.]

ežug-di, the day before yesterday (Bid.). Cf. *dī*.

bā, up to, as far as (III, 61); up (L. 86). [Cf. Psht. *bā*, with, by.]

be 1, m., a husband (Bid.). [? Cf. Skt. *vara-*; Sh. *barau*.]

be 2, without (Bid.). [Psht. *bē*.]

bī, adv., again (I, 35; III, 46; Bid.). [Cf. Skt. *dvitīya-*; Ksh. *biyĕ*, second, again; Psht. *biyā*, again.] Cf. *duyi*.

biū, N. of a certain tree; Sing. Gen. *biū-si* (II, 31).

bū, f. *bü*, deaf (Bid.). [? Cf. Skt. *badhira-*.]

buā, see *būūsa*.

bāba, a certain title, Bābā (II, 19, 22, 26, 35–7, 40, 42); Sing. Dat. *bāba-ye* (II 24); Gen. *bāba-si* (II, 33).

bĕbā, marriage (L. 225); *bēbā*, a wedding (Bid.). [Cf. Skt. *vivāha-*; Ksh. *vĕwāh.*]

bŏba, see *bāp*.

bebay, f., an apple. [? deriv.; B. *paṛṛ*, Kh. *pàlŏγ*, Sh. *phalā*, Ksh. *tsũṭ-*, *trēl.*]

bad (? *baḍ*), m., a stone (Bid.). [? Cf. Skt. *vṛtta-* round; B. *wōtt*, Kh. *bŏrt*, Sh. *baṭ.*]

bēḍū, see *baiyūsa*.

bid, f., fear (Bid.). [Cf. Skt. *bhīti-*; B. *wide-γ*, Sh. *biž-ōiki*, to fear.]

biad, timid (Bid.). [Cf. *bid.*]

bud, many, much (I. 30). [Cf. Skt. *bahu-*, *bahutva-*; Kh. *boh*, Sh. *bodu.*]

buḍ, *būḍ* (Bid. *bud*), all, whole, entire (*buḍ*, II, 49); *bud* (? *buḍ*) *māš*, everybody (Bid.); *būḍ māža-mī behter*, best among all men (L. 137); *būḍa-mē jīg* tallest of all (L. 137); *bud* (? *buḍ*) *siz*, everything (Bid.). [? Cf. Skt. *vaḍra-*; Hindī *baṛā*, great; Sh. *buṭu.*]

būda, see *būūsa*.

badaχšān-miā, from Badakhshān (II, 7).

baderōsa, to deceive (Bid.).

bādšāhī, f., kingship, ruling (III, 1, 61); Sing. Dat. *-ge* (III, 60). [Psht.] Cf. *pādšāhī*.

bàduškār, m., midday (Bid.).

baidāt, defeated (III, 16).

bāge nikūsa, to go out (Bid.). [If *bā-ge* is a Dative, cf. Skt. *bahiḥ*; B. *bē.*]

bogho [sic], m., a sheep (Bid.). [Cf. Skt. *barkara-*; Kh. *warkālū*, a ram; Ksh. (with metathesis) *gạb*[ü], a ewe.] Cf. *ē* 1 and *midhal*.

bogul, m., the cheek (Bid.). [Cf. Skt. *kapōla-*, with metathesis.]

biginūsa, to sell (Bid.). [Cf. Skt. *vikrīṇītē*; Ksh. *k*[a]*nun* to sell, Hindī *biknā*, to be sold.]

bagär, unless (Bid.). [Psht. *baγair*.]
bŏguvāl, m., a shepherd (L. 59). Cf. *bogho*.
bāγ, m., a garden (Bid.). [Psht.]
boγuz, m., hatred (Bid.). [Psht. *baγẓ*.]
bhā, (Bid.) *bā*, m., a brother, a cousin (see Bid., p. 76) (II, 39, 43, 46 ; L. 49, 231) ; Plur. Nom. *bhai* (I, 15, 31) ; Dat. *bhayā-gē* (I, 32). [Cf. Av. *brātar-*, Skt. *bhrātṛ-* ; B. *bṛoh*, W.T. *brā*, Kh. *brār*, G. *bliaia*, P. *lāī*, Sh. *jā*, Gār. *jā*, Ksh. *bāyᵘ*, V. *wayeh*.]
bⁱhai, *bⁱhī*, see *baiyūsa*.
bihũ, N. of a place, Bihun. Sing. Dat. *bihũ-ge* (III, 13, 14, 48, 51) ; Loc. *bihũ-mī* (III, 47).
bⁱhēṭh, see *baiyūsa*.
behter, better (L. 133). [Psht. *bihtar*.]
bijmot, m., lightning (Bid.). [Cf. Skt. *vidyut-* + *mān* ; Kh. *bilphak*, Sh. *bicuṣ̌*.]
bajūsa, *bažūsa*, to go (I, 19, 25, 27, 36, 41, 44–5, 49 ; II, 28 ; III, 13, 28, 31 ; L. 205–10, 217–18) ; to go away, be off (I, 52 ; L. 77) ; to walk (L. 238) ; to wander (Bid.). According to L. 77, this verb means rather "to go away", while √*til-*, q.v., means simply "to go".

Fut. (Old Pres.) *biži* (II, 28) ; *bižī* (I, 36, 44, 52) ; Impve. Sg. 2, *baž* (I, 25, 44–5 ; L. 77, 217, 238) ; Plur. 2, *buža* (I, 27) ; *baža* (I, 41) ; *boža* (III, 13).

Pres. Sing. Masc. *baže-dū* (I, 1, 45) ; *bažē-dū* (L. 205–7) ; Plur. Masc. *bažē-dī* (L. 208–10).

Conj. Part. *beš-te* (I, 19, 49 ; III, 28, 31).

Pres. Part. *bažunge* (L. 218).

The word *gā* 3, q.v., is used for the Past Participle of this verb.

[Cf. Skt. √*vraj-*, *vrajati* ; Sh. *bujä*, he will go ; Gār. √*bac-*, go.]

bujūsa, to hear (Bid.). [Cf. Skt. *budhyatē* ; Ksh. √*bōz-*. Cf. *būūsa*.]
bekū, m., stupidity (Bid.). [? Psht. *bēwuqūfī* ; Kh. *bekū*.]
būk, blunt (Bid.).

bekin, f., the arm (Bid.).

bāl, m., hair (L. 39; Bid.). [Skt. *bāla-*; Sh. *bālo*, T. *bāla*, Ksh. *wāl*; Europ. Gypsy *bāl*.]

balai, f., wind (Bid.). [Cf. Av. Skt. *vāta-*; Ksh. *wāv*, Psht. *bād*.]

bolu-di, to-morrow (Bid.)

būmel, m., an earthquake (Bid.). [Cf. Skt. *bhūmi-cala-*; Kh. *bŏlmaži*, Sh. *bũyāl*, Ksh. *būñulu*, an earthquake. ? the origin of the second member of the compound.]

bamandūr, m., a bridegroom (Bid.); *bamandir*, f., a bride (Bid.).

bandūsa, to order (Bid.). [Cf. Av. √*bañd-*, Skt. √*bandh-*; W. √*vand-*; Kh. √*bandē-*, to order; Sh. *band-ēš*, an order; Ksh. *band*, bound.]

banūsa, to say, speak; *sabak banūsa*, to say a lesson, to learn (II, 27). Pres. *banin* (§ 169) (I, 38–9); (Masc.) *bana-dū* (I, 7, 10, etc., 22, 25, 32–3, 41–2, 45, 47–9, 52; II, 10, 28, 35, 37–8, 40–1, 44, 46; III, 25 (bis), 28, 31, 34–5, 37, 40–1, 50, 52); (Fem.) *bana-žī* (III, 51, 53, 58); *bane-žī* (I, 44); Past (Masc.) *banū* (I, 20, 27; II, 8, 9; III, 7, 11–13); (Fem.) *banī* (I, 35); Pluperf. *banu-šat* (II, 27). [Cf. Skt. *varṇayati*; Ksh. √*wan-*.]

bāp, m., a father. Sing. Nom. *bāp* (II, 17, 29; L. 47, 101, 233); Dat. *bāp-ke* (L. 103); Abl. *bāpa-kĕjā* (L. 104); Gen. *bāp-si* (L. 223); Plur. Nom. *bāpe* (L. 106); *dū bāp* two fathers (L. 105); Dat. *bŏba-ge* (L. 108); Abl. *bŏba-mā* or *bŏba-kĕjā* (L. 109); Gen. *bŏba-sē* (L. 107). [Cf. Skt. *vapra-*; G. *bāp*, *bāb*, Sh. *bābo*, Ksh. (dial.) *babb*, Gypsy (Syrian) *bāb*.]

bār, f. *bär*, thick, fat (Bid.). [? Cf. Psht. *lwāṛ*.]

barai, victory (III, 8). [Psht.]

barābar, straight, level (I, 28); equal (Bid.). [Psht.]

bārdan, m., a bow (? the weapon) (Bid.). [? Cf. Skt. *dhanus-*; B. *drōn*, Kh. *drŏn*, Sh. *dānu*, Ksh. *dǭñ ü*.]

birārūsa, to search for (Bid.).

bariš, f., a side (Bid.). [? Cf. Skt. *pārśva-*; Kh. *praš*, a side.]

bàrīš, sloping (Bid.). [? Cf. Skt. *pārśva-*, as in the preceding; Kh. *praš*, sloping; Bur. Sh. *bēsko*, sloping.]

birāṭ, (Bid. *birat*), m., a he-goat (L. 150); Plur. *birāṭ* (L. 152). A nanny-goat is *chal* (L. 151; Bid. *cel*).

būūsa, to see (III, 43; Bid.); to look at (III, 31); to know (II, 25); Impve. Plur. 2, *buā* (III, 31); Past, Masc. Sing., *būda* (II, 25), *būdō* (III, 43). [Cf. Skt. √*budh-*, *bōdhati*, *buddha-*; Ksh. √*bŏz-*, hear < *budhyatē*. Cf. *bujūsa*.]

basān, m., spring (Bid.). [Cf. Skt. *vasanta-*; B. *wasnt*, Kh. *besun*, Ksh. *sŏt-*.]

besyāt, loot, plunder, booty (III, 8).

bīš 1, f., a flute (Bid.). [? Cf. Skt. *vaṁśa-* or *vādya-*; Sh. √*baš-*, to play (an instrument).]

bīš 2, Card. twenty (L. 11; Bid.); *nūm bīš*, nine times twenty (III, 17). [Cf. Av. *vīsaiti-*, Skt. *viṁśati-*; B. *vitsi*, W. *wišī*, K. *bišī*, G. *išī*, P. *wöst*, T. *biau*, Kh. *bišr*, Sh. *bī*, Ksh. *wuh*, European Gypsy, *bīš*.]

buš (? *buṣ*), m., hunger (Bid.). [Cf. Skt. *bubhukṣā*; Kh. *chūī*, hungry; Ksh. *bŏch*, hunger.]

bušā, m., summer (Bid.).

bušauhū, f. *bušaihī*, hungry. [See *buš*.]

bišat, clothes (Bid.). [? Cf. Psht. *bisāṭ*, show of things, display.]

bāt, m., language (Bid.); a word, words (f.) (I, 35). [Cf. Skt. *vārttā*; Ksh. *bāt-*. Probably borrowed from Panjābī.]

baṭhā, see *baiyūsa*.

batkūmā, f., a maid (Bid.).

bowūš, m., a nephew (Bid.); *beyīš*, f., a niece (Bid.). [Probably a compound of *bhā*, a brother, and *pūš*, a son. Cf. Skt. *bhrātṛ-putra-*; B. *nawōs*, nephew; Kh. *nōwēs*, nephew, niece; Sh. *ẓawai*, nephew; Ksh. *bāpath*ᵃ*r*, nephew, *bāw*ᵃ*za*, niece; all on the brother's side.]

baiyel, open (Bid.). [? Cf. Skt. *vyapâvṛta-* ; Sh. *bātu.*]

baiyim, out (prefix) (Bid.). [Cf. Skt. *bahiḥ* ; B. *bē*, Kh. *beri*. For the termination, cf. Ksh. *nĕb^a^rim^u^*, external.]

bayān, explanation, recital ; *b. kōsa*, to recite (II, 33, 35–6, 39). [Psht.]

baiyūsa, to sit (Bid.) ; *b^i^hai*, sit ! (L. 79) ; Fut. (Old. Pres.), Plur. 1 *b^i^hī* (I, 52) ; Past Part. *bēṭh*, he sat (I, 29) ; *b^i^hēṭh*, seated (L. 230) ; *bēḍū šū*, he was seated (II, 32) ; *baṭhā kī*, made (him) seated, made him sit down (III, 42). This last is a causal form. *bēṭh* and *b^i^hēṭh* are weak forms, and *bēḍū* is a strong form (§ 180.)

[Cf. Skt. *upaviśati, upaviṣṭa-* ; Sh. √*bai-*, Ksh. √*bĕh-*, Gypsy (Europ.) √*beš-*. Most Dardic languages use a word connected with Av. √*nihad-*, Skt. √*niṣad-*.]

beyīš, f., a niece (Bid.). [See *bowūš*.]

bizin, f., *bizīn*, broad (Bid.). [? Cf. Skt. *vistīrṇa-* ; B. *wištrī*.]

buzurg, reverend, venerable, a holy man (II, 17). [Prs.]

biž, f., seed (Bid.). [Cf. Skt. *vīja-* ; B. *bī*, Kh. *bīh*, Sh. *bi*, Ksh. *bīz*.]

cā (? *çā*) Card. three (L. 3 ; Bid.) ; *ca ḍe*, three parts (II, 10) ; *cā bīš*, sixty (Bid.) ; *cī-gona*, thrice (Bid.). [Cf. Av. *θri-*., Skt. *tri-* ; B.K. *trĕh*, W. *trē*, Kh. *troi*, Ksh. *trih*, Gypsy (Europ.) *trin*, G. *ṭhlē*, P. *hlē*, Gār. *ṭhā*, V. *chī*, Sh. *çei*.]

cai 1, m., a mountain (Bid.) ; a cliff (III, 57–9). [Kh. *cār*, a cliff, Sh. *char*, a mountain. Cf. *cāl*.]

cai 2, in *cai gā*, see *cōsa*.

cau (L. 4), *co* (Bid.), Card. four ; *co bīš*, eighty (Bid.). [Cf. Av. *caθwārō*, Skt. *catvāraḥ* ; P.Sh. *cār*, Kh. *cōr*, G. *tsūr*, Ksh. *tsōr*, B. *što*, W. *štā*, Gypsy (Europ.) *štār*.]

ci, see *tu*.

cī 1 (? *chī*), see *thū* ; in *di-cī*, see *thū*.

cī 2 (? *çī*), f., a woman, female, wife (Bid. ; L. 52. 53 ; I, 51, 53, *chī*). [Cf. Skt. *strī* ; V. *westi* ; Sh. (Ḍāh-Hanū) *tšrigā*, G. *šigāli* ; P. *šlika, hlika*, a wife ; Ksh. *triy*, Sh.

cāi, *çāi*, Gār. *īš*. The L.S.I. gives Tōrwālī *šī*, instead of *cī*.]

ciā-dū, he is grazing (cattle) (L. 229). [Cf. Skt. *cārayati*, with the usual Tōrwālī elision of intervocalic *r*. Sh. √*car-*.]

co, see *cau*.

cū, m., a dagger (Bid.). [Cf. Skt. *churikā*, with elision of intervocalic *r*.]

cūi, (Bid.) *cüi*, ord. third (II, 43, 47). [Cf. *cā*.]

cūī (? *çūī*), f., milk (Bid.). [Cf. Av. *χšīra-*, Skt. *kṣīra-*; Prs. *šīr*; B. *zu*, Kh. *cīr*. In Tōrwālī and B. there has been elision of intervocalic *r*.]

cude (? *cu ḍē*), a quarter (Bid.). [Cf. *cau*. The word seems to be a compound with *ḍē*, a share, q.v.]

cudo, m., a basket (Bid.).

cīdug-di, yesterday (Bid.). [? deriv. B. *dus*, Kh. *doš*. These two words probably have some connexion with Skt. *dōṣā*. Cf. Ksh. *rāt-*, yesterday. Cf. *cotug-di*.]

cāgū, m., a knife [Psht. *cāqū*.]

cigān, in *cigān gālūsa*, to shout (Bid.). [? Cf. Skt. *citkāra-*, **citkāraṇa-*, with elision of intervocalic *r*. Psht. *coγ*, clamour; B. *cō*.]

chī, see *cī* 1 and 2, and *tu*.

coh, away (Bid.).

chal (Bid. *cel*), f., a she-goat, nanny-goat (L. 151). A he-goat is *birāṭ*, q.v. Sg. Gen. *chal-si* (II, 18); Plur. Nom. *chal* (L. 152). [Cf. Skt. *chagalī*.]

cojol, m., a shadow (Bid.). [Cf. Skt. *chāyā*; B. *tsāwē*, Kh. *cāγ*, Sh. *chiżoṭ*.]

cujūsa, to learn (Bid.). [? Cf. Skt. √*śikṣ-*; Kh. √*cic-*, Sh. √*siç-*, Ksh. √*hĕch-*. Or else Skt. *śudhyatē*.]

cūjūsa, to teach (Bid.). [See the preceding. Kh. √*cicē-*, Sh. √*siçar-*, Ksh. √*hĕchanāv-*. Or cf. Skt. *śōdhyatē*, *śōdhayati*.]

cek, f., time (Bid.); *tet-cek*, then, when (rel.) (Bid.).

cuk, f., *cik*, acid (Bid.). [Cf. Skt. *cukra-*; B. *ceno*, Kh. *šut*, Sh. *curku*, Ksh. *tsạk*ᵘ.]

cal, m., an artifice, trick (I, 24); deceit (Bid.); [Psht.]

cāl, a rock; *cālā-bā*, up to the rock (III, 61). [Cf. Kh. *cār*, a cliff; Sh. *char*, a mountain. See *cai* 1.]

cel, see *chal*.

cele, in *me cele*, thus (Bid.). [? Cf. *cal*.]

cam, m., skin (Bid.). [Cf. Av. *careman-*, Skt. *carman-*; B. *camo*, Sh. *cŏm*, Ksh. *tsam*.]

cimu [Bid. *cimoh*], m., iron (L. 44). [Cf. Bur. *comar*, B. *cimeh*, W. *cimā*, V. *žema*, K. *cīmbar*, G. *tsimar*, P. Sh. Gār. *chimar*, Kh. *cumūr*, T. *tsimbar*, Ksh. *ts*[a]*mur*[u].]

√*cin-*, cut. Impve. Sing. 2, *cin*, cut thou (III, 58); Past Part. *cinū* (III, 38, 59). [Cf. Skt. √*chid-*, *chinatti*; Kh. √*cin-*, to cut; Ksh. √*tshĕnn-*, to be cut.]

cun, f. *cin*, narrow (Bid.). [? Cf. Skt. *kṣīṇa-*; Sh. *cuṇu*.]

cunū, f. *cene*, yellow (Bid.).

cir, much, very (II, 4; III, 27, 42; L. 224, 228; Bid.). [Cf. Ksh. *tsạr*[u], much.]

cēriḍ, a small bird [L. 76). A large bird is *pašīn*, see *pacin*. [Cf. Skt. *caṭikā*; Gār. *carōr*, Gypsy (Europ.) *ciriklo*.]

cōsa, to let go (Bid.); *cai gā*, he abandoned (I, 54). Cf. *cowūsa*. [Cf. Skt. √*cuṭ-*, *cōṭayati*, through *cōḍēi*, **cōṛēi*, with Tōrwālī elision of intervocalic *ṛ*.]

ceš 1 (? *ceṣ̌*), f., a circle (Bid.). [Cf. Av. *caχra-*, Skt. *cakra-*, with ordinary change of *kr* > *ç* > Tōrwālī *ṣ̌*.]

ceš 2 (? *çeš*), Card. thirteen (Bid.). [Cf. *cā* and Skt. *trayōdaśa*.]

ciš, the female breast (II, 18 bis, 21). [Cf. Skt. *cuci-*, *cūcuka-*; Sh. *cuci*.]

cat, in *cat kōsa*, to call (Bid.).

cit, f. *cīt*, low (Bid.). [Cf. Skt. *kṣudra-*, small; Ksh. *tsọṭ*[u], low.]

cotug-di, the day after to-morrow (Bid.). Cf. *cīdug-di*.

cōthum (II, 10. 46), *cotam* (Bid.), Ord. fourth. [Cf. Skt. *caturtha-*; Sh. *carmŏño*, Ksh. *tsūrịm*[u].]

cettiš, Card. fourteen (Bid.). [Cf. Skt. *caturdaśa*; B. *štrits*, Sh. *condai*, Ksh. *tsŏdāh*.]

cowūsa, to leave (Bid.). Cf. *cōsa*.
caiyõ, m., the neck (Bid.).

dā̆, f., the beard (Bid.). [Cf. Skt. *dāḍhikā*; B. *dāṛi*, Sh. *dā̃i*, Ksh. *dạ̄r*ᵘ.]
dai, see *dyūsa*.
daī, see *dhain*.
de 1, *dē* 1, see *dyūsa*.
de 2, f., a spoon (Bid.). [Cf. Skt. *darvī*; Kh. *dori*.]
dē 2, see *ḍhē*.
de 3, *dē* 3, see *te* 2.
dī, f., a day (Bid.); *ē dī*, one day (I, 18, 32); *ežug-di*, the day before yesterday (Bid.); *bolu-di*, to-morrow (Bid.); *cīdug-di*, yesterday (Bid.); *cotug-di*, the day after to-morrow (Bid.); *her-dī*, every day, always (Bid.); *sàtam-di*, a week (Bid.). [Cf. Skt. *div-*, *divasa-*; Sh. *dez*, Ksh. *dŏh*.]
diū, he fled (III, 16); he escaped (III, 45).
diū-šad, see *dyūsa*.
dō, see *dū* 5.
dū 1, see *dhū*.
dū 2, far (L. 89; Bid.); distance (L. 222). [Cf. Skt. *dūra-*; P.T.Sh. Ksh. Gār. *dūr*, G. *durae*, B. *dyuṛ*, Gypsy (Europ.) *dūr*.]
dū 3, see *dyūsa*.
dū 4, see *thū*.
dū 5, *du*, *dō*, Card. two; *du žāt*, two nights (I, 10); *dū* (II, 48; L. 2, 232; Bid.); *dū bīš*, forty (Bid.); *dū-gona*, twice (Bid.); *dō kāl*, two years (II, 47). [Cf. Av. Skt. *dva-*, Skt. *dvi-*; B. *diu*, Kh. *jū*, Ksh. *z*ᵃ*h*, W.G.Sh. *du*, K.G.Gār. *dū*, P.T. *dō*, Gypsy (Europ.) *dūī*, V. *lūe*.]
duī, see *duyī*.
di-ci, see *dyūsa*.
dād, m., a grandfather, ancestor (II, 1, 6, 7–10, 13, 34); Sing. Dat. *dād-ke* II, 8, 9); Gen. *dād-si* (II, 16). [? Cf. Skt. *tāta-*; Psht. *dādā*; Sh. *dādu*; Ksh. *dĕd*, a grandmother; Hindī *dādā*.]

did, see *dyūsa* 2.
dud, m., the lip (Bid.).
dadan, a fireplace ; Sing. Gen. *dadan-si* (III, 42). [Cf. Kh. *didaṅ*, Ksh. *dān*.]
dag, f., an old woman (Bid.). Cf. *derg*.
dugū, in *dugū-dut*, she was weaving (III, 18).
dhū (L. 56, 110), *dū* (Bid.), f., a daughter ; Plur. Nom. *dhī* (L. 114–5) ; Plur. Obl. *dhia* (L. 116–18). [Cf. Av. *duγδar-* Skt. *duhitṛ-*, Pr. *dhīdā* ; Psht. *lūr* ; Sh. *dī*, Ksh. (dial.) *dhī* Kh. *žūr*, G. *zū*, B.V. *jū*, K. *chū*.] Cf. § 18.
dhain dyūsa (L. 85), *daī dyūsa* (Bid.), to run. [Cf. Skt. √*dhav-* ; Prs. *davīdan* ; Kh. √*dē-*, Ksh. √*dav-*.]
dehqān, m., a cultivator (L. 58). [Psht. *dihqān*.]
dak 1, see *ḍāg*.
dak 2, m., a fight (Bid.). [? Cf. Hindī *ḍāknā*, to shout ; *ḍākū*, a robber.]
dukāndār, m., a shopkeeper ; Sing. Abl. *-kĕjā* (L. 241). [Psht. *dūkāndār*.]
del, shut (Bid.).
dīmi, f., smoke (Bid.). [Cf. Skt. *dhūma-* ; B. *dūm*, Sh. *dum*, Ksh. *dᵃh*.]
[The change of *ū* to *ī*, through *yū*, is not uncommon in Ksh.]
diumo, see *duyimo*.
dūmsa, m., a relation (Bid.).
dan 1, m., a handle (Bid.). [Cf. Skt. *daṇḍa-* ; B. *dōn*, Sh. *dŏṇu*, Ksh. *dan*.]
dan 2 (L. 37), *dān* (Bid.), m., a tooth. [Cf. Av. *dañtan-*, Skt. *danta-* ; B. *dut*, W. *dūt*, T. *dant*, K. *dandōriak*, G. *dãt*, P. *dānd*, Sh. *dōn*, Ksh. Gār. *dand*, Gypsy (Europ.) *dănd*, Ksh. also *dan-*.]
dāna, wise (Bid.). [Psht. *dānā*.]
dandak, m., a drum (Bid.) ; *dandak-o-bīši*, m., drum and flute (Bid.). [Cf. Skt. *dundhubhi-*, *ḍiṇḍima-* ; B. *dōtt*, Ksh. *ḍam-ḍam*, *ḍum-ḍum* (onomat.).]
dārū, m., gunpowder (Bid.). [Psht. So B. *dāru*.]

der, a door ; Sing. Loc. *derē* (III, 20, 22). [Cf. Av. Skt. *dvar-* ; B. *dū*, Kh. *duārt*, Sh. *dar*, Ksh. *bar*.] Cf. *derwāz*.

dērā, a house, dwelling (I, 14, 25, 27–8 ; III, 4) ; Sing. Loc. *dērā-mī* (I, 52). [Psht. *dēra*.]

dērī, Past Part. Masc. Plur., they remained (I, 31). [? Cf. Av. *darẹya-*, Skt. *dīrgha-* ; Prs. *dēr*, delay. Or ? cf. Skt. *dṛḍha-*, with which is connected the Ksh. √*dar-*, be firm.]

dur, m., mist (Bid.). [Cf. Phl. *dūt*, Prs. *dūd*, Psht. *dund*, *lū*.]

derg, m., an old man (Bid.). [? Cf. Skt. *dīrgha-*. For the connexion between "long" and "old", cf. Ksh. *z̤īṭh^u*, long, and *z̤iṭh^u*, elder.] Cf. *dag* and *jīg*.

darin, f., land (Bid.).

derwāz, m., a door (Bid.). [Psht. *darwāza*.] Cf. *der*.

dōs, m., a friend (Bid.). [Psht. *dōst*.]

dostī, f., friendship (Bid.). [Psht.]

dastūr, m., a custom (Bid.). [Psht.]

daš 1 (? *daṣ̌*) m., a grape (Bid.). [Cf. Skt. *drākṣā* ; B. *dros*, Kh. *drŏch*, Sh. *jaç*, Ksh. *dach*.]

daš 2, Card. ten (I, 15, 31 ; L. 10 ; Bid.) ; *daš o bīš*, thirty (Bid.) ; *daš o dū bīš*, fifty (L. 12 ; Bid.) ; *daš o cā bīš*, seventy (Bid.) ; *daš o co bīš*, ninety (Bid.). [Cf. Av. *dasa*, Skt. *daśa* ; K.G.Gār. *daš*, W. *dōš*, Kh. *još*, B. *duts*, V. *leze*, T.K. *dah*, Sh. *daii*, P. *dē*, Gypsy (Europ.) *deš*.]

diš, side, direction, in *phēm diše* (II, 3), *payim dišē* (III, 37), *payim diše-de* (III, 56), on the opposite (or far) side (of a river). [Cf. Skt. *diś-*, and the next.]

dišā, postpos. towards (Bid.). [Cf. Skt. *diś-*, direction, and the preceding.]

dušman, m., an enemy (I, 3 ; Bid.). [Psht.]

dit, see *dyūsa* 1.

dut, see *thū*.

dawa, m., medicine (Bid.). [Psht. *dawā*.]

duwā kōsa, to make a benediction, i.e. to grant in answer to a petition (II, 42, 44–5). [Psht. *du'ā*.]

dwāš (II, 4), *dūwāsh* (Bid.), Card. twelve. [Cf. Av. *dvadasa*, Skt. *dvādaśa* ; B. *dits*, Sh. *bāi*, Ksh. *bāh*.]

duyi (II, 39), *duī* (III, 25–6), Ord. second (II, 39) ; another (III, 25–6). [Cf. Av. *bitya-*, O.Prs. *duvitīya-*, Skt. *dvitīya-* ; Kh. *jūwum* ; Ksh. *dŏyimᵘ*, second, *biyĕ*, again.] Cf. *bī*.

duyimo (II, 11, 12), *diumo* (III, 15 ; § 56), both, the two (III, 15) ; *mō duyimo*, we two (II, 11) ; *ā duyimo*, those two (II, 12). [Cf. Sh. *dumŏṅo*, second, *baīĕ*, both.]

dyūsa 1, to give (Bid.) ; Fut. (Old Pres.), *dai*, I shall give (I, 49) ; *dē*, let us give (I, 36) ; Impve. Sing. 2, *dē* (I, 48 ; L. 84, 175, 234) ; *dū* (? *dē*) (I, 33 ; § 167) ; Imperf. Sing. 3, *diū-šad*, at end of sentence (I, 29) ; Past Part. Masc. Sing. *dit* (II, 48 ; III, 33) ; Fem. *dit* (I, 34–5, 38) ; Perf. Fem. Sing. *dī-cī* (for *dit-žī*, § 158) (I, 20).

[Cf. Av. Skt. √*dā-* ; K.Sh. √*de-*, Kh. Ksh. √*di-*, P.T. √*dē-*, G. √*thla-*, Gypsy (Europ.) √*dă-*, (Syrian) √*de-*.]

dyūsa 2, to strike, hit, beat ; Past Part. Sing. Masc. *did* (III, 44) ; Fem. *did* (III, 30), in both cases at the end of a sentence. [In many Dardic languages the √*dā-* is used for both " give " and " beat ". Thus, Kh. √*di-*, give, beat ; K. √*de-*, give, √*ti-*, beat ; Sh. √*de-*, give, (Cilāsī) √*ḍē-*, beat ; T. √*dē-*, give, beat ; G. √*thla-*, give, beat.]

ḍe, a share, portion, part (II, 10 (bis) ; Bid. *de*) ; Sing. Gen. *ḍē-si* (II, 25) ; *cu-de*, a quarter (Bid.).

ḍāg (L. 43), *dak* (Bid.), m., the back. [Cf. K. *ḍāk*, Sh. *ḍākī*.]

ḍhē (L. 42), *dē* (Bid.), f., the belly. [Cf. Lnd. *ḍhiḍḍh* ; Sh. *ḍēr*, Gār. *ḍār*, Ksh. *yĕḍ*, V. *iul* ; but the last two are probably connected with Bur. *yūl*.]

ḍiṭ, Past Part. Fem. Sing. she (was) seen (III, 23, 32, 49). [Cf. Skt. *dṛṣṭā* ; Ksh. √*ḍēš-*, past part. f. *ḍīṭhᵘ*.]

fikerdār, anxious (Bid.). [Psht. *fikrdār*.] Cf. *piger*, anxiety.

filankai (I, 12), *filankē* (I, 39, 43), a certain (man, etc.). [Psht. *falānkai*.]

gā 1, m., grass (Bid.). [Cf. Skt. *ghāsa-*; Kh. *gās*, Ksh. *gāsa.*]

gā 2, f., a cow (L. 69, 143; Bid.); Plur. *gai* (L. 145). [Cf. Av. Skt. *gāv-*; Ksh. *gāv*, B. *gảo*, Sh. *gào*, W.P.M. *gā*, K. *gak*; T. *gō*, a bull.]

gā 3, Past Part. gone. This word is used as the Past Part. and Past tense of *bajūsa* or *bažūsa*, to go, q.v. Past Part. Sing. Masc. *gā* (L. 219). Past Tense Sing. Masc. *gā*, (I) went (I, 43; L. 211); (thou) wentest (L. 212); (he) went (I, 2, 46, 54; III, 29 (bis), 38–9, 45, 48; L. 213); *gya*, in *karmā gya*, the army went (III, 14); Fem. *gā*, (she) went (I, 28); Plur. Masc. *gai*, (we) went (L. 214); (you) went (L. 215); (they) went (II, 47; III, 32; L. 216); Pluperf. Sing. Masc. *gā šū*, (thou) hadst gone (I, 39).

[Cf. Skt. *gata-*; B. *gwa*, W. *goā*, P. *gik*, G. *ga*, T.Gār·*gā*, Sh. *gōu*, Ksh. *ga-*, *gō-*, Gypsy (Europ.) *gelō.*]

ge, *gē*, see *ke* 2.

gō, m., a bull (L. 142; Bid.); Plur. *gō*144). (L. [See *gā* 2. Cf. T. *gō*, a bull.]

gud (? *guḍ*), m., a corner (Bid.). [Psht. *guṭ.*]

gadhō (L. 74), *gadō* (f. *gedē*) (Bid.), an ass. [Cf. Skt. *gardabha-*; W.G. *gadā*, Gār. *gada*, K. *gardōk*, Kh. *gardōγ*. The preservation of the aspirate is exceptional in Dardic. See § 3*e*.]

gedas, m., thunder (Bid.).

ghe, f., a mare (L. 139; Bid.); Plur. *ghai* (L. 141). Cf. the next.

ghō, m., a horse (L. 68, 138; Bid.); Sing. Gen. *ghō-sī* (L. 221, 226, 227); *ghō-se jada*, on a horse (L. 230); Plur. *ghō* (L. 140). [Cf. Skt. *ghōṭaka-*; W. *guṛ*, K. *gora*, P. *gōṛā*, Ksh. *gurᵘ*; Gypsy (Europ.) *khurō*, a colt, (Syrian) *gŏrā*, a horse. The elision of intervocalic *ṛ* is regular in Tōrwālī. The preservation of the aspirate is against Dardic custom, but is also found in Ksh. dialects (Kašṭawāṛī, *ghuṛᵘ*; Pŏgulī, *ghōṛᵘ*, and so on). See § 3*e*.]

gal, abuse (Bid., gender not mentioned); *gal dyūsa*, to abuse (Bid.). [Cf. Skt. *galda-*, speech; *gāli-*, abuse.]

gil, f., bread (I, 29; Bid.).

golē, in *nīlgolē*, f., a pigeon (Bid.). [? Cf. Sh. *kaṅgulī*, the black-throated ouzel, and Psht. *gulū*, throat.]

gōlī, m., a bullet (Bid.). [Psht. *gōlaī*.]

galla, m., a herd (Bid.). [Psht. f.]

gulām, m., a slave (L. 57). [Bid. and Psht. *γulām*.]

gām, m., a village (III, 16; Bid.); Sing. Dat. *gām-ke* (III, 45); *gām-ge* (III, 56, 60); Gen. *gām-si* (I, 30; L. 241); Loc. *gām-žet*, (rule) over the village (III, 1). [Cf. Skt. *grāma-*; B. *grām*, Ksh. *gām*.]

gomū, m., wheat (Bid.). [Cf. Skt. *gōdhūma-*; B. *gum*, Kh. *gom*, Sh. *gūm*.]

gan 1, m., a herd (Bid.). [Cf. Psht. *gaṇ*, crowded.]

gan 2, f. *gen* (Bid.), great, large, big (III, 22; Bid.). [Cf. Skt. *ghana-*; B. *gāno*, heavy; Ksh. *gan*, a log.]

gan 3, see *ganūsa*.

gani, big, grown up (II, 27). Cf. *gan* 2.

gona, see *ek-g°* (s.v. *ek*), *dū-g°* (s.v. *dū* 5), *cī-g°* (s.v. *cā*). The word is used with numerals to signify "fold". [Cf. Skt. *guṇa-*.]

gun, m., a family (Bid.). [Cf. Skt. *gaṇa-*, Ksh. *gan* (Ts.).]

ganūsa, to shut (Bid.); to bind, tie; Impve. Sing. 2, *gan*, bind (L. 236). [Cf. Skt. *√granth-*; Prs. *gira*, a knot; B. *√gīṛ-*, Sh. *√gaṇ-*, Ksh. *√ganḍ-*, all meaning "bind".]

ginūsa (this form of the Infinitive is without authority), to take; to buy; Fut. (Old Pres.) *ginī*, I will take (III, 53); Pres. *ginin* (§ 176), we take (i.e. we will take) (III, 8); Periphrast. Pres. Sing. Masc. *gina-dū*, I take (III, 25 (bis)); Fem. *gina-žī* I (f.) take (III, 51); she takes (III, 28); Impve. *gin*, take thou (III, 50; L. 235); Past Part. and Past Tense, Sing. Masc. Obj. *gin*, she took him (III, 55); *gin-thū* (Perf.), (a guitar) is held (I, 4); has been bought (L. 240–1); Conj. Part. *gin-de*, having taken (III, 44). The word *ginu* (III, 38) can only mean "having taken", but its grammatical form is uncertain.

[Cf. Skt. *gṛhṇāti*; Lnd. √*ghinn-*, Kh. √*gan-*, Sh. √*gin-*.]

garm, hot (Bid.). [Psht.]

garmī, f., heat (Bid.). [Psht.]

gašūsa, to take (Bid.); to capture; Conj. Part. *gaš-te*, having captured (III, 33, 36). [? Derivation. Cf. *ginūsa*. A reference to the Skt. √*gras-* is rendered unlikely by the fact that I know of no other case of *s* > *š*.]

gīt, f., singing (Bid.); *gīt dyūsa*, to sing (Bid.). [Cf. Skt. *gīta-*; Ksh. *gĕwun*, to sing.]

γule, silent (Bid. *ghule*). [Psht. *γalai*.]

γulām, see *gulām*.

γam, m., sorrow, worry (Bid.); Sing. Instr. *γame-de* (I, 11), *γamē-dē* (I, 55). [Psht.]

γamjān (Bid. *ghamžan*, f. *ghamžen*), sorry, worried (I, 11, 55). [Psht.]

γumāz, m., envy (Bid.). [Cf. Psht. *γammāz*, a tale-bearer.]

γāra, a bank, border; Sing. Dat. (for Loc.) *γāra-ye* (II, 4). [Psht. *γāṛa*.]

γora (I, 56; L. 236), *γŏra* (L. 119 ff., 132), (Bid. *ghōrā*, very well; *ghōrāh*, good); Fem. *γŏra* (L. 128); Plur. Masc. and Fem. *γŏra* (L. 123 ff., 130), good (I, 56; L. 119 ff., 128, 130, 132; Bid.); as Adverb, well, very, thoroughly (L. 236; Bid.); *e γŏra māš*, a good man, declined, L. 119 ff. [Psht. *γwara*.]

γarīb, in *hü γarīb*, humble (Bid.). [Psht.]

hü, f., the heart (Bid.); *hü γarīb*, humble (Bid.). [Cf. Skt. *hṛd-*, *hṛdaya-*; Kh. *herdī*, Sh. *hīu*.]

hubil, asleep (III, 43). [Cf. *hut*.]

hecerina, never (Bid.). [Cf. Psht. *hēcari*, never.]

hāda, in *hāda hōsa*, to produce (Bid.); to be able (Bid.).

hidej, f., pity (Bid.). [Apparently *hü*, heart + *dej*. With *dej*, compare Prs. *dard*, pain. Cf. Psht. *zṛa-swai*, heart-compassion.]

hagel, f., the chin (Bid.). [Cf. Skt. *hanu-*, Kh. *hunū*, Ksh. *hŏngañ*.]

hujā, f., *hüjä*, alert (Bid.). [Cf. the next.]

hūjā, m., knowledge (Bid.). [Cf. the preceding. ? Cf. Prs. *hōš*, understanding.]

hujrā, a guest-room; Sing. Loc. *hujrā-mē* (I, 18, 23). [Psht. *hujra*.]

hikū, m., courage (Bid.). [? Cf. Skt. √*śak-*, pass. *śakyatē*; Ksh. √*hĕk-*, be able.]

hukū, f. *hüki*, brave, generous (Bid.). [Cf. the preceding.]

hukum, an order (III, 13). [Psht. *ḥukm*.]

hilā, m., air (Bid.).

höl, m., a plough (Bid.). [Cf. Skt. *hala-*, *hāla-*; Sh. *hal*, Ksh. *ala*, *āla*.]

him, m., snow (Bid.). [Cf. Skt. *hima-*; Phl. *zam*; B. *zīm*, Kh. *hīm*, Sh. *hin*, Ksh. *šīn*.]

hum, and (L. 95). [Psht.]

hamal, m., the equinox (Bid.). [Ar. *ḥamal*.]

himāl, m., an avalanche (Bid.). [Cf. Skt. *himâlaya-*; Sh. *hināl*.]

himān, m., winter (Bid.). [Cf. Skt. *hēmanta-*.]

hamsōs, m., a sigh (Bid.). [Cf. Psht. *afsōs*, alas!]

har, m., a bone (Bid.). [Cf. Skt. *haḍḍa-*; Ksh. *aḍịl*ᵘ.]

her, every, in *her-dī*, every day, always (Bid.). [Psht. *har*.]

hōsa, to be, to become (Bid.); Fut. (Old Pres.) *ā hō*, I should be (L. 174); *hī*, let there be (II, 8); *e huī*, (we) shall become one (II, 11); Impve. Sing. 2 *hō* (L. 168); Periphrast. Pres. Sing. Masc. *ho-dū*, (thou) art (I, 11); (he) is (i.e. dwells) (L. 233); *mē hō-nin* (L. 172, translated "I may be"); Imperf. Sing. Masc. *hō-dut*, was, used to be (I, 23); Past Part. and Past Tense Sing. Masc. *hū*, became (I, 14, 54; II, 16, 19, 27, 36, 42–3, 49; III,

4 (bis), 42, 49); *hō*, became (I, 40 (bis), 46; II, 47 (the third year) became, i.e. came); Fem. *hī*, became (III, 20–1, 43, 46, 57, 60, 61); Plur. Masc. *hī*, became (III, 33); *hōi* (III, 22); *huī* (III, 15); Perf. Sing. Masc. *hō-thū* (I, 55); *hō-dū* (II, 20).

[Cf. Av. √*bav-*, Skt. √*bhū-*, *bhavati*; B. √*bu-*, Kh. Sh. √*bo-*; Ksh. √*bŏv-*.]

husai, m., a deer (L. 153); Plur. *husai* (L. 155); Fem. Sing. *husī* (L. 154). [Cf. Skt. *āśu-*; Psht. *hōsai*.]

hūsī, m., a hare (Bid.). [Cf. the preceding.]

hasūsa, to laugh (Bid.). [Cf. Skt. √*has-*, *hasati*; Kh. √*hŏss-*, Sh. √*ha-*, Ksh. √*as-*.]

hušā, intelligent (III, 27). [Cf. Psht. *hōṣ̌*, intelligence.]

hat (I, 4; III, 38), *had* (L. 32), *hāt* (Bid.), m., the hand; Sing. Instr. *hat-te* (III, 38); Loc. *hat-mē* (I, 4). [Cf. Skt. *hasta-*; K.P. *hāst*, G. *hast*, Kh. *host*, Sh. *hat*, Ksh. *atha*.]

hut, he slept (III, 43). No other forms of this verb have been noted. [Cf. Skt. *supta-*; Sh. *sutu*, he slept. Cf. *hubil*.]

haṭhiwāl-kĕjā, from a shopkeeper (L. 241). [Cf. Psht. *haṭaī*, a market.]

hwa, destitute (Bid.). [Cf. Psht. *χwār*.]

hažat, Past Part., driven away, driven back, repelled; Sing. Masc. III, 3; Plur. Masc. II, 15.

jib, m., the tongue (L. 41; Bid.). [Cf. Skt. *jihvā*; K.P. *jib*, G. *zib*, W. *jip*, Sh. *jīp*, Ksh. *zĕv*, Gypsy (Syrian) *jib*, (Europ.) *cib*.]

jabal, a pickaxe (III, 38, 44).

jūbal, f. *jūbel*, thin (Bid.). [Cf. Skt. *durbala-*; Hindī *dubla*. The change of *du*, through *d^vu*, to *ju* is common in Dardic.]

jabēr, N. of a place; Sing. Gen. *jabēya-si* (II, 7, 9, 13, 16).

jada, see *žet*.

juda, in *juda kōsa*, to separate (Bid.). [Psht. *judā*.]

jagō, the liver (Bid.). [Cf. Av. *yākar-*, Skt. *yakṛt-*; Psht. *jigar*.]

jīg (? *ẓīg*), high, tall (of men) (L. 135); *jik*, f. *jīk*, long (Bid.). [Cf. Skt. *dīrgha-*; M. *žiga* (through **drig*), Sh. *ẓīgu*, Gār. *līg*, Kh. *žaṅ*.] Cf. *derg*.

jama, collected (III, 33). [Psht. *jam'a*.]

jāma, clothes, a garment (I, 49, 50). [Psht.]

jamāldār, (I, 16), *jumāldār* (I, 35, 52), m., a head man (of a village, or the like). [Cf. Hindōstānī *jam'dār*.]

jan, m., a snake (Bid.). [Cf. Sh. *jŏn*. Can this word be connected with the Skt. *bhujaṅga-* ?]

jang, m., the leg (Bid.). [Cf. Av. *zañga-*, Skt. *jaṅghā*; B. *cōn*, Kh. *zang*.]

janūsa 1 (this form of the Infinitive is without authority), to make clean, make neat; Impve. Plur. 2 *janā* (I, 27); Past Part. and Past Tense, Masc. Sing. Obj. *janū* (I, 28). [? Cf. Ksh. *jān*, good.]

janūsa 2, to know (Bid.). [Cf. Av. √*zan-*, Skt. √*jñā-*, *jānāti*; B. √*zāṛḷ-*, Kh. √*jān-*, Ksh. √*zān-*.]

jōr, agreement; *jōr yōsa*, to come to agreement, to agree (III, 26); adj. prepared, ready (III, 11, 12). [Cf. Psht. *jōṛ*.]

juwāb, an answer. See *žuwāb*, which is the correct spelling.

jyūsa, to be born (Bid.). [Cf. Av. √*zan-*, Skt. √*jan-*, *jāyatē*; Sh. √*ja-*, Ksh. √*zĕ-*.]

ka (Pron. Inan.), what ? (II, 37, 40; L. 93, 220; Bid.); (Pron. Adj. Inan.) what ? (I, 9, 11, 24, 38); *ke χušālī*, what happiness ! (I, 20).

kām, who ? (L. 92; Bid.); somebody (Bid.); *kāme*, which ? (Bid.); *kāmē māš*, which man ? (III, 28); *kāme māš-se*, of what man ? (L. 239).

kis-kĕjā, from whom ? (L. 240); *kes-ke*, why ? (Bid.).

[Cf. Av. *ka-*; Skt. *ka-*, Dat. *kasmai*, Gen. *kasya*; B. *kū*, who ?; Kh. *kya*, what ?, *ki*, which ?, *kā*, who ?, *kŏs*, whose ? ; Sh. *ko*, Fem. *kä*, who ?, *käsä*, whose ? ; Ksh. *kus*, Fem. *kŏssa*, who ?, *kạmⁱ*, by whom ?, *kyā-*, what ?

kai (L. 94), *kē* 1 (I, 47), why ? [Cf. the preceding; B. *kyẽ*, *kai-kotē* ; Kh. *ko*, *kyo-te* ; Sh. *kē*, Ksh. *kyā-zi*.]

ke 1, see *khe*.

ke 2, or *kē* 2 (Bid. *kya*), Postpos. of Dat., to, for. After a semi-vowel or vowel it generally becomes *ge* (*gē*), *ye* (*yē*), or *e* (*ē*). See §§ 26–9. Bid. also gives *ke*, *ge*. [The origin of this postposition is dealt with in § 29.]

kē 3, when ? (Bid.). [Cf. *ka*, *kai*.]

kiau, because, therefore. [This is a variant form of *kai*, why ? (Cf. Kh. *kyo-te*, why ?) The use in this sense is not uncommon in Dardic. The full meaning, in this use, is "if you ask why, it is . . .", and hence "therefore".]

kū 1, see *χū*.

kū 2, *m*., a valley (Bid.). [? Cf. B. *gōl*, Kh. *gŏl*.]

kū 3, f. *kü*, hard (not soft) (Bid.). [Cf. Skt. *krūra-* ; Sh. *kuru*, with Tōrwālī elision of intervocalic *r*.]

kūī, a well ; Sing. Abl. *kūī-mā*, from the well (L. 237). [Cf. Skt. *kūpa-* ; Psht. *kūhai* ; Ksh. *krūrᵘ*, *kyūrᵘ*.]

kac (? *kaç*), near ; *kac-ke*, to near (I, 2). [Cf. Skt. *kakṣē*, in the armpit ; Bengali, *kāchē*, near ; Sh. *kaci*.]

kacis, something (Bid.). [? Cf. Skt. *kiṁcit*.]

keda, whence (Bid.). [Cf. B. *kōr-ste*, Kh. *kura-r*, Sh. *kōny-o*, Ksh. *kati*.]

kide, see *kadak*.

kud (? *kuḍ*), f. *küd*, lame (Bid.). [Cf. Skt. *khōḍa-* ; Psht. *guḍ* ; B. *kuttāt*, he is lame ; Kh. *kutū*, lame ; Sh. *khuṛo*.]

kadak, how much ? (L. 221 ; Fem. *kadak*, 222) ; *kadak*, how many ? (L. 223) ; *kede*, how many ? (Bid.) ; *kidat gen*, how much ? (Bid.). [Cf. Skt. *kiyat-* ; Kh. *kandūri*, how much ?, *kama*, how many ? ; Sh. *kacāk*, how much ?, how many ? ; Ksh. *kūtᵘ*, how much ?, Plur. how many ?]

kuḍūsa, to beat (Bid.). The root of this verb is *kuṭh-*, in which the *ṭh* becomes *ḍ* when between vowels (see § 3*d*). The verb is conjugated in L. 175–204. The principal parts there given are :—Impve. Sing. 2 *kūṭh* (175) ; Fut. (Old Pres.) *kuḍī* ; Fut. *kuḍī-yā* (195–200) ; Pres. *kuḍe-dū* (179–184) ; Imperf. *kuḍe-šū* (192) ; Past Masc. Sing. *kuḍū* (185–190) ; Perf. *kuḍū-dū* (228) ; Pluperf. *kuḍū-šū* (193). [Cf. Skt. √*kuṭṭ-* ; Sh. (dial.) √*kut-* (? *kuṭ-*), beat ; Ksh. √*kuṭ-*, crush.]

kāfir, an unbeliever (II, 29). Cf. *kupār*.

kufār, see *kupār*.

kugū, m., a cock (L. 72) ; Bid. *kugū*, f. *kügī*). [Cf. Skt. *kukkuṭa-* ; hence Tōrwālī **kukuṛ*, *kugū* ; G. *kukuṛ*, P. *kukūr*, Kh. *kūkū* (fowl), Sh. *kūkurōco*, Ksh. *kŏkur*, Gypsy (Syrian) *gukări*.]

kāgh [sic], m., a crow (Bid.). [Cf. Skt. *kāka-* ; B. *koṛṛ*, Kh. *kāg*, Sh. *kā̃*, Ksh. *kāv*.]

khē, (Bid. *ke*), f., a rope. Sing. Instr. *khē-de* (L. 236).

khujūsa, see *kujūsa*.

khanḍ, Sing. Loc. *khanḍ-mē*, translated "on the top of the hill" (L. 229).

khowūsa (Bid. *kowūsa*), to eat ; Impve. Sing. 2 *khō* (L. 78). [Cf. Skt. √*khād-* ; Sh. √*kha-* (Bid. √*ka-*), Ksh. √*khĕ-*, Gypsy (Europ.) √*χă-*.]

kĕjā, postpos. of Abl., from (II, 38 ; L. 231, 235 (Abl. of comparison), 238–41). [For the use and derivation of this word, see §§ 31–3.]

kujū, *kužū*, m., a dog (L. 70, 146 ; Bid.) ; Plur. *kujū* (L. 148) ; Fem. *kijī*, a bitch (L. 147 ; Bid.) ; Plur. *kijī* (L. 149). [? Cf. Skt. *kaulēya-*, with the common change of *l* to *j* ; B. *kuṛi*, V. *kirukh*, Gār. *kūcur*.]

kujūsa (? *khujūsa*), to ask (Bid.). [Cf. Skt. *kṣudhyati*, he is hungry ; H. *khōjē*, he asks ; Sh. √*khoj-*.]

kal, *kyul*, how ? (Bid.).

kala, if (L. 97). [See § 206.]

kalā, m., a fort (Bid.). [Psht. *qil'a*.]

kāl, m., a year (II, 47 ; Bid.) ; *panjam kālō*, in the fifth year (III, 9). [Cf. Skt. *kāla-*, time ; Psht. Sh. *kāl*, a year.]

kilē, a village ; Sing. Loc. *kilē-mē* (II, 19). [Psht. *kilai*, a corruption of *qil'a*. See *kalā*.]

kol, f. *kel*, crooked (Bid.). [? Cf. Skt. *kuṭila-*, through **kuṛila-*, with elision of intervocalic *ṛ*. B. *škoṛī*, Kh. *koli*, Sh. *kōlu*, Ksh. *hạl*^{u}.]

kulekule, f., frost (Bid.).

kalimā, The Moslem creed (II, 33, 35–6, 46). [Psht.]

kam, m., work, business (I, 67) ; *kam kōsa*, to work (Bid.). [Cf. Skt. *karma* ; Kh. *kŏram*, Sh. *krŏm*, *kŏm*, Ksh. *kạm*^{ü}.]

kām, a tribe, sept (II, 49) ; Sing. Dat. *kām-gē* (II, 33) ; Gen. *kām-si* (II, 51). [Psht. *qām*, *qaum* ; cf. Ksh. *krām* (with intrusive *r*, which is common in Ksh.), a sept ; possibly this explains Sh. *rom* (low rising tone), a tribe.]

kambai (II, 6) ? (taxes) were (not) paid. See § 193.

kamādar, f. *kamādir*, industrious (Bid.). [Cf. *kam*.]

kamal, f. *kemel*, soft (Bid.). [Cf. Skt. *kōmala-* ; Ksh. *kamạl*^{u}.]

kaman, m., a master (II, 25). [? a corruption of Psht. *χāwand*.]

kīmat, price (L. 232). [Psht. *qīmat*.]

kāmwāl, m., relationship (Bid.). [Cf. *kām*.]

kamzōr, f. *kamzer*, weak (Bid.). [Psht.]

kamzortyā, m., weakness (Bid.). [See the preceding.]

kan 1, m., the ear (L. 38 ; Bid.). [Cf. Skt. *karṇa-* ; B. *kōr*, W. Kh. *kār* K. *kuṛō*, Sh. *kŏn*, Ksh. *kan*, Gypsy *kān*.]

kan 2, *ken*, in *kan-ke*, to near (III, 29) ; *ken-ta*, by the side (of) (III, 42). [This word is the same as *kan* 1, ear, in a special meaning. Cf. *kyũ* (Bid.).]

kan 3 (III, 30), *kān* 1 (Bid.), m., an arrow ; Sing. Instr. *kan-de* (III, 30). [Cf. Skt. *karṇi-* ; Sh. *kōn*, Ksh. *kān*.]

kan 4, m., a cough (Bid.). [? Cf. Skt. *kāsa-* ; B. √*kas-*, Kh. √*kop-*, Sh. √*khu-*.]

kān 2, m., the shoulder (Bid.). [Cf. Skt. *skandha-*.]

kanbel, N. of a place; Sing. Dat. *-ge* (III, 36); Loc. *-mī* (III, 2).

konīm, in (Bid.). According to Bid., it is prefixed (i.e. apparently not a postposition.]

kupār (III, 2), *kufār* (II, 11, 12, 13, 15, 17), a Kāfir (the tribe); Sing. Dat. *kufār-ke* (II, 11); Plur. Nom. *kufār* (II, 17). Cf. *kāfir*. [Cf. Ar. *kuffār*, Plur. of *kāfir*.]

kera, f., a knife (Bid.). [Cf. Skt. *kartari-*; B. *kato*, Kh. *kutēr*, Sh. *khaṭār*.]

kir, f., a solstice (Bid.).

kur (? *kuṛ*), m., a wall (Bid.). [Cf. Skt. *kuṭa-*, a fort, or *kuḍya-*, a wall; Sh. *kuṭ*.]

kure, m., the knee (Bid.). [? Cf. Skt. √*kuṭ-* be bent; Sh. *kuṭo*, Ksh. *kǒṭh*[u].]

koroda (? *-ḍa*), m., a whip (Bid.). [Cf. Psht. *karōṛa*.]

karmā, an army (III, 7, 9, 14 (bis)); Sing. Dat. *karmā-ye* (III, 13).

karran, f. *keren*, short (Bid.). [Cf. Sh. *khuṭo*.]

koror, f. *kerer*, round (Bid.).

kairat, m., health (Bid.). [Cf. Prs. *χairīyat*.]

karwanda, cultivation (II, 2). [Cf. Psht. *kar*, cultivator.]

kōsa, to do (Bid.); to make; Fut. (Old Pres.) *kī*, I will make (III, 28), we will do (III, 8 (bis)); *keī*, I may do (I, 24), we may make (II, 29); *kuwē*, he may do or make (II, 48; III, 35); Impve. Sing. 2 *kō* (I, 25; II, 35, 44); *ku*, (III, 11); Plur. 2 *kuwa* (III, 5, 28);

Periphrast. Pres. *kō-dū*, Sing. 1 (I, 8, 10, 56 (bis); II, 9); Sing. 2 (I, 9); Sing. 3, *kō-nin* (I, 37); Imperf. *kō-dut* (III, 1); *kao-dud* (I, 19);

Past Part. and Past Tense, Masc. Sing. Obj. *kī* (I, 5, 24; II, 2, 14, 33, 36, 39, 47, 50; III, 3, 13, 15, 16 (bis), 42); Masc. Plur. Obj. *kī* (I, 28); Fem. Sing. Obj. *kī* (I, 51; II, 6, 42, 45; III, 5); some of these genders are doubtful; Perf., Masc. Sing. Obj. *kī-dū* (L. 225); Fem. Sing. Obj. *kī-jī* (L. 224).

[Cf. Av. √*kar-*, Skt. √*kṛ-*, *karōti*; B. √*ka-*, Kh. √*kŏr-*, Ksh. √*kar-*. In Tōrwālī, note the usual elision of *-r-*. The same occurs in B., but only in some forms.]

kasab, employment, work (III, 35). [Psht. *kasb*.]

kāsim, N.P. (II, 19, 22, 24, 26, 28, 32, 36–7).

kišun, f. *kišen*, black (Bid.). [Cf. Skt. *kṛṣṇa-*; Sh. *kinu*, Ksh. *krĕhạn^u*.]

kēt, where ? (Bid.); Gen. *kēt-si*, of where ? (I, 6). [Cf. Skt. *kutra*; B. *kett*, *kōr*, Kh. *kura*, Sh. *kōni*, Ksh. *kạt^u*.]

kutub, m., the North (Bid.). [Psht. *quṭb*.]

katār, N. of a place; Abl. *-miā* (II, 1).

katernāk, dangerous (Bid.). [Psht. *χaṭarnāk*.]

kūtsā, a lane (I, 14). [Psht. *kūtsa*.]

kūṭh, see *kuḍūsa*.

kōwūsa, to eat (Bid.). See *khowūsa*.

kya 1, perhaps (Bid.).

kya 2, postpos., for (Bid.). See *ke* 2.

kye, ever (Bid.).

kyū, alongside (Bid.). Cf. *kan* 2.

kyul, see *kal*.

χū, (Bid. *kū*), m., the foot (L. 33). [Cf. Psht. *pχa*.]

χādī, f., happiness (Bid.). [N. Psht. *χādī*.]

Xodā (II, 48), *Xudā* (I, 20), *Xudāe* (L. 60), m., God. [Psht. *Xudāe*.]

χalak, people (I, 30); Sing. Dat. *-ke* (III, 5), *-kē* (III, 6). [Psht. *χalq*.]

χān, m., a Khān (I, 7, 9, etc., 47, 49, 54); Sing. Abl. *-mi* (I, 5); Gen. *-se* (I, 12); *-sē* (I, 39, 43, 46 (bis), 53). [Psht.]

χāna, N. of a place; Sing. Gen. *-si* (II, 34).

χānī, f., Khānship (I, 54; II, 38). [Psht.]

χūnza, f., a queen (Bid.). [? Derivation. Perhaps the word should be spelt *khūnza*.]

χuš, f. *χeš*, happy (Bid.). [Cf. Prs. Kh. *χuš*, Sh. *khuš*. The existence of the feminine form shows that the word can hardly be borrowed. For the derivation, see Horn, GNPE, 508.]

χušāl, pleased, happy (III, 42, 60). [Cf. H. *χušāl*, a corruption of *χuš-ḥāl*.]

χušālī, f., happiness (II, 20, 22). [See the preceding.]

χušūsa, to please (Bid.). [See *χuš*.]

χyāl, m., thought (Bid.). [Psht. *χiyāl*.]

χužā, pleased (Bid.); *χuža hōsa*, to be pleased (Bid.). [Cf. *χuš*.]

lā, in *lā talūsa*, to throw down (Bid.); *la-dūt*, down (Bid.). Cf. *lar*.

lēb, a bed-cover (I, 28). [Corruption of Psht. *liḥāf*.]

lobo, m., a lie (Bid.). [Cf. B. √*lar-*.]

lobyāt, m., dawn (Bid.).

lud, see *luṭ*.

la-dūt, down (Bid.). See *lā*.

lāḍa, see *lāṭ*.

liḍe, see *liṭ*.

lagū, in *šir-ke lagū*, he entered the house (III, 29). [Cf. Skt. √*lag-*, Pass. *lagyatē*, to be attached.]

lagur, in *lagur zar* (L. 45), *lur zar* (Bid.), red precious metal, gold. [Cf. Psht. *sra zar*. See *lohūr*.]

ligūsa, to write (Bid.). [Cf. Skt. √*likh-*; Sh. Ksh. √*likh-*. Cf. *lekūsa*.]

lehī, she was asked for (I, 39). [This may perhaps be two words, *le hī*.]

lohūr, f. *lihīr*, (Bid.), *lehir* (II, 18), red. Cf. *lagur* and *lur*. [Cf. Skt. *rudhira-*; B. *lui*, blood; ? Kh. *krūi*, Sh. *lōlyu*, red.]

loj, m., light (subst.) (Bid.). [Cf. Skt. *ruci-*; B. *ruc*, Kh. *rŏšti*, Sh. *lo*.]

lajin, old (Bid.).

lēkin, but (L. 96). [Psht.]

lekūsa (? *lekhūsa*), to count (Bid.). [Cf. Skt. √*likh-*; H. *lēkhā*, an account. Cf. *ligūsa*.]

lamād, m., a tail (Bid.). [Cf. Av. *duma-*, Prs. *dum*, Psht. *lam*; B. *dumrī*, Ksh. *dumba*.]

lāmōsa, to swim (Bid.). [Cf. Psht. *lānbō*, swimming.]

langī, they crossed (a river) (II, 12). [Cf. Skt. √*laṅgh-*; ? Cf. B. √*palang*, to march.]

lar, in *lar bajūsa*, to fall (Bid.). [Cf. Psht. *lar*, below. See Geiger, ELA, No. 91.] Cf. *lā*.

lur, see *lagur*.

lāš (Bid. *laš*, f. *laž*), bad; *e lāš saran*, a bad girl (L. 131). [? Cf. Skt. *rūkṣa-*; Ksh. *l*ᵃ*ch*ᵘ, rough-natured.]

lāt, in *lāt kōsa*, to tell (Bid.). [? a misprint for *bāt*.]

lāṭ, (Bid. *lāt*), m., a fight, quarrel (II, 12; III, 15); *lāṭ kōsa*, to fight (II, 12; III, 5, 8, 28); Sing. Dat. *lāṭ-ke* (III, 11, 12); Loc. *lāṭ-mi* (III, 16); Obl. *lāḍa šit*, aware of the fight (III, 19, 21). [Cf. Skt. √*raṭ-*, Beames, C.G. I, 228; H. etc. √*laḍ-*.]

liṭ, small; an infant (Bid. *lit*); *pāe liḍe širē*, in that small house (L. 233). [Cf. the next.]

lūṭ, small, young (I, 13); *lud* (? *luḍ*), f. *lid* (? *liḍ*), small (Bid.). [Cf. Ksh. *lŏkaṭ*ᵘ, small, which Paṇḍits connect with Skt. *laghu-*.]

lewānai, mad (I, 54). [Cf. Psht. *lēwānai*.]

loyi, proud (Bid.); *loyicār*, pride (Bid.). [Cf. Psht. *loe*, great.]

ma (also Bid.), *mā*, *miā* 1, (Bid. also *ama*, i.e. *-a*, the termination of the Oblique case, + *ma*), postpos. of Abl., from; by (Bid.). [See § 31.]

√*mā-*, see *mowūsa*.

mē 1, *mē*, *mi*, *mī* 1 (L. 229), *mō*, postpos. of Loc., in. [See §§ 39, 42.]

me, *mē* 2, *mī* 2, *miā*, pronoun, this, see §§ 85–95. *me-de*, but (Bid.); *mhēda*, from here (Bid.).

miā 2, a Miyā̃, a friar (II, 19, 22, 24, 26, 28, 32, 36, 37). [Psht.]

maī, *mau*, *mō*, *mū*, *muī*, see *maiyūsa*.

mubārakī, f., congratulation (I, 36, 38); Sing. Dat. *mubārakiye* (I, 40). [Psht.]

mid (? *miḍ*), sweet (Bid.). [Cf. Skt. *miṣṭa-*; B. *macī*, Ksh. *mīṭh*[u].]

midhal (sic), a ram (Bid.). Cf. *ē*, a ewe, *boγo*, a sheep. [Cf. Av. *maēša-*, Skt. *mēṣa-*; Sk. *màul* (Geiger, GIP. I, ii, 305); B. *mažurala*.]

miḍē-dē, (beaten) with (many) stripes (L. 228).

magrib, f., the West (Bid.). [Psht. *maγrib*.]

màh, m., a month (Bid.). [Cf. Av. *māh-*, Skt. *māsa-*; B. *mōs*, Kh. *mas*, Sh. *mā̃s*, *mā̃z*, Ksh. *mās*, *mah*, *māh*.]

mih, f., fat (subst.) (Bid.). [Cf. Skt. *mēdas-*; Sh. *mī̃*.]

mhēda, from here, see *me*.

maj, m., a fish (Bid.). [Cf. Av. *masya-*, Skt. *matsya-*, Pr. *maccha-*; B. *matsa*, Kh. *mātsi*.]

mūj, see *mū̃š*.

majlis (I, 10), *majlas* (I, 18), *manjlas* (I, 21, 23), an assembly, party, entertainment; Sing. Loc. *manjlas-mē* (I, 21). [Psht. *majlis*.]

mek (? *mekh*), f., hail (Bid.). [? Cf. Skt. *maigha-*, descended from clouds.]

mukadima, f., a quarrel (II, 6). [Cf. Psht. *muqaddama*, a cause at law.]

māl, cattle (L. 229). [Psht.]

māil, see *mowūsa*.

mēl, here (II, 2). [Cf. *me*, this, *mēlī*, and *met*.]

mēlī, adj., fem., the same (I, 35). [Perhaps connected with *me*, this. [Cf. Kh. *hess*, he, *hassa*, the same. Cf. *mēl*.]

malandē, m., a bridle (Bid.). [Cf. Psht. *mlūna*.]

milūsa, to touch (Bid.). [Cf. Skt. √*mil-*; Ksh. √*mēl-*, to be joined.]

melāštōp, a visit (III, 48). [Cf. Psht. *mēlmastiyā*. See *malāž*.]

māliyā, tax, tribute (II, 5). [Cf. Prs. *māliyat*.]

malāž, a guest (I, 46); Plur. Dat. *malāž-ge*. Cf. *melāštōp*. [Cf. Av. *miθnāiti*, he abides (Horn, GNPE, 1002), Prs. *mĕhmān*, Psht. *mēlma*, Kh. *mēnū*.]

mām, m., a maternal uncle (Bid.). Cf. *māšo*. [Cf. Skt. *māma-*; Psht. *māmā*; B. *mam*, Sh. *māmu*, Ksh. *mām*.]

mīm, f., the brain (Bid.).

mī-mī, between (near) (Bid.). Cf. *may-mo*. [? Connected with *mē* 1.]

mingaora, N. of a place; Sing. Dat. *mingaore-ye* (I, 1).

mere (I, 24, 52; Bid.), now. [Cf. *me*.]

merg, m., death (Bid.). [Psht. *marg*.]

mās, m., meat (Bid.). [Cf. Skt. *māṁsa-*, Pr. *māsa-*; Sh. *mos*, Ksh. *māz*.]

musulmān, m., a Musalmān (II, 36, 43, 47, 49); Plur. Nom. *musulmān* (II, 29).

massam, this much (Bid.). [? *mas-sam*, for *me-sam*, see *me*; cf. *es-sam*, s.v. *ē* 3.]

māš, (before a vowel, *māž*), a man (Bid. gives *meš*, a man, and *māš*, mankind) (I, 4, 5, 8, 10 ff., 25, 56; III, 10, 27–31; L. 51, 230); *māž* (I, 3); Sing. Dat. *māš-ke* (III, 12; L. 121); Abl. *māš-ma* (I, 24); *māš-mā*, or *-kĕjā* (L. 122); Gen. *māš-si* (L. 120, 225); *māš-se* (L. 228, 231, 239); Plur. Nom. *māš* (III, 22; L. 123–4); Dat. *māža-ge* (L. 126); Abl. *māža-mā*, or *-kĕjā* (L. 127); Gen. *māža-si*, (or *-se*) (L. 125).

[Cf. Skt. *manuṣya-*; W. *manaš*; G. *manuš* (homo). B. *manci* (vir), *mōc* (homo); K. *mōc*, *moc*; V. *muš*; Kh. *mōš*; Sh. *mušā* (vir), *manūẓo* (homo); Ksh. *mahaniv*ᵘ; Gār. *mēš* (cf. Bid. *meš*, ab.); Gypsy (Europ.) *mānuš*.]

māšo, f., a maternal aunt (Bid.). Cf. *mām*. [Cf. Skt. *mātr̥-ṣvasr̥-*; Ksh. *mās*.]

mūš (? *mūṣ*), m., a mouse (Bid.). [Cf. Skt. *mūṣ-*, *mūṣaka-*; Prs. *mūš*; B. *mussā*.].

mūš (Bid.), *mūj*, (L. 90, 238), before (postpos.) (Bid.) (*mē-kĕjā mūj*, before me (L. 238)); first (ordinal) (Bid.); before (adv.) (L. 90, *mūj*); *mūšā*, before (adv.) (I, 3);

mūš-ke, in front (adv.) (III, 57); *muš-ke*, in front (of) (governing Genitive) (II, 31).

[Cf. Skt. *mukha-*; Psht. *maχ*; B. *pa-myuk*, V. *ti-mik*, Sh. *muço*, Gār. *mūka*, M. *mūṭhō*. The Skt. *mukha-* can hardly represent the original of *mūš* or of the Sh. and M. forms. We seem to require some such original as **muχša-*.]

miśku, N. of a place; Sing. Gen. *-si* (III, 61).

maškulā, business, a business-talk (I, 56). [Psht. *mašγūlā*.]

muškil, difficult (Bid.). [Psht.]

muššrikh, the East (Bid.). [Psht. *mušriq*.]

met, here (Bid.). [Cf. *me*, *mēl*, and *mēlī*.]

mewā, m., fruit (Bid.). [Psht. *mēwa*.]

mowūsa, to kill (Bid.). Cf. *maiyūsa*. Impve. Sing. 2, *mā* (III, 35); Periphrast. Pres. Sing. 1, *mā-dū* (III, 34, future meaning); Plur. 3, *mā-nin*, they (will probably) kill (I, 44); Past Part. fem. *māil*, killed (III, 32). [The root is evidently √*mā-*. Cf. Skt. *mārayati*, with the usual elision of intervocalic *r*; Kh. √*màr-*, Sh. √*mar-*, Ksh. √*mār-*.]

mayō, N. of a place, and of the clan inhabiting it; Sing. Dat. *mayō-ye* (III, 34); Gen. *-si* (III, 22); Loc. *-mi* (III, 4).

may-mo, between (remote) (Bid.). [Cf. *mī-mī*.]

mayin, fond of, loving, in love with (III, 49). [Psht. *mayan*.]

maiyūsa, to die (Bid.). Cf. *mowūsa*. Impve. Sing. 2, *mō* (L. 83); Past Sing. Masc. *mū*, he died (I, 13); *mau* (III, 45); Fem. *muī*, she died (I, 53); *maī* (III, 30). [Cf. Av. √*mar-*, Skt. √*mṛ-*, *mriyatē*; V. √*o-mo-*, G. √*mī*, P. √*lī*, B. √*mṛe-*, W. √*mṛī-*, Kh. √*bri-*, T.Sh. √*mir-*, (Sh. p.p. *mūu*), Ksh. √*mar-* (p.p. *mūd*[u]), Gār. M. √*mar-*, Gypsy √*mer-*.]

miz, thus (III, 7).

na (Bid. *nā*), *ne*, Negative, no (L. 99, Bid.); not (*na*, I, 34–5; II, 9, 18, 21, 46, 48; III, 19, 57; *ne*, II, 6; III, 26); Prohibitive Negative (*na*, III, 28, 35; *ne*, I, 44–5). [Cf.

Av. Skt. *na*; P.T.Ksh. *na*, Gār. *nā*, Sh. *nā*, *nāi*, B. *nei*, W.G. *nai*, Kh. *no*, Gypsy *nā*.]

niō (Bid. *nyū̃*), near (L. 87). [Cf. Skt. *nikaṭa-*; G. *neṛa*, Ksh. (Kaštawāṛī) *niōṛ*ᵘ, Gār. *nīaṛ*, Ksh. *nīṛ*ᵘ (pronounced *nyūr*ᵘ). In Tōrwālī, there has been the usual elision of intervocalic *ṛ*.]

ned (Bid. *nad*), m., a river (Bid.); Sing. Abl. *nedā phēm diše*, on the opposite side of the river (II, 3). [Cf. Skt. *nada-*; Ksh. *nadī*, *nad*, both fem.]

nidā, in *nidā kōsa*, to look at, view, watch (I, 19). [Cf. Prs. *dīda*, Psht. *līda*.]

nigālūsa, (no authority for this infinitive form), to draw out, take out, extract (L. 237); to dig out, excavate (III, 51–4); Fut. (Old Pres.), Sing. 1, *nigālī* (III, 52); Impve. Sing. 2, *nigāl* (III, 51); *nīgal* (L. 237); Past Part. (Past tense), Fem. Sing. Obj. *nigālī* (III, 53–4). [Cf. Skt. *niṣkālayati*; H. √*nikāl-*; Sh. √*nikhal-*.]

nigāt, see *nikūsa*.

najurtya, m., illness (Bid.). [Psht. *nājōṛtiyā*.]

nēk, good (L. 132). [Psht.]

nōk, m., a finger-nail (Bid.). [Psht. *nūk*.]

nakāmna, nobody (Bid.). Cf. *nokoyna*.

nākāra, bad (L. 129, 131 ff.). [Psht.]

noker, m., a servant (Bid.). [Psht. *nōkar*.]

nikūsa, to come out, go out (Bid.); Past Sing. 3 *nigāt* (III, 31); Plur. 1, *nigāt* (I, 52). [Cf. *nigālūsa*.]

nokoyna, nothing (Bid.). Cf. *nakāmna*.

nīl, blue (Bid.). [Cf. Skt. *nīla-*; Sh. *nīlu*, Ksh. *nīl*ᵘ.

nilau, m., the South (Bid.).

nīlgolē, f., a pigeon (Bid.). Cf. *golē*.

nam, new (Bid.). [Cf. Skt. *nava-*; B. *noi*, Kh. *noχ*, Sh. *nāwu*, Ksh. *nạw*ᵘ.]

nām, m., a name (II, 26; III, 2; Bid.). [Cf. Skt. *nāma*; B. *nām*, B. Sh. *nom*, Kh. *nām*, Ksh. *nāv*.]

nem, f., the new moon (Bid.).

nimā, in *nimā-dū*, I desire (II, 38, 41); thou desirest (II, 37, 49).

nōm, *nūm* (Bid. *nom*), Card., nine (L. 9 *nōm*); *nūm-bīš*, nine times twenty (III, 17). [Cf. Av. Skt. *nava*; W. *nū*, P. *nō*, Sh. *nau*, B. *noh*, K. *nŏh*, V.G. *nūh*, T. *nab*, Ksh. *nav*, Gypsy (Syrian) *nā*.]

nin, Suffix of Periphrast. Pres. See §§ 169, 170, 176.

nīn, f., sleep (Bid.); Sing. Abl. *nīnā* (III, 43); *nīn bàjūsa*, to sleep (Bid.). [Cf. Skt. *nidrā*; Sh. *nir*, Ksh. *nẹ̆ndᵃr*.]

ningōlī, N. of a place; Sing. Gen. *-se* (I, 2).

nār (? *nāṛ*), m., dancing (Bid.); *nār kōsa*, to dance (Bid.). [Cf. Skt. *nāṭya-*; B. *nōl*, Sh. *naṭĕ*; Ksh. *naṭ-*, palsy.]

nariā, N. of a place, Narēr (with elision of intervocalic *r*); Sing. Gen. *-si* (II, 1, 6, 8–10).

nurī, in *pade-ge nurī*, they turned backwards (II, 14). [? Cf. Skt. *nivṛtta-*.]

nàrina, m., a male (Bid.). [Cf. Psht. *nārīna*.]

nerer, m., play (Bid.). [? Cf. *nār*. See the next.]

norūsa, to play (a game) (Bid.). [See the preceding.]

narāz, idle (Bid.). [Cf. Psht. *nārāst*, confounded with *nārāz*.]

nat (Bid.), *natkel* (L. 24), m., the nose. [Cf. Skt. *nasta-*; P. *nast*, M. *nathūr*, B. *nazuṛ*, Gār. *nōzōr*, Sh. *nato*, W. *nasū*, G. *nāsi*, V. *nes*, Ksh. *nas*, Ksh. (Kaṣṭawāṛī, *nasth*, K. *nātcur*, Kh. *naskār*.]

na-tsāba, unexpected (III, 20). [Cf. Psht. *nāṫsāpā*.]

nyū, see *niō*.

neyūsa, to take away (Bid.); Imperf. (? Pluperf., §§ 178, 191, 201) Sing. 3, *neyu-dut* (II, 5); Past Part. (Past Tense), Masc. Sing. *nū* (II, 23; III, 36). [Cf. Skt. $\sqrt{}$*nī-*, *nayati*; Kh. $\sqrt{}$*nī-*, Ksh. $\sqrt{}$*ni-*.]

nyašām, m., evening (Bid.). [Cf. Psht. *māṣ̌ām*.]

pāē, *paigā* (Bid. *paga*), Dem. Pron., he, that; Sing. Dat. *pāyis*; Plur. Nom. *paiyē*; *?* Sing. Obl. *pātē* (§ 127). [See §§ 122 ff.]

paï, in *paï dyūsa*, to kick (Bid.). [Cf. Skt. *pāda-*; B. *pâ vīsth*, to kick.]

pō, *po*, m., a boy (*pō*, I, 26, 29, 41, 46; II, 20, 23, 27; L. 239; *po*, Bid.); a child of either sex (*pō*, L. 54); a son (*pō*, II, 16; L. 225, 228); Sing. Ag. *pōē* (I, 24); *puē* (L. 225); *pō* (I, 41, 45, 48; II, 18, 28); Dat. *pō-gē* (I, 33); *pōē* (I, 25); Gen. *pō-si* (I, 44; II, 26). [Cf. Av. *puθra-*, Skt. *putra-*; Mj. *pūr.*; V. *piē*, G. *pola*, beside several forms such as B. *pitr*, etc. The nearest relation to *pō* is Mj. *pūr*, with the usual Tōrwālī elision of *r*. See also *pūc*.]

poa, m., skill (Bid.). [Cf. Ksh. *pav*, dexterity.]

pabī, f., a paternal aunt (Bid.). Cf. *peži*. [Cf. Skt. *pitṛ-ṣvasṛ-*; Sh. *phapi*; Ksh. *pŏph*.]

pūc (? *pūç*), *puš* (? *puṣ̌*), (Bid. *puž*), m., a son; *pūc* (L. 55, 225, 228); Plur. Nom. *pūc* (L. 223); *puš* (II, 4). [Cf. Av. *puθra-*, Skt. *putra-*; T. *putr*, K. *pūtr*, W. *piutr*, B. *pitr*, G. *pult*, P. *puṭhlē*, Gār. *pūṭ*, Ksh. *pūtᵘ*, Sh. *puç*. See also *pō*.]

pacin (? *paçin*) (Bid.), *pašīn* (? *paṣ̌īn*) (L. 76), f., a bird. [Cf. Skt. *pakṣin-*; Ksh. (Kaṣṭawāṛī) *pachaṇ*, G. *picin*, K. *pachīyek*. According to L. 76, *pašīn* is a large bird, and *cēriḍ* (q.v.) is a small bird.]

pade, see *pat*.

paidā, produced, born (II, 16, 20). [Psht.]

pid, f., a point (Bid.). [Cf. Ksh. *pẹtᵘ* (pronounced *pyotᵘ*).]

pādšāh, m., a king (Bid.). [Psht.]

pādšahī, f., kingship, ruling (III, 46). Cf. *bādšāhī*. [Psht.]

pīḍ, the back (L. 227, of a horse). [Cf. Av. *paršti-*, Skt. *pṛṣṭha-*; B. *pṭi*, W. *yā-paṭī*, G. *pišṭi*, Sh. *piṭu*, Ksh. *piṭhᵘ*, Gypsy (Syrian) *pišt*.]

pa-ga, *pai-ga*, see *pāē*.

piger, m., anxiety (Bid.). [Cf. Psht. *fikr*.]

pugūsa, to blow (Bid.). [Cf. Psht. √*puk-*; Skt. *phūt* + √*kṛ-*; Kh. √*phū-*; Sh. *phū*, blowing; Ksh. √*phuk-*.]

pihīl, green (Bid.). [? Cf. Skt. *pālāśa-*, with metathesis; ? B. *poṛ*.]

phēm, see *payim*.

pāji, see *pāš*.

puχtuā, enmity (I, 52). [? connected with Psht. *puṣ̌tēdᵃl*, to ask.]

pallas, m., dew (Bid.).

pel, f., an ant (Bid.), [Cf. Skt. *pipīla-*; Kh. *pilīli*, Sh. *ṛhilīli*.]

pām, m., wool (III, 18; Bid.). [Cf. Skt. *pakṣman-*; Prs. *pašm*; Kh. *pŏšp*, Sh. *paṣ̌*, Ksh. *phamb*.]

pan (L. 224, *pand*; Bid. *pān* 1), m., a road (III, 37–8, 40–1, 57). [Cf. Av. *pañtan-*, Skt. *pathin-* (*panth-*); B. *pott*, Kh. *pon*, Sh. *pŏn*.]

pān 2, see *panj*.

pin, f., the full moon (Bid.). [Cf. Skt. *pūrṇa-*, full.]

panj (Bid. *pān* 2), Card., five (L. 5); *panj bīš*, a hundred (L. 13). [Cf. Av. Skt. *pañca*; P.G. *panj*, K.Kh. *pōnj*, G.T. *pants*, Ksh. *pōnts*, B. *puc*, W. *pūc*, V. *uc*, Sh. *puš*, Gypsy *pănc*, *pănj*.]

panjam (Bid. *pānjam*), Ord., fifth (III, 9). [Cf. Skt. *pañcama-*; Prs. *panjum*.]

punkā, N. of a place; Sing. Loc. *-mī* (II, 3).

pūnil, full (Bid.). [Cf. Skt. *pūrṇa-* + *illa-*; B. *puru*; Sh. √*pur-*, fill; Ksh. *pūrᵘ*.]

puṅš, Card., fifteen (Bid.). [Cf. Skt. *pañcadaśa*; B. *pacits*, Sh. *panzai*, Ksh. *pandāh*.]

pēṛia, a generation (II, 48). [Cf. Skt. *pīṭhikā*; H. *pīṛhī*; Psht. *pēṛaī*.]

pīr, N. of a village (II, 19).

pōrē, till, until (II, 48). [Psht.]

pergūsa, to move (trans.) (Bid.). [Cf. Skt. *parigamayati*.]

puran-gām, the Old Village, N. of Old Braniāl; Sing. Dat. *-ge* (II, 56, 60), *-ke* (III, 45); Loc. *-žet* (III, 1).

porōsa (? *poṛōsa*), to break (trans.) (Bid.). [Cf. Skt. *sphōṭayati*, cf. the next; B. √*peṛ-*, √*peṭ-*; Sh. √*phuṭ-*; Ksh. √*phuṭᵃr-*, secondary formation from √*phuṭ-*.] Cf. the next.

pūrūsa (? *pūṛūsa*), to break (intrans.), to become broken (Bid.). [Cf. Skt. *sphuṭati*; B. √*peṛ*-, √*peṭ*- (trans. and intrans.); Sh. √*phuṭiž*-, secondary formation; Ksh. √*phuṭ*-. The optional Prakrit form *phuṭṭaï* accounts for the preservation of the intervocalic *ṛ*.]

pūsa, to drink (Bid.); Periphrast. Pres. *pō-dū* (II, 21); Imperf. *pō-šat* (II, 18 (bis)). [Cf. Skt. *pibati*; Wkh. *pöwam*, I drink; B. Kh. Sh. √*pi*-. For the vowel of *pō*-, cf. Wkh. and also **pōišn*, thirst, in Horn, GNPE *168*.]

paš, *pāš*, *pāji*, *piyāj*, *paiž*, behind, following (Bid. *pāš*); *ēs paš*, after this (I, 20); *telā pāš*, after then, after that time (II, 49; III, 47); *saran paš*, after (i.e. in order to get) the daughter (I, 43); *pāš*, second (Bid.); *pāji*, afterwards (II, 39, 43, 46); *piyāj*, behind (L. 239); *paiž*, behind (L. 91). [Cf. O. Prs. *pasā*, Av. *pasca*, Skt. *paśca*-, Prs. *pas* (Horn, GNPE. 315); P. *paškin*, Gypsy (Syrian) *păci*.] Cf. *pat*.

pašū, m., a flower (Bid.). [Cf. Skt. *puṣpa*- or (?) *puṣya*-; B. *piš*, Ksh. *pōš*. The Ksh. form suggests an original **pauṣya*-.]

piš, a cat (L. 71). [Cf. Prs. *pušak*, Psht. *pišō*, Wkh. etc. *piš*, Ōr. *pus*; B. *pišaš*, W. *pišā̆*, G. *psāsi*, V. *pšikh*, K. *phušak*, P. *pīšōṇak*, Kh. *puši*, Sh. *būši*, T. *pišē*, Gār. *pīšīr*, Gypsy (Syrian) *pišīkā*. ? Cf. Khērwārī (Austro-Asiatic) *pūsī*.]

puš, see *pūc*.

pūš, m. (f. *pīš*), a fox (Bid.).

pišul, f. *pišel*, smooth (Bid.). [Cf. Skt. *picchila*-; Sh. *phicīlu*, Ksh. *pišaḷ*^{u}.]

pašīn, see *pacin*.

pašūsa, to look at (Bid.). [Cf. Skt. *paśyati*; Kh. √*poš*-, see; Sh. √*paš*-, see; Old Ksh. √*paš*-, see.] Cf. the next.

pašat, they quarrelled (III, 24). [Possibly a Past Part. of *pašūsa*, in the sense of " looking menacingly ".]

pušt, ancestry, lineage, a generation, hence, a descendant (I, 12). [Psht.]

pat, *pad*, back, behind; *pat-gē* (I, 26), *pata-ge* (III, 16, 39); *pade-ge* (II, 13, 14, 15), *pade-gē* (I, 50), to back, backwards, back again; *pad-ge būsa*, to return (Bid.). [Cf. Av. *paršti-*, Skt. *pṛṣṭha-*; B. *pṭī*, W. *yā̃-paṭī*, Sh. *piṭu* all meaning "the back"; W. *pat*, G. *pata*, Gār. *patā*, M. *patō*, Sh. *phatu*, Ksh. *pat-*, T. *patī-kana*, K. *pišṭō*, all meaning "behind".] Cf. *paš*.

pātē, see *pāē*.

pet, m., a feather (Bid.). [Cf. Skt. *pattra-*; Kh. *pŏc*; Sh. *phurgū*, feather, *phaçāli*, wing; Ksh. *paṭᵃr*.]

pöt, *pot*; *pöt*, m., a place (Bid.); *e-pot*, together (Bid.). [? Cf. Skt. *paṅkti-*; Ksh. *pŏt-*, a line, a row of people.]

pattang, m., a butterfly (Bid.). [Cf. Skt. *pataṁga-*; Sh. *phaṭōi*, Ksh. *patang*.]

powūsa, to receive (Bid.). [Cf. Skt. *prâpayati*; H. √*pā-*. This root hardly occurs in Dardic, being crowded out by forms akin to Ksh. *pāwun*, to fell.]

paiyē, see *pāē*.

piyāj, see *paš*.

payim, *phēm*, across, on the other side; *payim dišē* (III, 37), *payim diše-de* (III, 50), *phēm diše* (II, 3), on the other side (of a river). [Cf. Skt. *parē*, *pāra-*; B. *pā̆r*, Kh. Sh. *pār*, across; Ksh. *pāṛimᵘ* (*pöryumᵘ*), belonging to the other side. The suggested derivation involves elision of intervocalic *r*.]

pyūsa, to send (Bid.); Impve. Sing. 2, *pai* (I, 49); Past Part. (Past Tense) Masc. Sing. *pewū* (I, 50); *peyū* (II, 22); *piyū* (III, 10). [Cf. Skt. *prêrayati*, with elision of intervocalic *r*; B. √*pre-*, give, send.]

pāyis, see *pāē*.

paiž, see *paš*.

puž, see *pūc*.

peži (Bid.), *pižī* (L. 225), a paternal uncle; Sing. Gen. *pižī-si* (L. 225). Cf. *pabī*. [Cf. Skt. *pitṛvya-*.]

rabaṛ, a fight (III, 3); Sing. Dat. *-ke* (III, 13). [Cf. Psht. *rabaṛ*, toil, trouble.]

rājgana, f., a queen (III, 47, 49, 55–6, 58, 61); Sing. Dat. *rājgana-ye* (III, 50); Loc. *-žet* (III, 49). [? A corruption of Skt. *rājñī*.]

ruksat, in *ruksat kōsa*, to allow to depart, send away (II, 51). [Cf. Psht. *ruχṣat*.]

rāng, m., colour (Bid.). [Cf. Psht. *rang*; B.Kh.Ksh. *rang*, Sh. *rŏṅ*.]

reza, m., a wish (Bid.); *reza kōsa*, to wish (Bid.). [? A corruption of Psht. *ārzū*.]

sā, m., life (Bid.). [Cf. Aryan **šuši-*, Av. *suši-*, Wkh. *šuš*, lung; Skt. *śvāsa-*, breath; B. *šus*, Sh. *ṣā*, Ksh. *šāh*, breath. The final *h* of the Ksh. form shows a derivation from **śvāša-*, not *śvāsa-*. The form **śvāša-* is borne out by the Eranian forms. So also the dental *s* of Tōrwālī *sā* points to Av. *suši-*. Cf. also Tōrwālī *šīš* 1, breath, below.]

sai, in *sai kōsa*, to find (Bid.).

se 1 (Bid.), *sē* 1 (II, 13), f., a bridge; Sing. Instr. *sē-dē* (II, 12). [Cf. Skt. *sētu-*; B. *sū*, Sh. *sau*, Kh. *sair*.]

se 2, *sē* 2, termination of the Genitive. See §§ 34 ff.

sē 3, that (not within sight), he, she, it. Noted only in the Nominative Singular and Plural (see §§ 117 ff.). Sing. Nom. *sē*, § 118; Plur. Nom. *sē*, § 119 (written *sēh* in L. 29); as Pron. Adj. §§ 120–1.

sī, f., the sun (L. 62, Bid.). [Cf. Skt. *sūrya-*; K. *sūri*, Sh. *sūrī*, G. *suri*, T. *surī*, Ksh. *sirĕ*, B. *su*, W. *sōi*, V. *isikh*, M. *swīr*, Gār. *sīr*. In Tōrwālī, there has been the usual elision of intervocalic *r*.]

so (Bid. *soh*), card, a hundred. [Cf. Psht. *saw-*.]

sabā, *sabat*, *sabāt*, forms of a verb, for the infinitive of which I have no authority. The verb means, to "prepare," "arrange," "set in order." Impve. Sing. 2, *sabā* (III, 7); Past Part. (Past Tense) *sabāt* (III, 6); *sabat*, I made (a road) (III, 41); thou madest (III, 40); he made (III, 38); *lāṭ sabat* they joined fight (II, 12). [Cf. Skt. *saṁbhārayati*; Psht. *sambālaw^{a}l*; H. *sãwārnā*; Ksh. *sambālun*.]

sabak, a lesson, reading ; *sabak banu-šat*, said lessons (II, 27). [Psht. *sabaq*.]

suban, in *suban hāt*, m., the right hand (Bid.). Cf. *aban*.

sād, see *sāt*.

sēd, see *set*.

siga, m., lead. [Psht. *sika*.]

sugā, f. *sugä*, easy (Bid.). [Cf. Skt. *sukara-*, with elision of intervocalic *r*.]

sigal, m., sand (Bid.). [Cf. Skt. *sikatā* ; Kh. *šuγūr*, Sh. *sigal*, Ksh. *sĕk-*.]

saj, m., truth (Bid.). [Cf. Skt. *satya-*, Pr. *sacca-* ; Sh. *sū̃çu*.]

sulaimānik, m., N. P. (III, 1) ; Sing. Voc. *Sulaimānig-a* (III, 40 ; § 15) ; Ag. *Sulaimānike* (III, 12–3, 59) ; *Sulaimānige* (III, 54) ; Obl. *Sulaimānike-sāt*, with S. (III, 3) ; Dat. *Sulaimānik-kē* (III, 11, 58) ; *Sulaimānike* (*bhāvē prayōga*) (III, 16) ; *Sulaimānige* (id.) (III, 55) ; Gen. *Sulaimānik-si* (III, 14, 23, 46, 61).

sam, in *es-sam* s.v. *ē* 3, and *massam*, qq.v.

semū, m. N. P. (III, 2) ; Sing. Dat. *Semū-ye* (III, 7, 33) ; *Semū-ge* (III, 35) ; Gen. *Semū-se* (III, 12) ; *-si* (III, 14, 39, 44).

sen, f. a dream (Bid.). [Cf. Skt. *svapna-*, Pr. *siviṇa-* ; Sh. *sā̃çi*.]

sung, m., earth, soil (Bid.).

sipad, m., praise. (Bid.). [Psht. *ṣifat*.]

saran, f., a girl (L. 56) ; I, 39 ; III, 17, 25–6, 30–2 ; Bid.) ; a daughter (L. 110, in Chil-darra ; I, 39, 48 ; III, 23) ; *saran paš*, after (in order to get) a daughter (I, 43) ; Sing. Dat. *-gē* (L. 112) ; Abl. *-ma* (III, 28 ; L. 113) ; *-kĕjā* (L. 113) ; Gen. *-se* (L. 111) ; *-si* III, 29, 30) ; Loc. *-žet*, on (concerning) the girl (III, 24) ; Plur. Nom. *saran* (L. 115) ; *saranē* (III, 17) ; Dat. *saran-gē* (L. 117) ; Gen. *-si* (L. 116). [? Cf. Ksh. *šur*ᵘ.]

sūrat, m., the body (Bid.). [Psht. *ṣūrat*.]

sat, Card. seven (L. 7, Bid.). [Cf. Skt. *sapta* ; K.G.P.T. Gār. Sh. *sat*, Ksh. *sat-*, B. *sut*, W. *sōt*, Kh. *sot*, V. *sete*.]

sāt (Bid. *sat*), *sāth*, *sād*, with ; *Sulaimānike-sāt*, (fight) with Sulaimānik (III, 3) ; *mē-sāt*, (fight) on my side (III, 5) ; *Semū-sāt*, together with Semū (III, 9) ; *te-sāt*, with thee (II, 9 ; III, 7) ; *te-sād*, id. (before *m*) (I, 56) ; *tiyi-sāt*, with her (III, 17) ; *dui-sāt*, (agree) with the other (III, 26) ; *kufār-sāth*, (fight) with the Kāfir (II, 12). [Cf. Skt. *sârtha-* ; Pr. *sattha-* ; Sh. *sāti*, H. *sāth*.]

set, *sēd*, with ; *te-set*, (quarrel) with thee (II, 6) ; *šū-sēd*, (marriage) with the sister (L. 225) (at end of a sentence). [Cf. Skt. *sahitē* ; Ksh. *süt*ⁱ.]

sot, f., *söt*, slow (Bid.). [? Cf. Psht. *sust* ; Sh. *sūs*, lazy ; Ksh. *sọt*ᵘ slow.]

sitār, a guitar (I, 4) ; Sing. Gen. *-sē* (I, 5, 8, 10, etc.). [Psht.]

satāš, Card. seventeen (Bid.). [Cf. Skt. *saptadaśa* ; B. *sapits*, Sh. *sataĩ*, Ksh. *sadāh*.]

sattam, Ord. seventh (II, 48). Bid. has *satam di*, f., a week. We should expect it to mean " seventh day ". [Cf. Skt. *saptama-* ; Sh. *satmŏṅo*, Ksh. *satịm*ᵘ.]

*s*ᵃ*wāl*, a request (I, 8, 9) ; a report, complaint (I, 56). [Psht. *sawāl*.]

šā (Bid. *šōh*), m., the head (L. 40) ; *šā-si did*, hit the head (III, 44). [Cf. Skt. *śiraḥ* ; P. *šīr*, B.W. *šei*, T. *χār*, Ksh. *hīr*ᵘ, Gypsy (Europ.) *šērō*. The vowel changes are remarkable. In Tōrwālī, as usual, there has been elision of intervocalic *r*.]

šai, a thing ; Sing. Gen. *šai-se* (L. 232). [Psht.]

šī, see *šū*.

šō (? *ṣō*) (Bid. *šo*), Card. six (L. 6). [Cf. Av. *χšvaš*, Skt. *ṣaṣ-* ; B. *šo*, W. *šū*, V. *ušū*, T. *χō*, P. *š*ᵃ, Gār. *šō*, Sh. *ṣā*, K. *šōh*, G. *šoh*, Ksh. *šĕ-*, Gypsy (Syr.) *šās*, (Europ.) *šŏv*.]

šū 1, f., a sister (L. 50 ; I, 28, 33–5, 44 ; Bid.) ; Sing. Dat. *šī-ge* (I, 27) ; *šī-yē* (I, 42) ; Abl. *šū-kĕjā* (L. 231) ; *šū-sēd*, (marriage) with the sister (L. 225). [Cf. Skt. *svasā*, *svasār-*; Kh. *ispusār*, T. *spaz*, Gār. *išpō*, B. *sus*, W. *sōs*, V. *siusu*, G. *sase*, P. *sāī*, Sh. *sà*.] Cf. § 18.

šū 2, for *ašū*, q.v., when used as an auxiliary verb. See §§ 157 ff., 177, 201.

šad, see *šat*.

šid, see *šit*.

šidàhū, f., *šidaihi*, cold (adj.) (Bid.). [Cf. the next. The origin of the termination is obscure. It is apparently an adjectival ending. See other examples under § 49.]

šidal, m., cold (subst.) (Bid.). [Cf. Skt. *śītala-*; B. *šillā*, Sh. *šidalu* (adj.), Ksh. *šĕhạlᵘ* (adj.).]

šugil, dry (Bid.). [Cf. Skt. *śuṣka-*, dry, *śuṣkala-*, dry flesh; Pr. **sukkhala-*; Kh. *cucō*, Sh. *šūku*, *šušī*, Ksh. *hǫkhᵘ*.]

šōh, see *šā*.

šijo, f., *šije*, beautiful (Bid.); *šijū*, f., *šiji*, clean (Bid.). [Cf. Skt. *śuci-*, clean; Ksh. *šŏts-*, purity.]

šijūsa, to fly (as a bird) (Bid.).

šukur, m., gratitude (Bid.). [Psht. *šukr*.]

šēχ, m., a title given to converts to Islām, the disciple of a Moslem Missionary (II, 22–3). [Psht.]

šella, m., wood (Bid.).

šālmī, a rupee (L. 234); Plur. Nom. *šālmī* (L. 232, 235).

šulan, in *šulan dyūsa*, to curse (II, 48). [Cf. Psht. *ṣarā*, *ṣēra*; ? cf. Skt. *śrathana-*, see Morgenstierne in EVP., p. 78.]

šen a bedstead (I, 28). [Cf. Skt. *śayana-*; Kh. *žen*.]

šāng, m., the throat (Bid.).

šīr (L. 67), *šir* (Bid.), f., a house; Sing. Dat. *šir-kē* (I, 27, 42); *šir-ke* (II, 15; III, 29, 39); Abl. *širā* (I, 50); *šira* (III, 31); Loc. *širē* (III, 18; L. 223, 226, 233). [Cf. Gār. *šiṭ*, a house.]

šuru, in *šuru kōsa* (III, 15; Bid. *šurū*), to begin. [Psht. *šurūʿ*.]

šĕrīkat, in *šĕrīkat kōsa*, to divide (II, 8, 9). [Psht. *šarīkat*.]

šerm, m., shame (Bid.). [Psht. *šarm*.]

šerunke, exiled, deposed, expelled (III, 4). [Psht. *šaṛūnkai*.]

šeš (? *ṣeš*) Card., sixteen (Bid.). [Cf. Skt. *ṣōḍaśa*; B. *šēṣ*, Sh. *ṣōī*, Ksh. *šurāh*.]

šīš 1, f., breath (Bid.). [See *sā*.]

šūš, f. *šīš* 2, straight, upright (Bid.). [? Cf. Skt. *sidhra-*, perfect; Sh. *sūçu*, Ksh. *šẹdᵘ* (pronounced *šyodᵘ*). There may have been contamination with the √*śudh-*. Probably the Tōrwālī word is really *šūṣ*.]

šat, *šad*, an Auxiliary Verb, used to form the Imperfect and the Pluperfect. See §§ 169, 179, 200, 201.

šet, m., autumn (Bid.). [Cf. Skt. *śarat*, with the usual elision of intervocalic *r*; B. *šāra*, Kh. *šōroh*, Sh. *šarō*, Ksh. *harud*. The preservation of the initial *š* in most of these is noteworthy.]

šit, (I, 40) *šid*, aware of (I, 40; II, 19; III, 19, 21). [Cf. O.Prs. √*χšnās-*, Prs. *šināχtan*, see Horn, GNPE, 793; B. *šū*, knowledge; Sh. *šūyōiki*, to know.]

šaitān, m., a devil (L. 61). [Psht. *šaiṯān*.]

šāṭ, in *šāṭ hū*, (house) became ruined (I, 14).

šawam, Ord., sixth (Bid.). [Cf. Skt. *ṣaṣṭha-*; Sh. *ṣamōño*, Ksh. *šĕyịmᵘ*.]

šeyat, Past Part., in *pade-ge šeyat*, he drove them back (II, 13).

ta 1, Postpos., till, to (Bid.). [Psht.]

ta 2, *tā* 1, see *tu*.

tā 2, (Bid.) *ta* 3, m., a star. (Cf. Av. *star-*, Skt. *tārā*, *tāraka-*; P. *tārā*, Sh. *tārū*, Ksh. *tāruk-* (for **tāraku*), K. *tāri*, Gār. *tār*, W. *tarā*, G. *tare*.]

tai, see *tu*.

tē 1, (Bid.) *tiya*, Pron., he, she, it, that; Sing. Ag. *ti*, *te*; Acc. *tes*; Obl. *te*, *tes* (*tez*); Gen. *tesi*; Plur. Nom. *tiyā*; Ag. *tihē*; Obl. *tiyā*. For these, and variant forms, see §§ 96 ff.

te 1, *tē* 2, see *tu*.

te 2, *tē* 3, or, between vowels, *de* (*dē*), postpos. of Instrumental (see §§ 23 ff.), and also the suffix of the Conjunctive Participle (§ 202).

ti, see *tē* 1.

tiā, ready (Bid.). [Psht. *taiyār*, with loss of final *r*.]

tō, see *tu*.

tu, *tū*, (Bid.) *tūh*, Pron., thou; Sing. Ag. *ta*, *tā*, *tai*; Obl. *te*, *tē*; Gen. *chī*, (Bid.) *ci*; Plur. Nom. *tō*, *thō*; Ag. *tahī*; Obl. *to*; Gen. *tun*, *thun*. For these, and variant forms, see §§ 69 ff.

tid, f. *tīd*, bitter (Bid.). [Cf. Skt. *tikta-*; H. *tītā*, Ksh. *ṭĕṭhᵘ*. Other Dardic languages have words allied to Psht. *trīχ*.]

tofān, m., a storm (Bid.). [Psht. *ṭūfān*.]

tāgat, m., strength (Bid.). [Psht. *ṭāqat*.]

thā (Infinitive not noted); Impve. Sing. 2 *thā*, put!, place! (L. 227); Past Part. Sing. Masc. *thāu* (II, 26); *thalū* (I, 28) (see § 195). [Cf. Skt. *sthāpita-*; Ksh. √*thāv-* or √*thav-*.]

thō, see *tu*.

thū, Verb Substantive, Pres. Masc.; Plur. Masc. *thī*; Fem. Sing. and Plur. *cī* (? *chī*). See §§ 163 ff. As an Auxiliary Verb—and hence usually following a vowel—it becomes *dū*, Plur. *dī*; Fem. Sing. and Plur. *žī* or *jī* (§ 168). In one case, *dit-žī* becomes by contraction *dī-cī* (§ 168). The Past of *dū* is *dut* or *dud*, which (§ 178) is used to form an Imperfect or (?) a Pluperfect. [Cf. Skt. *sthita(ka)-*. See § 154.]

tahī, see *tu*.

tih, f., the elbow (Bid.).

tihē, see *tē* 1.

thalū, see *thā*.

thām, (Bid.) *tām*, m., a tree (II, 31); Sing. Gen. *thām-si ṭin*, under a tree (L. 230). [? Cf. Skt. *stambha-*, a post. But Bur. Sh. *tŏm*, a tree; Ksh. *tham*, a pillar.]

thun, see *tu*.

tlūi (? *ṭlūi*), Ord., third (Bid.). [Cf. Skt. *tṛtīya-*; Kh. *troiyum*, Sh. *ċĕmŏño*, Ksb. *trĕmiyu*.]

talā, then (III, 51) (§ 147). [Cf. Skt. *tadā*; Kh. *tà*, Ksh. *tĕli*.]

tel 1, f., a roof (Bid.). [Cf. Skt. *tala-*, the flat roof of a house; Sh. *tal*, a lower ceiling; Ksh. *tālav*.]

tel 2 (II, 12; Bid.), *til* (I, 19; II, 19), there; *tel-te*, there (II, 12); *telā*, from there, thence (II, 30); *telā pāš*, after there, thereafter (II, 49; III, 47). Cf. § 145. [Cf. Skt. *tatra*; Ksh. *tati*; but some word like *tadā* (see *talā*) is to be expected as the origin.]

telī (Infinitive not noted); Past Part. (Past Tense) Sing. Fem. in *sē telī*, the bridge was broken (II, 13). [? Cf. Skt. *trōṭayati*; H. √*tōṛ-*, break; Sh. *ṭar*, a piece.]

tìl (Infinitive not noted); Impve. Sing. 2, *til* (L. 77), go!; Plur. 2, *tila*, go ye! (III, 13); Old Pres. (Fut.), Plur. 1, *tilai* (I, 52), *tili* (II, 28), let us go. [Cf. Psht. *tlal*, to go; Sk. *tīd-ao*, to go; Shg. *tuid*, gone. According to L. 77, this verb means simply "to go", while *bajūsa* (q.v.) means rather "to go away".]

talχ, active (Bid., possibly a misprint for acrid; but cf. *talaχ*). [Cf. Psht. *talχ*, acrid.]

talaχ, swift (Bid.). [Cf. *talχ*.]

tàlūsa, to throw, to pour (Bid.); *lā tàlūsa*, to throw down (Bid.). [? Cf. Skt. *tata-*, extended, spread; B. √*atl-*, fall, Causal √*attalā-*; Kh. *tor*, fallen.]

tambā, m., copper (Bid.). [Cf. Skt. *tāmra-*; Ksh. *trām*.]

tambū, m., a window (Bid.). [? Cf. H. Psht. *tambū*, a tent.]

tamām, in *tamām kōsa*, to finish (Bid.). [Psht.]

tanu, *tanū*, (one's) own; (Bid.), self. [See §§ 133–5; cf. Kh. *tan*, self; Sh. *tomu*, (one's) own; Ksh., see § 129.]

tīn 1, f., an edge (Bid.).

tīn 2, sharp (Bid.). [Cf. Skt. *tīkṣṇa-*, Pr. *tiṇha-*; Sh. *tīṇu*.]

tun, see *tu*.

tandergyat, m., an eclipse (Bid.). [Cf. Psht. *tandar*, an eclipse ; Ksh. *gaṭa*, darkness.]

tongū (? *ṭongū*), m., a pear (Bid.). [Cf. Skt. *ṭaṅka-phala-* (used by Ksh. Paṇḍits for the fruit) ; Psht. *ṭāngā*, B. *tōng*. Kh. *tŏng*, Ksh. *ṭang*.]

tunōl, m., rice (Bid.). [Cf. Skt. *taṇḍula-* ; Ksh. *tŏmul*.]

tunger (? *ṭunger*), m., an axe (Bid.). [Cf. Skt. *ṭaṅka-*.]

tapōs, m., a question ; *tapōs kōsa*, to ask (I, 5, 24, 37 ; III, 28). [Psht.]

terbel, f., a sword (Bid.). [Cf. Skt. *taravāri-* ; B. *tarwac*.]

tes, *tesi*, see *tē* 1. *tisi-kya*, therefore (Bid.).

tiš (? *tiṣ̌*), f., thirst (Bid.). [Cf. Skt. *tṛṣā* ; Kh. *trušni*, thirsty ; Ksh. *trēš*.]

tūš, empty (Bid.). [Cf. Skt. *tucchya-*; Psht. *taš* (EVP.).]

tišauhū, f., *tišaihi*, thirsty (Bid.). [See *tiš*. Cf. Ksh. *trēšĕ-hạt*ᵘ, thirsty.]

tūt, m., the mulberry (Bid.). [Psht. Cf. Ksh. *t*ᵃ*l*, *tul*.]

tetcek, then (Bid.) ; when (relative) (Bid.).

tatašūsa, to creep (Bid.).

tōwāl, Tōrwāl ; Sing. Abl. *tōwāl-miā* (II, 5) ; Gen. *tōwāl-si* (II, 31, 51) ; Loc. *tōwāl-mē* (II, 2) ; *tōwāl-mī* (II, 20, 29). [Intervocalic *r* elided as usual.]

tiyā, see *tē* 1.

tīyū, m., a sneeze (Bid.). [? Cf. Sh. *jī*.]

tēyis, f., a charm (Bid.). [? Cf. Psht. *t'awiz̤*.]

tez, see *tē* 1.

ṭubak, (Bid.) *tūbūk*, m., a gun, a rifle ; Sing. Gen. *ṭubak-si* (II, 44–5). [Psht. *ṭōpak*, with intervocalic *p* > *b*.]

ṭhin, see *ṭin*.

ṭin, (Bid.) *ten*, Postpos., under, below ; down (L. 88) ; *thām-si ṭin*, under a tree (L. 230) ; *tisi ṭin*, under it (II, 32). In III, 16, *gām ṭin kī* is translated, the village was taken. Probably *ṭin kī* means, was made under, was subjugated.

wā, adv., down (L. 88); Postpos. *wa*, down (from, abl.) (III, 61); *wa*, to (Bid.). [Cf. Av. Skt. *ava*; Psht. *wa*, to; B. *wā*, down.]

wai kōsa, to promise (Bid.). [Cf. Psht. *ōē*.]

wadān, in good order (I, 17, 25).

wek, apart (Bid.).

wālī (Infinitive not noted), Past Part. Fem., she was brought (III, 56). [Cf. Skt. *avapādayati*; B. √*awē-*, Past *awāṛā*, bring; Sh. √*wal-*, bring; Ksh. √*wāl-*, bring down.]

wōsa, to dismount (Bid.). [? Cf. Skt. *avarōhati*, with elision of intervocalic *r*; but Ksh. √*was-*, descend.]

wat (Infinitive not noted), Past Part. Masc. (Past Tense), he came, he arrived (II, 34, 43; III, 14); Fem., she came (III, 56, 60). [Cf. Skt. *avâpta-*; Sh. √*wa-*, come; Ksh. √*wāt-*, arrive.]

watan, (Bid.) *wattan*, m., a country; Sing. Dat. *watan-gē* (I, 46; II, 1, 7); Abl. *watana* (III, 3); Gen. *watan-sē* (I, 12); *-si* (II, 8, 42); Loc. *watan-mī* (II, 10; III, 8, 46). [Psht. *waṯan*.]

wazīr, m., a Wazīr (II, 42). [Psht.]

wazīrī, the office of a Wazīr (II, 41). [Psht.]

ya, or (Bid.). [Psht. *yā*.]

yū, see *ō* and § 206.

yai, (Bid.) *yē*, f., a mother (II, 17, 29; L. 48); Sing. Dat. *yai-ge* (I, 27); Gen. *yai-si* (II, 18, 21). [Cf. W. *oie*, K. *āya*, G. *jai*, P. *āī*, Sh. *āje*, Sh. (of Ḍāh-Hanū) *āi*, Ksh. (Dōdā Sirājī) *ī*, Ksh. (Pōgulī) *yēī*, Gār. *yai*.]

yo, m., barley (Bid.). [Cf. Skt. *yava-*; Sh. *yō*.]

yādūsa, to remember (Bid.). [Cf. Psht. *yād*, memory. See *yāt*.]

yun, m., the moon (L. 63; Bid.). Cf. *nem* and *pin*. [Cf. Skt. *jyōtsnā*, Pr. *joṇhā*; Sh. *yūn*, Ksh. *zūn*, Gār. *yasūn*.]

yāp, a canal (III, 51–4). [? Cf. Prs. *jō* < O.Prs. *yauvⁱyā-* (GIP. I, ii, 43).]

yār, m., love (Bid.). [Psht. *yār*, a lover.]

yarak, a jirga, tribal council (III, 6). [? A corruption of Psht. *jirga*.]

yōsa, to come (Bid.); Impve. Sing. 2, *yē* (L. 80); Plur. 2, *yā* (I, 33, 36); Periphrast. Pres., *ye-dū* (III, 26; L. 239); *ya-nin* (? *yā-nin*), we shall come (III, 7; §§ 170–1); Past Part. (Past Tense), Masc. Plur. 3, *ai*, they came (II, 15; III, 10, 22). [Cf. Skt. *ā* + √*i*-, *ā* + √*yā*-, p.p. *āyāta*-; K.P. √*ī*-, T.Sh. (Drās) √*ē*-, Ksh. √*yi*- (p.p. *ā*(*v*)), Gār. √*ya*-.]

yāt, m., remembrance (Bid.). [Cf. Psht. *yād*, and *yādūsa*, ab.]

zucūsa, to grieve (Bid.). [Cf. *žingūsa*.]

zōg, f., a noise (III, 20). [Psht. *zwag*.]

zigh (? *zig*), rough (Bid.). [Psht. *zīg*.]

zālim, powerful (Bid.). [Psht. *ẕālim*.]

zamīdār, m., a cultivator (of his own plot) (L. 58). [Psht. *zamīndār*.]

zīn, a saddle (L. 226–7). [Psht.]

zinās, m., a corpse (Bid.). [Cf. Psht. *junāza*, a funeral.]

zer, Card., a thousand (Bid.). [Psht. *zar*.]

zaror, strong (Bid.). [Cf. Psht. *zōrāwar*.]

zuwā̃ (Bid.), *zuwān*, m., a youth, young man; Sing. Voc. *zuwān* (I, 47). Psht. *d̲z̲wān*.]

žed, f., blood (Bid.). [Cf. Skt. *rakta*-, Pr. *ratta*-; Ksh. *rat*-. For the Dardic interchange of initial *r* > *ž*, see my *Piśāca Languages*, p. 121. Cf. § 4.]

žigalūsa, to pull (Bid.). [Cf. Skt. *kr̥ṣṭa*-; Psht. *kṣ̌ᵊl*, *ṣ̌kᵊl*, to pull (EVP. p. 34); B. √*kšō*-, Kh. √*žingē*-, Sh. √*ẓakal*-.]

žujūsa, to overthrow (Bid.). [? Cf. Skt. *rujati*, he destroys.]

žem, f., a widow (Bid.). [Cf. *žon*.]

žamung, m., a bean (Bid.). [Cf. Bur. *rabong*, Sh. *rabuṅ*.]

žon, m., a widower (Bid.). Cf. *žem*. [Cf. Skt. *raṇḍa-*; Ksh. *rọṇ^u* (pr. *rūn^u*), a husband.

žingūsa, to weep (Bid.). [? Cf. Skt. √*ru-*, √*rud-*; B. √*žu-*, Sh. √*rō-*, Ksh. √*riw-*. Cf. *zucūsa*.]

žōš, angry (Bid.); *žōš kowōsa* (? *khowōsa*), to be angry (Bid.). [Cf. Skt. *rōṣa-*, anger; Sh. *rōṣ̌*, anger, angry; Ksh. √*rōš-*, be angry.]

žōšil, f., anger (Bid.). Cf. the preceding.

žat, m., morning (Bid.). [? Cf. the next. In Ksh. *rāt-* means both "night" and "yesterday".]

žāt, m., night (III, 43; Bid.). [Cf. Skt. *rātri-*; B. *rōtr*, Sh. *rāti*; Ksh. *rāt-*, f.]

žet, *jada*, on (Bid.), over, concerning. [See §§ 40–2.]

žit, f., brass (Bid.). [Cf. Skt. *rīti-*; Sh. *rīl* ($t > l$).]

žuwāb, in *žuwāb dyūsa*, to answer (Bid.). [Cf. Psht. *d̲z̲awāb*.]

INDEXES

Of Words in Other Languages Quoted in the Foregoing Vocabulary

In the case of Avesta and Sanskrit, the order of words is that usually employed for these languages. For all other languages, the order is that followed in the Vocabulary. That is to say, for each language, words beginning with vowels are placed first, and, after them, the order of the English alphabet is followed, only consonants being taken into consideration.

Each word is followed by the word or words in the Vocabulary under which it is quoted, the two being separated by a colon (:).

CONTENTS

Aryan

**šuši- : sā.*

Eranian

Old Persian

duvitīya- : duyī.
√χšnās- : šit.

pasā : paš.
yauvⁱyā : yāp.

Avesta

az : ā 2.
añgušta- : àngut.
ava : wā.
awra- : agā.
ašta : aṭ.

āp- : ū 2.

uta : o.
uštra- : ud.

ka- : ka.
√kar- : kōsa.

χšīra- : cūī.
χšvaš : šō.

gāv- : gā 2.
gouru- : ūgū.

caχra- : ceš 1.
caθwārō : cau.
careman- : cam.

zanga- : jang.
√zan- 1 *: jyūsa.*
√zan- 2 *: janūsa* 2.

θri- : cā.

dañtan- : dan 2.
darẹγa- : dērī.
dasa : daš 2.
√dā- : dyūsa 1.
duγδar- : dhū.
duma- : lamād.
dva- : dū 5.
dvadasa : dwāš.
dvar- : der.

na : na.
nava : nōm.

pañca : panj.
pañtan- : pan.
paršti- : pīḍ, pat.
pasca : paš.
puθra- : pō, pūc.

√bañd- : bandūsa.
√bav- : hōsa.
bitya- : duyī.
brātar- : bhā.

maẹša- : ē 1, *midhal.*

Pahlavī

Persian

Balōcī

Paṣ̌tō

'ādat : āded.
afsōs : hamsōs.
agar : aχir.
agarci : agarki.
āχūn : āχūn.
āχir : aχir.
ūχ́ : ūχ.
aulād : aulād.
imām : imām.
'umr : umu.
armān : armān.
'ārẓī : arzī.
ārzū : reza.
āsmān : àzmān.
aš̌āṛai : ašay.
ata : aṭ.
awwal : awal.
āwāz : awās.

bā : bā.
bē : be 2.
bād : balai.
bādšāhī : bādšāhī.
bāγ : bāγ.
baγair : bagār.
baγẓ : boγuz.
bihtar : behter.
barai : barai.
barābar : barābar.
bisāṯ : bisāt.
bēwuqūfī : bekū.
biyā : bī.
bayān : bayān.

coγ : cigān.
cal : cal.
cāqū : cāgū.

du'ā : duwā kōsa.
dādā : dād.
dihqān : dehqān.
dūkāndār : dukāndār.
dānā : dāna.
dund : dur.
dārū : dārū.
dēra : dērā.
darwāza : derwāz.
dōst : dōs.
dōstī : dōstī.
dastūr : dastūr.
dušman : dušman.
dawā : dawa.

d̲z̲awāb : žuwāb.
d̲z̲wān : zuwā̃.

fikr : piger.
fikrdār : fikerdār.
falānkai : filankai.

guḍ : kud.
gōlaī : gōlī.
gulū : golē.
galla (f.) *: galla* (m.).
gaṇ : gan 1.
garm : garm.
garmī : garmī.
guṭ : gud.

γalai : γule.
γulām : gulām.
γam : γam.
γamjān : γamjān.
γammāz : γamāz.

mēwa : mewā.
mayan : mayin.

nūk : nōk.
nājōṛtiyā : najurtya.
nākāra : nākāra.
nōkar : noker.
nārīna : nàrina.
nārāst : narāz.
nārāz : narāz.
nātsāpā : na-tsāba.

paidā : paidā.
pādšāh : pādšāh.
pādšāhī : pādšāhī.
√puk- : pugūsa.
pχ́a : χū.
pōrē : pōrē.
pēṛaī : pērīa.
pišō : piš.
puṣ̌tēdᵃl : puχtuā.

qil'a : kalā, kilē.
qām : kām.
qaum : kām.
qīmat : kīmat.
quṯb : kutub.

rabaṛ : rabaṛ.
ruχṣat : ruksat.
rang : rang.

sabaq : sabak.
sika : siga.
sambālawᵃl : sabā.
sra zar : lagur.

sust : sot.
sitār : sitār.
saw : so.
sawāl : sᵃwāl.

ṣifat : sipad.
ṣūrat : sūrat.

šai : šai.
šukr : šukur.
šēχ : šēχ.
šurū' : šuru.
šarīkat : šĕrīkat.
šarm : šerm.
šaṛūnkai : šerunke.
šaiṯān : šaitān.

ṣ̌kᵃl : žigalūsa.
ṣ̌ēra : šulan.

ta : ta.
talχ : talχ.
tlᵃl : til.
tambū : tambū.
tamām : tamām.
tandar : tandergyat.
tapōs : tapōs.
trīχ : tid.
taš : tūš.
t'awīẕ : tēyis.
taiyār : tia.

ṭāngā : tongū.
ṭōpak : ṭubak.

ṯūfān : tofān.
ṯāqat : tāgat.

Iškāšmī

Munjānī

Šiγnī

Sarīkolī

Waχī

INDO-ARYAN

Sanskrit

aṣṭadaśa : *atāš*.
aham : *ā* 2.

√*āp*- (Vedic), *āpnōti* : *abōsa*.
√*āp*, *prâpnōti* : *abōsa* ; *prâpayati* : *powūsa* ; *avâpta*- : *wat* ; *āpita*- : *abāt*.
āśu- : *husai*.
ās- : *aī*.
āsya- : *aī*.

√*i*-, *ā* + √*i*- : *yōsa*.
indradhanus- : *inhān*.

√*īr*-, *prêrayati* : *pyūsa*.

ujjvala- : *ūjul*.
uta : *ō*.
uṣṭra- : *ud*.

ēkādaśa : *agāš*.
ēna- : *ē* 3.

ka- : *ka*.
kakṣē : *kac*.
kapōla- : *bogul*.
karṇa- : *kan* 1.
karṇi- : *kan* 3.
kartari- : *kera*.
karma : *kam*.
√*kal*-, *niṣkālayati* : *nigālūsa*.
kasmai : *ka*.
kasya : *ka*.

kāka- : *kāgh*.
kāla- : *kāl*.
kāsa- : *kan* 4.
kiṁcit : *kacis*.
kiyat- : *kadak*.
kukkuṭa- : *kugū*.
√*kuṭ*- : *kuḍūsa*, *kure*.
kuṭa- : *kur*.
kuṭila- : *kol*.
kuḍya- : *kur*.
kūpa- : *kūī*.
kutra : *kēt*.
√*kṛ*-, *karōti* : *kōsa* ; *phūt* + √*kṛ*- : *pugūsa*.
√*kṛṣ*-, *kṛṣṭa*- : *žigalūsa*.
kṛṣna- : *kišun*.
kōmala- : *kamal*.
kaulēya- : *kujū*.
√*krī*-, *vikrīṇītē* : *biginūsa*.
krūra- : *kū* 3.
√*kṣip*-, *utkṣipati* : *ucūsa*- ; *utkṣipta*- : *ušūsa*.
kṣīṇa- : *cun*.
kṣīra- : *cūī*.
kṣudra- : *cit*.
√*kṣudh*-, *kṣudhyati* : *kujūsa*.

√*khād*- : *khowūsa*.
khōḍa- : *kud*.

gaṇa- : *gun*.
√*gam*-, *gata*- : *gā* 3 ; *parigamayati* : *pergūsa*.
gardabha- : *gadhō*.
galda- : *gal*.

dundhubhi- : dandak.
durbala- : jūbal.
duhitṛ- : dhū.
dūra- : dū 2.
dṛḍha- : dērī.
√dṛś-, paśyati : pašūsa ;
dṛṣṭā : ḍiṭ.
d ṣā : cidug-di.
drākṣā : daš 1.
dva- : dū 5.
dvar- : der.
dvādaśa : dwāš.
dvi- : dū 5.
dvitīya- : bī, duyī.

dhanus- : bārdan.
√dhav- : dhain dyūsa.
dhūma- : dīmī.

na : na.
nada- : ned.
nava : nōm.
nava- : nam.
nasta- : nat.
nāṭya : nār.
nāma : nām.
nikaṭa- : niō.
nidrā : nīn.
√nī-, nayati : neyūsa ;
ānayati : anūsa.
nīla- : nīl.

pakṣin- : pacin.
pakṣman- : pām.
paṅkti-: pöt.
pañca : panj.
pañcadaśa : puṅš.
pataṁga- : pattang.
pattra- : pat.
pathin- (panth-) : pan.
√pad-, avapādayati : wālī.
parē : payim.
paśca : paš.
√pā-, pibati : pūsa.
pāda- : paī.
pāra- : payim.
pārśva- : bariš, bàrīš.
pālāśa- : pihīl.
picchila- : pišul.
pitṛ-ṣvasṛ- : pabī.
pitṛvya- : peži.
pipīla- : pel.
pīṭhikā : pērīa.
putra- : pō, pūc.
puṣpa- : pašū.
puṣya- : pašū.
pūrṇa- : pin.
pūrṇa + illa- : pūnil.
pṛṣṭha- : pat, pīḍ.
**pauṣya- : pašū.*
phūt + √kṛ- : pugūsa.

badhira- : bū.
√bandh- : bandūsa.
barkara- : bogho.
bahiḥ : bāge, baiyim.
bahu- : bud.
bahutva- : bud.
bāla- : bāl.
√budh-, bōdhati, buddha-,
budhyatē : būūsa, bujūsa.
bubhukṣā : buš.

√śak- : hikū.
śayana- : šen.
√śikṣ- : cujūsa.
śiraḥ : šā.
śītala- : šidal.
√śudh-, śudhyatē : cujūsa ; śōdhyatē, śōdhayati : cūjūsa.
śuṣka- : šugil.
śuṣkala- : šugil.
śuci- : šijo.
śrathana- : šulan.
√śrī-, ucchrayati : ucūsa.
śvāsa- : sā.

ṣaṣ- : šō.
ṣaṣṭha- : šawam.
ṣōḍaśa : šeš.

satya- : saj.
√sad-, niṣad- : baiyūsa.
sapta : sat.
saptadaśa : satāš.
saptama- : sattam.
sahitē : set.
sârtha- : sāt.
sikatā : sigal.
sukara- : sugā.
sūrya- : sī.
sētu- : se 1.
stambha- : thām.
skandha- : kān 2.
√stṝ-, vistīrṇa- : bizin.
strī : cī 2.
√sthā-, sthita(ka)- : thū ; sthāpita- : thā ; adhiṣṭhita- : eṛī ; uttiṣṭhati : ušūsa ; utthita- : ūtal.
√sphuṭ-, sphuṭati : pūrūsa ; sphōṭayati : porōsa.
√svap-, supta- : hut.
svapna- : sen.
svasā, svasār- : šū 1.

haḍḍa- : har.
hanu- : hagel.
hala- : höl.
√has-, hasati : hasūsa.
hasta- : hat.
hāla- : höl.
hima- : him.
himâlaya- : himāl.
hṛd- : hū.
hṛdaya- : hū.

Prakrit

**āvaï : abōsa.*
utthaï, utthida- : ušūsa.
joṇhā : yun.
tiṇha- : tīn.
dhīdā : dhū.
pāvaï : abōsa.
maccha- : maj.
māsa- : mās.
ratta- : žed.
sacca- : saj.
siviṇa- : sen.
**sukkhala- : šugil.*

Bengali

Lahndā

Hindōstānī

Dardic

Bašgalī

camo : cam.
cimeh : cimu
ceno : cuk.
cōn : jang.

diu : dū 5.
dū : der.
dūm : dīmī.
dumrī : lamād.
dōn : dan 1.
dāru : dārū.
drōn : bārdan.
dros : daš 1.
dāṛī : dä.
dus : cidug di.
dits : dwāš.
duts : daš 2.
dut : dan 2.
dōtt : dandak.
dyuṛ : dū 2.

gåo : gā 2.
gōl : kū 2.
gum : gomū.
gāno : gan 2.
grām : gām.
√gīṛ- : ganūsa.
gwa : gā 3.

jū : dhū.

√ka- : kōsa.
kai-kotē : kai.
kū : ka.
kōr : kēt.
kōr : kan 1.
kōr-ste : keda.
kuṛi : kujū.
koṛṛ : kāgh.
√kas- : kan 4.
√kšō- : žigalūsa.
kato : kera.
kett : kēt.
kuttāt : kud.
kyē̃ : kai.

lui : lohūr.
√lar- : lobo.

macī : mid.
mōc : māš.
mam : mām.
manci : māš.
√mṛe- : maiyūsa.
mōs : màh.
mussā : mūš.
matsa : maj.
myuk : mū̃š.
mažurala : midhal.

nei : na.
noi : nam.
noh : nōm.
nām : nām.
nom : nām.
nōt : nār.
nawōs : bowuš.
nazuṛ : nat.

på vīsth. : paī dyūsa.
√pi- : pūsa.
puc : panj.

Gārwī

√bac- : bajūsa.

chimar : cimu.
carōr : cēriḍ.

dū : dū 5.
dand : dan 2.
dūr : dū 2.
daš : daš 2.

ḍār : ḍhē.

gā : gā 2.
gada : gadhō.

kūcur : kujū.

līg : jīg.

mā : ā 2.
mūka : mū̃š.
√mar- : maiyūsa.
mēš : māš.

nā : na.
nīaṛ : niō.
nōzōr : nat.

pīšīr : piš.
patā : pat.
pūṭ : pūc.

sīr : sī.
sat : sat.

šō : šō.
šiṭ : šīr.

tār : tār.

ṭhā : cā.

√ya- : yōsa.
ya : ā 2.
yai : yai.
yāsūn : yūn.

Gawarbati

ā : ā 2.
aū : ū 2.
amōna : ā 2.
angār : angā.
aṛi : ār.
išī : bīš 2.
√ušṭ- : ušūsa.

bāb : bāp.
bliaia : bhā.
bāp : bāp.

du : dū 5.
dū : dū 5.
durae : dē 2.
daš : daš 2.
dāt : dan 2.

ga : gā 3.
gadā : gadhō.

hast : hat.
jai : yai.
kukuṛ : kugū.

Khōwār

dori : de 2.
drŏch : daš 1.
drŏn : bārdan.
drŏnanū : inhān.
duart : der.
doš : cidug-di.

gŏl : kū 2.
gom : gomū.
√gan- : ginūsa.
gardōγ : gadhō.
gās : gā 1.

hīm : him.
hunū : hagel.
herdī : hü.
√hŏss- : hasūsa.
host : hat.

jū : dū 5.
√jān- : janūsa 2.
jŏš : daš 2.
još-ī : agāš.
jūwum : duyī.

kā : ka.
ki : ka.
ko : kai.
kāg : kāgh.
kūkū : kugū.
koli : kol.
kama : kadak.
kandūri : kadak.
√kop- : kan 4.
krūi : lohūr.
kār : kan 1.
√kŏr- : kōsa.
kura : kēt.
kŏram : kam.
kurar : keda.
kŏs : ka.
kutū : kud.
kutēr : kera.
kya : ka.
kyo-te : kai, kiau.

χuš : χuš.

mēnū : malāž.
√màr- : mowūsa.
mas : màh.
mōš : māš.
mātsi : maj.

√nī- : neyūsa.
no : na.
noχ : nam.
nām : nām.
naskār : nat.
nōwēs : bowūš.

√pi- : pūsa.
pŏc : pet.
√phū- : pugūsa.
pàlŏγ : bebay.
pelīli : pel.
pon : pan.
pōnj : panj.
pār : payim.
praš : bariš, bàrīš.
√pōš- : pašūsa.
puši : piš.
pŏšp : pām.

Kalāšā

piṣṭō : *pat.*
pūtr : *pūc.*

rang : *rāng.*

sūri : *sī.*
sat : *sat.*

šōh : *šō.*

tāri : *tār.*
trĕh : *cā.*

yōz : *ōš.*

Kāšmīrī

aũ (dial.) : *ā* 2.
ī (dial.) : *yai.*
ạch[i] : *achī.*
ạdur[u] : *öž.*
aḍ : *ar.*
aḍịl[u] : *har.*
ala : *höl.*
āla : *höl.*
√*an-*, *anun* : *anūsa.*
ạn[u] : *an.*
ạng[u]*j*[ü] : *āngī.*
√*as-* : *hasūsa.*
ạ̄s[ü] : *aī.*
atha : *hat.*
öṭh : *aṭ.*
ā(v) : *yōsa.*
az : *aj.*

babb (dial.) : *bāp.*
bŏch : *buš.*
bāh : *dwāš.*
√*bĕh-* : *baiyūsa.*
band : *bandūsa.*
būñul[u] : *būmel.*
bāpath[a]*r* : *bowāš.*
bar : *der.*
bāt- : *bāt.*
√*bŏv-* : *hōsa.*
bāw[a]*za* : *bowuš.*
bạ̄y[u] : *bhā.*
biyĕ : *bī, duyī.*
bīz : *biž.*
√*bōz-* : *būūsa, bujūsa.*

√*di-* : *dyūsa* 1.
dach : *daš* 1.
dĕd : *dād.*
dhī (dial.) : *dhū.*
d[a]*h* : *dīmī.*
dŏh : *dī.*
dumba : *lamād.*
dan : *dan* 1.
dan- : *dan* 2.
dān : *dadan.*
dand : *dan* 2.
dọ̄ñ[u] : *inhān, bārdan.*
√*dar-* : *dērī.*
dạ̄r[ü] : *dä.*
√*dav-* : *dhain dyūsa.*
dŏyịm[u] : *duyī.*

ḍam-ḍam : *dandak.*
ḍum-ḍum : *dandak.*
√*ḍēš-* : *ḍiṭ.*
ḍīṭh[ü] : *ḍiṭ.*

niōṛ^u (dial.) : niō.
nĕṇd^{a}r : nīn.
nas : nat.
nasth (dial.) : nat.
naṭ- : nār.
nav : nōm.
nāv : nām.
nạw^u : nam.
nyŏṭh : àngut.

pachaṇ (dial.) : pacin.
√phuk- : pugūsa.
phamb : pām.
√phuṭ- : pūrūsa.
√phuṭ^{a}r- : porōsa.
pāna : aban 2.
pandāh : puṅš.
pönts : panj.
pŏph : pabī.
pūr^u : pūnil.
pạ̄rịm^u : payim.
√paš (old) : pašūsa.
pōš : pašū.
pišạl^u : pišul.
pat- : pat.
pẹ̆t^u : pid.
pŏ̃t- : pöt.
pūt^u : pūc.
patang : pattang.
pạt^{a}r : pet.
pịṭh^u : pīḍ.
pav : poa.
pāwun : powūsa.

rọ̄n^u : žon.
rang : rāng.
√rōš- : žōš.
rāt- : cidug-di, žat, žūt.
√riw- : žingūsa.

sadāh : satāš.
sĕk- : sigal.
sambālun : sabā.
sirĕ : sī.
sat- : sat.
sŏ̃t- : basān.
sọ̆t^u : sot.
sū̃t^i : set.
satịm^u : sattam.

šĕ- : šō.
šẹ̆d^u : šūš.
šāh : sā.
šĕhạl^u : šidal.
šīn : him.
šur^ü : saran.
šurāh. : šeš.
šŏts- : šijo.
šĕyịm^u : šawam.

thạd^u : ūtal.
tham : thām.
√thav- : thā.
√thāv- : thā.
t^{a}l : tūt.
tĕli : talā.
tul : tūt.
tālav : tel 1.
tŏmul : tunōl.
trih : cā.
tāruk- : tā 2.
trēl : bebay.

Maiyā̃

Pašai

gōṛā : ghō.

hlē : cā.
hlikā : cī 2.
hamā : ā 2.
hāst : hat.

jib : jib.

kukūr : kugū.
χō : šō.

lai : bhā.
√lī- : maiyūsa.

na : na.
nō : nōm.

nast : nat.

panj : panj.
paškin : paš.
pīšōṇak : piš.
puṭhlē : pūc.

sai : šū.
sat : sat.

š[a] *: šō.*
šlika : cī 2.
šīr : šā.

tārā : tā 2.

wöst : bīš 2.

Ṣiṇā

ãi (dial.) *: yai.*
ã̄i : aĩ.
ē : ē 3.
√ē- (dial.) *: yōsa.*
ō : ē 3.
açi : achī.
agui : āngī.
agār : angā.
aguru : ūgū.
aguṭo : àngut.
āje : yai.
akāi : agāš.
√amuš- : amašūsa.
èsai : ē 3.
aš : aj.
aṣṭāī : atāš.
ūṭ : ud.

√uth- : ušūsa.
uthalu : ūtal.
āzī (dial.) *: aĩ.*
ež : ē 1.
aẓu : agā, öž.

√bai- : baiyūsa.
bāi : dwāš.
baĩĕ : duyimo.
bi : biž.
bī : bīš 2.
√bo- : hōsa.
bābo : bāp.
bicuṣ : bijmot.
bodu : bud.
bujä : bajūsa.
bālo : bāl.

ko : ka.
kaci : kac.
kacāk : kadak.
√*kha : khowūsa.*
√*khu- : kan* 4.
√*khoj- : kujūsa.*
khuṛo : kud.
khuš : χuš.
khuṭo : karran.
khaṭār : kera.
kũkurōco : kugū.
kāl : kāl.
kōlu : kol.
kŏm : kam.
kinu : kišun.
kŏn : kan 1.
kōn : kan 3.
kōni : kēt.
kōnyo : keda.
kaṅgulē : golē.
kuru : kū 2.
krŏm : kam.
käsä : ka.
√*kut-* (? *kuṭ-*) (dial.)*: kuḍūsa.*
kuṭ : kur.
koṭo : kure.

lo : loj.
√*likh- : ligūsa.*
lōlyu : lohūr.

mai : ā 2.
mī (dial.) *: ā* 2.
mī̃ : mih.
mūu : maiyūsa.
muço : mū̃š.
māmu : mām.
manūẓo : māš.
√*mar- : mowūsa.*
√*mir- : maiyūsa.*
mas : mās.
mā̃s : màh.
mušā : māš.
mā̃z : màh.

nā : na.
näi : na.
nau : nōm.
√*nikhal- : nigālūsa.*
nīlu : nīl.
nom : nām.
nir : nīn.
nata : nat.
naṭĕ : nār.
nāwu : nam.

√*pi- : pūsa.*
puç : pūc.
phū : pugūsa.
phicīlu : pišul.
phaçāli : pet.
phalā : bebay.
philīli : pel.
phapi : pabī.
phurgū : pet.
phatu : pat.
phaṭōi : pattang.
√*phuṭ- : porōsa.*
√*phuṭīž- : pūrūsa.*
pŏn : pan.
panzai : puṅš.
pār : payim.

Tirāhī

gā : gā 3.
gō : gā 2, *gō*.

χō : šō.
χār : šā.

√mir- : maiyūsa.
myāna : ā 2.

na : na.
nab : nōm.

uc : panj.
iul : ḍhē.

√omo- : maiyūsa.
isikh : sī.
iš : aī.
ušū : šō.
√išt- : ušūsa.
āveh : ū 2.

chī : cā.
jū : dhū.
kirukh : kujū.
leze : daš 2.

mik : mū̃š.
muš : māš.

ao : ū 2.
oie : yai.
ōli : eṛi.
āri : ār.
āš : aī.
√ōšt- : ušūsa.

pants : panj.
pišē : piš.
patī-kana : pat.
putr : pūc.

spaz : šū 1.
surī : sī.
sat : sat.

tsimbar : cimu.

Veron

nūh : nōm.
nes : nat.

pič : pō.
pšikh : piš.

√ro- : žingūsa.

siusu : šū 1.
sete : sat.

ti-mik : mū̃š.

weste : cī 2.
wayeh : bhā.

yē : ā 2.

žema : cimu.

Wai-alā

brā : bhā.

cimā : cimu.

du : dū 5.
dōš : daš 2.
dū̃t : dan 2.

Gypsy

Gypsy (European)

Gypsy (Syrian)]	TORWALI
khurō : ghō.	*šerō : šā.*
√χa- : khowūsa.	*štār : cau.*
	šŏv : šō.
mānuš : māš.	*trin : cā.*
	GYPSY (Syrian)
bāb : bāp.	*nā : nōm.*
√de- : dyūsa 1.	*păci : paš.*
gukări : kugū.	*pišīkā : piš.*
gŏrā : ghō.	*pišt : pīḍ.*
jib : jib.	*šās : šā.*
	BURUŠASKĪ
bēsko : bàrīš.	*tŏm : thām.*
comar : cimu.	*yūl : ḍhē.*
rabong : žamung.	
	KHĒRWĀRĪ
pūšī : piš.	
	ARABIC
ḥamal : hamal.	*kāfir : kupār.*
kuffār : kupār.	

ERRATA

Pp. 32, l. 21; 43, l. 16; 46, l. 7; 49, l. 10; 66, l. 16; 70, l. 21; 85, l. 19; 86, l. 9; 105, col. 2; 118, ll. 13, 17. Read "*šĕrīkat.*"

Pp. 41, l. 13; 43, l. 12. Read "*ḍe*", and correct the Index on p. 93 accordingly.

P. 64, l. 4 from bottom, for "*šat* "to be", read "*šat*, to be".

P. 93. The entry "*ḍhē*" is in wrong alphabetical order.

P. 163, Art. *χūnza*. Add "Cf. Gār. *hȧnza*, Kh. *χunza*", and add these words in their proper places on pp. 202 and 204.